Program Architecture

Business executives consider what is necessary to protect the company. It comes down to people, process and technology, organized within an information security program. Everything has its place within the program, including business processes, assets and the right blend of controls to protect them.

This book describes program architecture, the discipline of designing, implementing and leading information security programs.

- Prove Yourself Ready Now
- Team Development and Retention
- Program Maturity
- Influence Support and Funding
- Cyber Threat Intelligence
- Third Party Risk Management
- Metrics and Reporting
- Insider Risk Monitoring and Response
- Threat Landscape and Controls Analysis
- Conduct an Assessment
- Crisis Communications
- Control by Governance

This book provides practical advice in the areas of cybersecurity and operational risk management. The goal is to provide readers with practical advice they can use upon return to work.

Security, Audit and Leadership Series
Series Editor: Dan Swanson, Dan Swanson and Associates, Ltd., Winnipeg, Manitoba, Canada.

The scope and mandate for internal audit continues to evolve each year, as does the complexity of the business environment and speed of the changing risk landscape in which it must operate. The fundamental goal of this exciting series is to produce leading-edge books on critical subjects facing security and audit executives and practitioners. Key topics addressed include Leadership, Cybersecurity, Security Leadership, Privacy, Strategic Risk Management, Auditing IT, Audit Management and Leadership, and Operational Auditing.

Members, Methods, and Measures: Unlocking the Secrets of IT Leadership
By Thomas E. Armstrong

Philosophy.exe: The Techno-Philosophical Toolkit for Modern Minds
By Matthias Muhlert

Guardians of the Digital Age: Securing the Future
By Elçin Biren

Ironwill 360° Leadership: A Blueprint for Level 5 Unicorn Leadership
By Douglas P. Pflug

Behavioral Insights in Cybersecurity: A Guide to Digital Human Factors
By Dustin S. Sachs

Integrated Assurance: Unified Risk Strategy
By Patrick Hayes

Preparing for Sustainability Audits: A Practical Guide for IT Sector
By Mahsa Fidanboy

Scaling Pyramids: Leadership Lessons from a Mid-Level Bureaucrat
By Christopher Stitt

Program Architecture: Fight the Good Fight
By Gideon T. Rasmussen

Program Architecture

Fight the Good Fight

Gideon T. Rasmussen
CISSP, CRISC, CISA, CISM, CIPP

CRC Press
Taylor & Francis Group
Boca Raton London New York

CRC Press is an imprint of the
Taylor & Francis Group, an **informa** business

Designed cover image: Gideon T. Rasmussen

First edition published 2026
by CRC Press
2385 NW Executive Center Drive, Suite 320, Boca Raton FL 33431

and by CRC Press
4 Park Square, Milton Park, Abingdon, Oxon, OX14 4RN

CRC Press is an imprint of Taylor & Francis Group, LLC

ISBN: 978-1-032-84233-2 (hbk)
ISBN: 978-1-032-89600-7 (pbk)
ISBN: 978-1-003-54361-9 (ebk)

DOI: 10.1201/9781003543619

Typeset in Sabon
by SPi Technologies India Pvt Ltd (Straive)

Contents

Figures

Author biography

Gideon T. Rasmussen is a cybersecurity leader with over 20 years of experience in corporate and military organizations. Gideon has designed and led programs including Information Security (CISO), PCI - Payment Card Security, Third Party Risk Management, Application Security and Information Risk Management. He has diverse cybersecurity industry experience within banking, startups, insurance, pharmaceuticals, DoD/USAF, aerospace and defense, state government, advertising and talent management.

Gideon is a sought-after speaker, addressing audiences at conferences, universities and corporate events. He has authored the book *Program Architecture: Fight the Good Fight.* A veteran of the United States Air Force, Gideon has completed the Bataan Memorial Death March four times.

Gideon T. Rasmussen
Cybersecurity Leader | Speaker | Author | Veteran
CISSP, CRISC, CISA, CISM, CIPP

Introduction

I started my career in the United States Air Force, where you gain skills and experience from apprentice up through journeyman and beyond. Each team member raises others up by their boot straps.

This book was written for college students, individual contributors and leaders. It is the book I wish was available to me years back and my attempt to give back to the InfoSec community.

I'm grateful to leaders that mentored me and gave me stretch roles. I have designed and implemented information security programs with many talented professionals. We learned from each other. This book is my effort to pass years of experience on to others, an attempt to repay a debt.

On a personal note, I want to thank my wife Mary. She has been with me through countless tough times. Mary is the secret to my success.

I want to thank my children Kaeli and Hunter for their support and understanding over the years. They are both working in the InfoSec career field. I am very proud of them.

I challenge you to stretch yourself, to put yourself at risk, to have professional courage.

Are you ready? Let's go on an intense, hard-charging journey into cybersecurity.

Chapter 1

Prove yourself ready now

1.1 INTRODUCTION: CAREER AND PROFESSIONAL DEVELOPMENT

This chapter provides practical advice to prove yourself 'ready now' for a cybersecurity management role. The journey begins with a view from the executive's side of the table and how to speak in terms of risk. There is an overview of risk management, with tips for influencing risk mitigation. Focus transitions to how a communications plan can make you more effective as a leader. There is practical advice for developing presentation skills with limited stress and anxiety through a four-step approach. With that skill in-place you can communicate program statuses to executives. Professional development and C-Level presentation round out the chapter.

1.2 UNDERSTAND EXECUTIVES' PERSPECTIVES

If you have a goal of being promoted from individual contributor to manager, it is very important to align with executives. You have to understand their perspectives. That starts with reviewing their mission and vision statements before meeting with them. Mission describes the purpose of the organization that the executive leads. Vision is how they are going to accomplish those priorities. When you think about the motivations of an executive try switching sides of the table and see where they are coming from. In many cases they are focused on providing a product or service and either generating revenue directly or supporting revenue generation. All of them need to have a budget and must keep to that budget. If you are planning to start a new initiative that has requirements for them, give them advance notice to plan for resources within their budget. Executives will not support an unfunded mandate in mid-budgetary cycle. Executives are focused on cost savings, on efficiency and doing more with their current resources. The information security program's impact on their productivity matters. Executives will call you out if program initiatives are wasteful, duplicative or unnecessary. Executives and information security professionals share a desire to manage and mitigate operational risk. While we align from that perspective, note that is a goal further down on their list of priorities. Think in terms of how executives are rated on performance, how they get their bonuses and how they get promoted. Their ratings are more focused on products and services and how they are generating revenue than how they are mitigating operational risk.

Be mindful of existing security and business processes when kicking off a new initiative or implementing emerging technology. Communications flow more smoothly when inserted into an existing process. Be mindful of impact to productivity. If you will be asking for significant resources and support, start by communicating that one-on-one with the executive rather than sending an e-mail or blindsiding them with a slide deck.

DOI: 10.1201/9781003543619-1

Be aware of pain points when taking over leadership of an existing program. Determine if there have been challenges working with the security team with respect to communications or productivity impact. Be sensitive to that and own up to that up-front during your initial conversations with that business executive or that IT leader.

There may be perspectives of we are separate teams and it is 'us versus them'. Collectively business, IT and information security have gotten better at that over time. However, it is important to emphasize when having conversations with business and IT executives that ultimately we all are one team. Our organization has an overarching mission and vision. We are all working toward those goals. We may have differing roles in our teams but at the end of the day we have those same goals. It is important for information security to run with the business and to block and tackle to help make them successful. We may need to change information security processes; change the way we work to support our business partners.

1.3 SPEAK IN TERMS OF RISK

Operational Risk: Replace the word 'security' with 'risk' in conversations with business and IT executives. Consider the view from the other side of the table. Many employees view security as a binary term, either something is secure or it is not. Managers and executives lead in an environment of operation risk, some issues will be mitigated and others will be accepted. Risk is the Rosetta Stone between security professionals and business management. As security professionals we are trying to mitigate risk just like the business. Be mindful of those subtleties in the way that you express yourself and the way that you represent your program.

Reputation Risk: Executives often refer to reputation risk as headline risk. If there is a significant event such as a data breach, there is the potential for that to impact the brand of your organization. That may be the decision point that cause our clients to transition to a competitor.

Strategic Risk: When a risk issue causes financial damage, that may affect the ability to execute on strategic goals. For example, cancelation of a new product launch could have a negative impact on profit for the year.

Compliance Risk: There are many regulatory and contractual obligations that can have impact on an organization. Substantial fines and penalties may be assessed for failure to adhere to requirements within the healthcare and payment card industries. The Federal Trade Commission is known for citing companies with data breaches with unfair or deceptive trade practices, significant financial penalties and a requirement for independent privacy assessments over the next 20 years.

1.4 RISK EXISTS...

Business as Usual: Risk exists when we plan for business as usual. This issue occurs within process design. People design processes in the way they expect activities to occur under normal circumstances. The problem is things do not go normally. It is necessary to mitigate risk within process execution.

Control Deployment: Risk exists when controls are not in place. When there is a risk issue that will cost significant money to address, there may be a decision to push it off to the next budgetary cycle. While that may make sense to meet near-term business objectives, the organization is accepting risk until mitigating controls are implemented.

Complexity: Risk exists when there is complexity. When a technology environment is complex and is not well understood, that may result in security incidents or service outages.

Data Location: In order to protect data, you need to know where it is. Modern enterprises must have data discovery tools and inventories. That enables control deployment and migration of unstructured data to systems of record.

Data Control: Risk exists when data leaves our control. The transition to another party can be the cause of a security incident or a data breach. It is necessary to evaluate the security posture of service providers through a Third Party Risk Management Program.

New Technology: Risk exists in the adoption of new technology. Deploy new software and hardware thoughtfully and deliberately with appropriate design, testing and change management in place. Implement security configurations and monitoring. Test security controls with vulnerability scanning and penetration testing.

Awe of Rank: Risk exists when a senior leader asserts their influence on a subordinate. Document risk issues within an appropriate business process such as a risk register. That provides risk transparency to senior executives.

1.5 RISK MANAGEMENT (HIGH LEVEL)

Information Security Framework: Have a focus on risk management within your information security program. Start with a control framework such as the NIST Cybersecurity Framework or ISO 27001. A control framework provides coverage of foundational controls.

Laws, Regulations and Contracts: Compliance requirements provide additional risk mitigation. Layer on controls required by laws, regulations and contractual obligations.

Risk Management: Risk management is where the rubber meets the road. Every information security framework speaks of having a risk assessment and risk management in place. Identify controls to protect business products, services and assets. Risk management is also necessary to adapt to emerging threats and changes in technology. Compliance focused organizations still need these forms of operational risk management to meet business objectives.

Residual Risk: Residual risk can be viewed as the potential for a threat actor to circumvent in-place controls, gaining access to data assets. Risk tolerance statements and a risk register process are effective techniques to help foster risk transparency to executives. That enables them to make informed decisions (Figure 1.1).

1.6 RISK RESPONSE

When it comes to risk management, there are four options to select from. Here are examples:

Risk Acceptance: It makes sense to sign off on risk acceptance with issues that pose a low risk to the organization.

Risk Avoidance: A business unit may decide to avoid doing business in a region with few customers, where the cost of compliance and potential impact of fines is high. The risk versus reward calculation does not favor that scenario.

Risk Mitigation: Information security professionals strive to mitigate risk business-as-usual. The goal is to act in accordance with the risk tolerance of the organization.

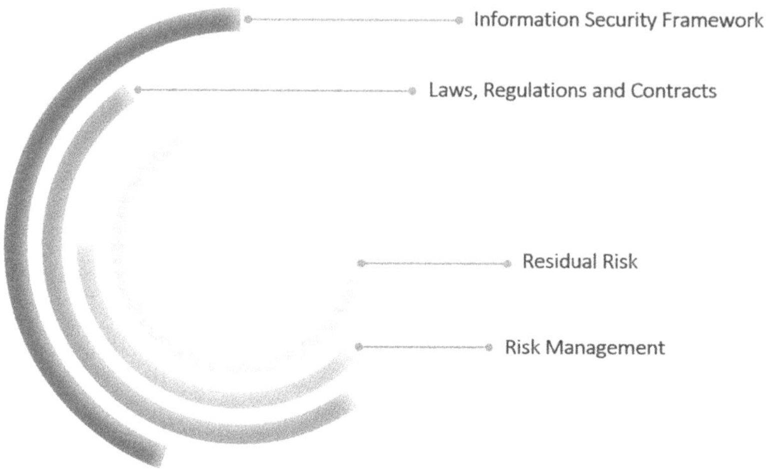

Figure 1.1 Risk management (High Level).

Risk Transference: Most organizations have cybersecurity insurance in place to transfer risk to the insurance company in the event of a data breach. A risk register is an internal form of risk transference. Register entries provide risk transparency to senior executives, who make the decision to mitigate or accept risk.

1.7 HAVE COMMUNICATIONS ROUTINES

Communications are an area of professional development for many of us within the information security career field. Here is a simple methodology to help ensure you are communicating effectively, which is an absolute must to transition into a leadership position.

To establish your own Communications Plan, start with a standard-sized sheet of paper. Draw a circle in the middle and put your initials where ABC appears in Figure 1.2. Draw three circles that go outward. Those are your primary, secondary and tertiary stakeholders. The first circle is your primary stakeholders, the people that you work with every day or every week. The second circle are also within your processes, typically support and business partners. IT and risk partners fall within this category as well. The third circle are optional and infrequent contacts such as meetings with your mentor, mentees and professional contacts.

When you have a communications plan in a visualization like this, you start to see activity all in one place. Jot down communications routines on this piece of paper over a week or two. Review your calendar a few weeks out to capture meeting routines. Leave the paper on your desk and flesh it out as you go.

The real value comes in within the second and third circle. Identify areas where communications are missing or are no longer necessary. There are intersections between information security, privacy management and fraud prevention. Data governance ties them all together. Have touch base meetings with other teams to foster collaboration and to prevent duplicate efforts (Figure 1.3).

Push and pull from your professional network. Give support and guidance freely. There are times where all of us are pulled into a situation where we are not a subject matter expert and are a bit challenged. In that event, it is good to have friends with dark circles around their eyes who are willing to advise you and perhaps give you an artifact to help you fulfill the need.

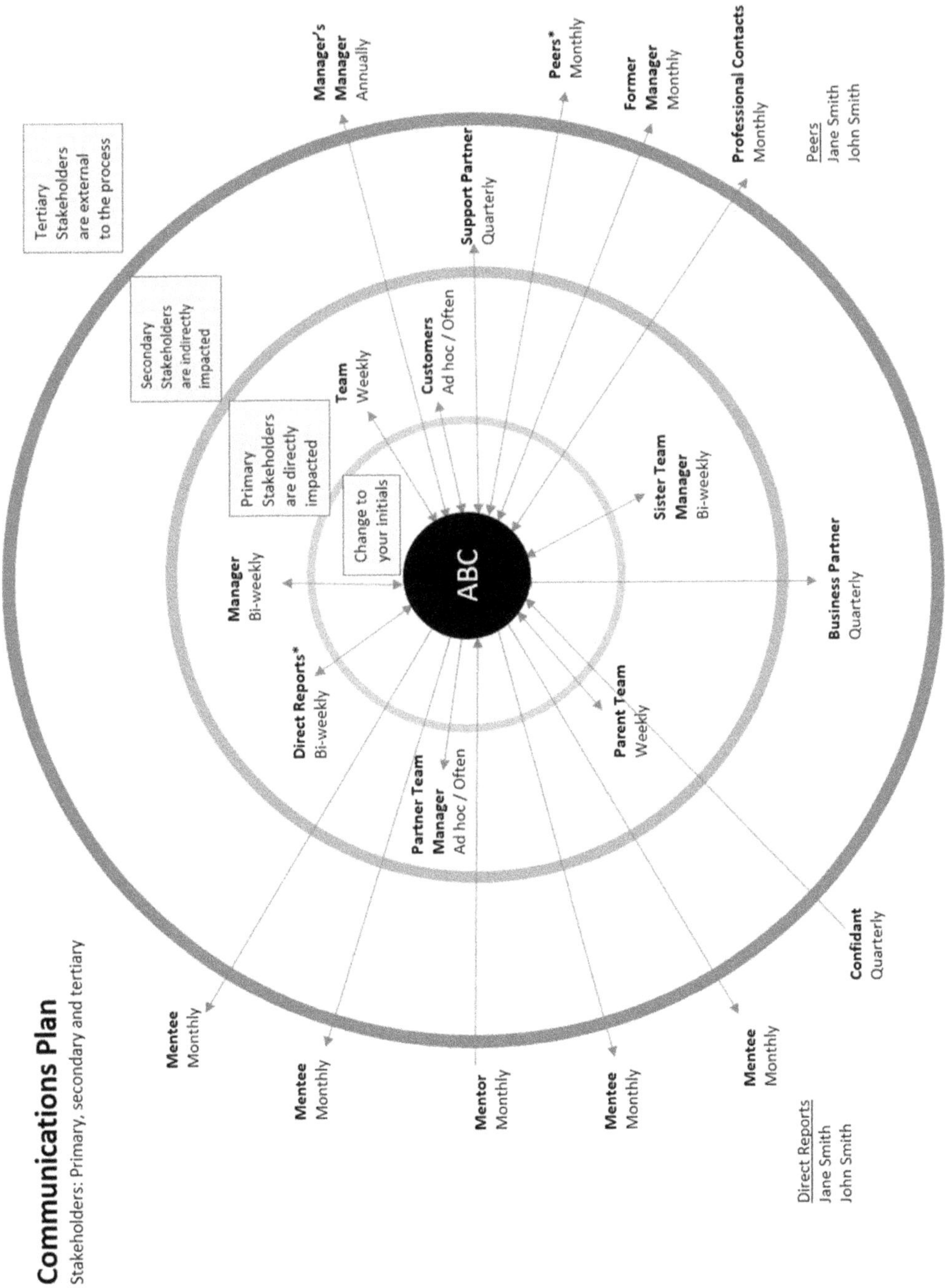

Figure 1.2 Communications plan.

Figure 1.3 Operational risk intersections.

Meet periodically with a Mentor to identify areas of professional development and drive your career forward. Mentor others as a matter of being a professional. As you transition into management, meet one-on-one with each of your direct reports at least every week or two. While information security takes us into nights and weekends, you must be passionate about your people. They require care and feeding as professionals.

1.8 DEVELOP PRESENTATION SKILLS

Managers are called upon to present a few times a year. That frequency increases with the transition to an executive role. Most people experience anxiety when thinking about their first presentation. That is a normal reaction. A healthy bit of anxiety is good for you. Generations back it would keep you safe from wild animals. In a modern context it warns you to 'pay attention', such as the need to rehearse for a presentation.

When creating for your first presentation, start with a bulleted list of topics you want to discuss. Those will be your slide titles. Now just fill in the details. Creating a slide deck helps reduce anxiety. You know the content. You created the content. It is right there in front of you when you present.

Here is a second way to reduce anxiety. Rehearse your presentation three times before you are scheduled to present. The first day will be nerve wracking. The second day you will be much more comfortable. At the start of the third rehearsal, you will feel ready to present, like you are going through the motions. When you start to speak on the day of the presentation, the thoughts and words will flow through you. That is because it is your fourth day presenting that deck. At the end you will be very happy and will feel accomplished.

Here are tips to gently work your way into presenting. In the beginning it all comes down to the size of the audience.

- Lead a meeting: Create a slide deck with the title of the meeting and a purpose slide. Create slides to lead the conversation. Leverage industry resources for content. Embed questions for the team as appropriate. Conclude with a Meeting Minutes slide. Work with the team to create bulleted action items at the end of the meeting. Include a References slide at the end with links to source material.

- Present in a webinar: Presenting in a webinar is less stressful than leading a meeting. The slides are displayed on your computer screen in front of you. Speak to the bullets. If you have rehearsed three days before, this will be easy. You will gain confidence in the process.
- Present at a chapter meeting: This will be your first in-person presentation. Address the causes of anxiety head-on. You will have rehearsed three days in advance. During those sessions, stand and use a wireless remote to advance the slides. Keep in mind the audience is focused on what they learn, what they come away with after the presentation. You have that in your deck and you know the material from rehearsals. Finally, keep in mind this is a small audience of 30-50 people. They will clap and cheer for you at the end.

1.9 COMMUNICATE PROGRAM STATUSES

Communicating progress is another aspect of proving yourself ready now. As an individual contributor, identify an opportunity to identify or mitigate risk and volunteer to lead a project. From there, provide weekly or monthly project statuses. Strive to use existing meeting routines and communications channels. See if you can slip into the team meeting that your manager hosts or another meeting that makes sense. Know your audience. Your manager will be open to an informal update and will be receptive to lower-level detail.

Executives want a more concise update that answers the 'so what' question. If you present to them, it needs to make sense from their side of the table. Providing them with information so they can make a decision or where you need their guidance or support. If there is a problem, executives expect a proposed solution. They are also open to concise progress updates and want to know planned activities for the months ahead.

When you begin to speak to senior executives such as the CISO, CIO or COO, be mindful that they consume information very quickly. Be prepared to communicate 60 minutes of information if you have a 30 minute 1:1 with them. If an executive responds with something concise like 'uh-huh', that's a good thing. Keep going! Match their pace to retain their attention. It's all about their side of the table. When you are preparing for a meeting like that, get a good night's sleep and you will be fine. They are welcoming you and want you to succeed.

You will be called upon to provide a program update in a reoccurring management meeting with the executive. If the format is 5–10 minutes per team, one slide can be a very effective method to communicate. Start with Progress Updates. Consider what your team is doing that adds value to the organization. That section has utility at the end of the year when the executive asks for team accomplishments. You already have that content in program status updates. Include Issues and Challenges in your update. It's good to have these because it shows you're actively managing your program. If you raise a problem, have a solution or even better, two or three options. Be mindful that the leader you're presenting to is also thinking, 'well, what do you need from me'. So if you need something ask for it. Include Next Steps at the bottom of the slide. Provide an informal timeline with activities that will take place over the next three months.

Having attention to detail is very important. Avoid have formatting problems that will distract executives from your message. For example, when there are different bullet types between slides, executives notice it. The problem is when they see it, they are focusing on it and they are looking for what else is out of place and you have lost them. They may consider if this leader is presenting to me and there is something out of place, what other quality issues do they have? It is also important to have accuracy in data and reporting to maintain credibility.

Slide decks should stand alone. When you're presenting program statuses or information to your leadership, there will be times when an executive is not in the meeting and they review it later. Be mindful that your deck may 'get legs' and be forwarded along to another audience.

Have supporting detail in the deck appendix. It is important to anticipate and influence if you want to be effective. Anticipate the type of questions people are likely to ask. For example, if you are presenting a heat map visualization with dots that represent high risk vendors, anticipate that someone will ask, 'who are those high risk vendors'. Have a list in the appendix to refer to.

1.10 HAVE A FOCUS ON THE PROGRAM

It is necessary to have a focus on Program Architecture to build new programs or to take existing programs and make significant changes to them. When you come into a new situation, have a conversation with the executive to ensure you are on the same page. A good way to do that is to create a Mission and Vision Statement. Ask does this resonate with you? Do you have any issues with this? Is there anything we need to change? You're on the right path when you have a mission/vision statement that resonates with your executive. Bring one or two process diagrams to the next conversation. Review those high level processes to go one step deeper with them. It's safe for you to start moving forward when the executive agrees on mission/vision and process.

Continue program design with procedures and a system of record. Typically you will be reporting out security and risk issues. You need a system of record to do that. In the beginning a content management application like SharePoint can provide an interim solution that helps you identify requirements for a formal system of record later. Reporting and metrics provide a certain degree of maturity in the program at this point. When you consider an information security program, there is adherence to frameworks. You need to comply with laws, regulations and contractual obligations. Then you have added risk management controls. There is a high degree of complexity at this point. Layer on quality assurance (QA) to help ensure consistency and process execution. Build in QA at critical control points within processes. That helps ensure activities function in the way that we expect them to.

Establish a Welcome Packet to communicate effectively with the people that are subject to our program. Explain the program's purpose and what their role is. Include mission/vision at the beginning. Transition to the common roles that interact with the program. For each role, explain the person's responsibility what is reasonably expected from them. Then much of the document is how can we help make them successful in doing those things. People will have challenges completing tasks. Provide training and links to supporting documents hosted on your site. The goal is to provide an orientation so people can quickly adapt to your program and know what they need to do. The Welcome Packet is a great resource when onboarding a new contact to your program. Discuss their role and responsibilities. Reference resources in the Welcome Packet to help make them successful. Offer a connection to answer questions and to help them in the future.

Assessments are necessary and they provide value. Assessments are a critical component of information security programs, whether it is the program on the whole or a sub-program such as vulnerability management. Beyond QA, it is necessary to conduct assessments because they identify issues from a different risk lens. When coming to a new organization, it is a good practice to conduct a program assessment based on reputable practices such as the NIST Cybersecurity Framework. Research threat actors that are targeting your organization and their tactics, techniques and procedures. If you want to focus on a given function, the NIST 800 series documents drill down into specific areas of focus such as incident response. Reference the 'Conduct an Assessment' chapter for additional details.

A risk assessment can reveal threats and countermeasures that have not been considered. Controls thought to be in place may not be. Commissioning an assessment is a proactive approach, a sign of ownership. You will have identified control gaps arising from the assessment. That enables you to proactively mitigate risk, which prevents business impact. That activity adds value from an executive's perspective. Focus on maturity and continuous improvement will serve you well.

Use research and analysis to increase program maturity. There are many reputable methodologies available throughout information security domains. At least once per year identify a source document that can be used to evaluate your program. Distill requirements down to bullet points in a slide deck. Meet with your team to discuss which practices should be adopted within your program. Determine 'just do it' initiatives that can be done in the near term with limited effort. Remaining work efforts should be added to next year's annual program goals. That leaves time for resource and funding allocation. Research and analysis should be a positive experience for the team, not something that incurs unnecessary stress or working nights and weekends.

1.11 USE EXECUTIVE TOOLS

Failure Mode and Effects Analysis (FMEA): FMEA is an executive tool that can be used to influence support and funding. Review a critical process where a cybersecurity incident or fraud could occur. Start with a process diagram that has 15-20 steps in it. Ask six people to review the process diagram by this methodology. They review the process diagram off on their own with the FMEA spreadsheet. They determine how each process step could fail. For each failure mode, what would be the severity, rate of occurrence and rate of detection. The numeric values of those three elements multiplied together is the Risk Priority Number (RPN). Give the team two weeks. All six people can e-mail their content in to have it combined into one spreadsheet, sorted by the RPN. Have a meeting with the team to discuss ways to reduce the risk. There are a variety of techniques to do that, add a process step, add a tool or add quality assurance for example. Choose three or four FMEA entries to solve for. Have a meeting with executives to quickly provide an overview of FMEA, with a slide for each issue. Discuss how we plan to mitigate the risk of each issue. Conclude with how risk has been reduced in total reduction of RPN. For example, we have reduced risk by 32%. That measurement can be very compelling. If there is a strong positive reaction from management, consider conducting FMEA with other processes over the next few years (Figure 1.4).

Process Step or System Component	Potential Failure Mode	Potential Effect (s) of Failure	Severity	Potential Cause (s) of Failure	Occurrence	Current Process Controls	Detection	RPN
High risk escalation	High risk issue is not escalated	Acme is exposed to significant risk	4	Employee does not follow established procedure	2	Quality assurance inspection	1	8

Potential Failure Mode: How could a failure occur?
Potential Effect(s) of Failure: What are the consequences of failure?
Severity: How severe would the impact be on a scale of 1 to 5?
Potential Cause(s) of Failure: What would be the cause of the failure?
Occurrence: What is the probability of failure occurring on a scale of 1 to 5?
Current Process Controls: What controls are in place to detect failure?
Detection: What is the probability of failure being detected on a scale of 1 to 5?

FMEA calculates a Risk Priority Number (RPN) for each process step or system component using this simple technique:

Risk Context:

- FMEA is a practical way to conduct a process risk assessment
- Failure modes are rated by Severity, Occurrence and Detection. That results in a Risk Priority Number
- Use RPN scores to prioritize remediation. The highest RPN values correspond to issues with the greatest potential for business impact
- Gives voice to known/suppressed risk issues

Figure 1.4 Failure mode and effects analysis (FMEA).

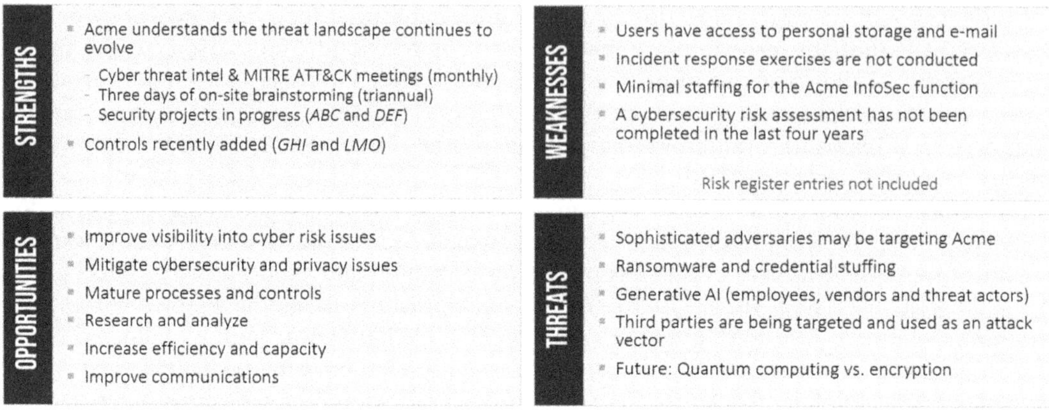

Figure 1.5 SWOT analysis (Strengths, Weaknesses, Opportunities and Threats).

SWOT Analysis: SWOT analysis is a powerful, simple tool that is used by executives. SWOT provides risk transparency at a high level. It can be used to present a program summary when a new executive joins the team. As an example, here's where we are strong, here's where we have some challenges, here is where I could use some support. SWOT also has utility at the end of an assessment report meeting to provide an overview of current state. SWOT is often used within annual updates for C-level executives and boards of directors. Introduce SWOT into your program communications and use the precedence to make it an annual occurrence. SWOT highlights opportunities for improvement, which may result in increased support and funding (Figure 1.5).

1.12 FOCUS ON PROFESSIONAL DEVELOPMENT

If you want to prove yourself ready now for promotion, it's important for you to identify areas of professional development and gain the skills necessary for your next role. Each of us should always have a mentor. It is best to have a mentor within your organization. Use performance and development plans to focus your efforts. None of us are meant to keep the lights on. The performance plan helps highlight your contributions to drive the program forward. When you attain those goals it should be obvious how you made significant changes that identify or mitigate risk. Have three to five goals, with at least two tough goals where you push and drive change in a good way, to benefit the company.

On January 2nd (the start of the performance year), you have one of three choices. Choice # 1 is you are going to stay in your current role as an individual contributor. Choice # 2 is you want to move laterally to another team. Choice # 3 is you want to pursue leadership (no promises). If you want to pursue promotion to leadership, welcome to the long and painful road. It is a difficult path. You must demonstrate leadership over time before an executive will have faith in giving you a team. They do that out of care and to protect emerging leaders against failure. Having selected one of those three choices, you can now begin work on a development plan. If you want to stay in your current role, how could you be more effective in that position? If you want to move to another team, perhaps a call to that manager is in order. What new skills do you need to be considered when a position opens on that team? Is there an opportunity to work on a project or to fulfill an alternate duty on that team? If you want to pursue leadership, that begins with consistent high performance in your current role.

From there, it is necessary to create performance and development plans that help prove you ready now for promotion. You will need advice and coaching to establish those plans. Ask your supervisor 'what behaviors do I need to prepare for my next role'.

Ask your mentor to help identify your areas of professional development with 'Stop, Start, Continue' feedback. Most of us do not have the self-awareness that we need. We have blind spots and therefore cannot improve in those areas. This is a simple methodology. Ask someone that is separate from your team to send an e-mail to people that you select and to consolidate the responses into anonymous feedback. There are three simple questions in that message:

- What should *name* start doing?
- What should *name* stop doing?
- What should *name* continue doing?

Once you have that agreement in place, reach out to your contacts and ask them to give constructive criticism to support your professional development. Good candidates to provide feedback include business partners, people that work within your process and people that may not be entirely a fan of yours, but you can tell it is not personal. Those are good people to get feedback from. Requesting 'Start, Stop, Continue' feedback is a sign of professional courage. When the survey e-mail arrives, prepare yourself for negative feedback. Remember that you asked your contacts to please be honest and give constructive criticism in areas where they see that you need to develop professionally. Two of the three survey questions are negative. By simple math, you will receive 66% negative feedback. Meet with your mentor soon after receiving that e-mail. Do not take that feedback as a 'to do' list. Your mentor will help you identify themes and trends that you should be addressing.

If you have consistent performance year-over-year, you will build momentum. Strong performance and recognition awards lead to promotion. Keep that in mind as you are writing your performance plans. It's a marathon, not a sprint.

Put yourself at risk. If you go through a year and do not feel stressed out and anxious about one or more goals you have signed up for, you are not stretching yourself enough.

Keep learning! That is part of the information security career field. Wherever you are today, you will need to pick up on new techniques and technologies as you move through your career. There will be continuous change.

Here are leadership attributes you should be exhibiting:

- Focus on program maturity and risk transparency
- Be proactive, anticipate management routines and requirements
- Anticipate problems and questions
- Act with a sense of urgency, drive projects and issues to closure
- Be a Mentor, known for coaching and developing employees

1.13 BE KNOWN

There is a Performance Calibration process within most organizations. At the end of the year each employee is assigned a rating such as 'Exceptional', 'Meets' and 'Does not meet'. There are a small percentage of people that can achieve that highest rating. As you would suspect, leaders are going to rate too many employees in aggregate to fit into that percentage. Therefore it is necessary to have a meeting to calibrate or to determine which of those exceptional candidates are actually going to receive that rating.

In some cases a performance calibration session will not go well for an employee. The leader gets up and says 'let me tell you about my exceptional candidate, he or she has done *X*, *Y* and *Z* and there's been the following benefits'. At that point, one of the executives reacts and sheepishly says 'I'm sorry. I don't really know who that is'. From that example it's easy think 'well that's not a very good manager. they should have let people know what this person was doing, what value they were providing within communications routines throughout the year'. That is true. However, if the candidate got that far and people don't know who they are then there is a problem there too. That may rest with the candidate being introverted. Everyone needs to be their own advocate. To prove yourself ready now for promotion, you are challenged to become known within your company as a change agent, as a partner. It is important for information security leaders to be considered part of the solution with IT and business unit executives.

Gain validation through certifications, articles and presentations. Be social. If you work remotely, travel into the office. Get out of the cubes. Get out of the conference rooms. Have coffee and lunch with people. If you have a one-on-one scheduled, consider meeting outside or on a walk. Go to company events. If there is a company Town Hall, stay there for that social networking period afterward. You have friends and colleagues at a minimum that you can spend time with. You can have a conversation with your manager. Have a conversation with his/her peer managers. Go to local information security chapter meetings and conferences. Most of them are very reasonably priced. Ask your manager, often times they will fund it. Go to conferences. You should know everyone in your local security community. Post articles and cybersecurity resources on LinkedIn. Check the web statistics and see how many people from your organization are reading it. What's strange is you can become known through an external service. It's like a boomerang.

1.14 PREPARE FOR C-LEVEL PRESENTATION

If you think of all the activity that you have been through earlier in this chapter, presenting to executives does not seem so daunting. You are ready to go to the 50th floor of an office building and to sit across a table from a C-level executive. You are much more prepared now. Obviously you need to be mindful of the audience. When you are speaking with a C-level executive, they speak very quickly and they consume information very quickly. For example, they may say 'OK, OK'. Pick up on those cues to deliver information much more quickly. Have a risk-based focus. Present a straightforward message. Often times you will present a program status or a problem and a solution such as a very significant high risk issue that needs to be remediated now and it costs money. Then you want to give the executive information to make a decision. Ideally you are not coming and saying here's what we need to do, you're saying here's a few options that you can choose from.

Leadership will gauge you by executive presence and emotional intelligence. Provide context. Tell a story. Speak in terms of 'here's the threat landscape and adversaries that are targeting us. As a result of that we had the following incident. Here is what we have done to correct that and to prevent reoccurrence'. Walk them down a road. Provide details like trend reporting if you are trying to make a point. Include narrative so the deck stands alone if forwarded to another audience. Do not forget these themes when it really matters. Anticipate questions. Have hip pocket material in the appendix of the deck. Have a sounding board. Ask leaders to preview your deck. You may even have a dry run.

1.15 PREPAREDNESS

The secret to success is to be prepared. Develop the skill set you need to get the job done. Continue to learn and build experience to prepare you for the next role. Set a high standard for yourself, continuous improvement. Your peers are a distraction.

Anticipate new requirements by considering what senior management or business partners are likely to do. Here are sample responses to a spontaneous request, with corresponding ratings:

- 'I'll get on that right away'. - Acceptable
- 'I have already started working on it'. - Good
- 'I've got it. Here it is...' - Great!

Base estimates on known data and business cycles (e.g. the fiscal year). Take note of unanticipated requirements for next year and prepare accordingly. When a new senior manager is assigned, ask what their management routines are (Figure 1.6).

Be a Change Agent. Each of us is hired to drive change. C-level executives do not want employees to stay static, to merely keep the lights on. Embrace change, thrive on it, benefit from it. Adapt and overcome. Architect a plan, lead and influence change. Drive change in yourself, in your program, in others around you. Senior executives will recognize you, promote you, give you bonuses and stock options. Know what you want and close on it.

Strong performance requires consistency and hard work. Don't let a day go to waste. Learn new skills, have professional courage and lead change. **Your actions define you.**

Figure 1.6 Professional courage.

Chapter 2

Team development and retention

2.1 INTRODUCTION

This chapter provides leaders with practical advice for developing employees in their current role, with tips to help them move laterally or to pursue promotion to management. The focus shifts to management routines throughout a calendar year, including performance and development plans, communications, financial acumen, talent review and program architecture. The chapter begins to conclude with performance calibration, succession planning, promotions and retention risk.

If you are an individual contributor with a goal of being promoted to leadership, there is a significant value in this chapter. There are also activities behind the scenes that you should know about in your current role.

2.2 GETTING TO KNOW YOUR REPORTS

When transitioning to lead an existing team, it is a good practice have a meeting with the prior leader. Left to their own devices, they will typically provide an overview of the program and which projects are underway. Ask the prior leader to provide an overview of each employee, their strengths and areas of professional development. It can be helpful to get his or her opinion and learn of experiences with each of the employees.

Next, access the Human Resources web application and review each employee's performance and development ratings from last year. Within a week of taking over the team have 1:1 meetings with each of your new reports. It is important to have those conversations quickly after taking over the team. Think about the other side of the table. It is a stressful time for employees when new supervisor is assigned to lead the team. Before that time, the team is stable and now there is uncertainty. It is a good approach to have an open conversation with each person and to help ease that stress and to start to get to know each other.

Develop an understanding of each employee's current state of professional development in that first meeting. These are people we are responsible for and quickly grow to care about. Determine what stage they are in their career. A recent college graduate may have only been with the organization for a year or two. A mid-term individual contributor has three to five years of experience. A senior staff member has five or more years of experience. Consider who is sitting across from the other side of the table. Determine their background and experience. We need to treat all employees the same, fairly and equitably. With that being said, people have differing areas of professional development that must be accounted for and nurtured. It is important for a leader to have that focus.

DOI: 10.1201/9781003543619-2

Next, focus on the motivations of each employee. Some team members are hard charging and career oriented. That becomes apparent when you first sit down with them. They want to prove themselves ready now for promotion. Other team members may be technology focused and are highly-qualified professionals. Some employees may want to remain in technology, with no desire to pursue a leadership position. It is important to understand the motivations of each employee to support their career aspirations.

Understand the person at the other side of the table. There are phases of life to account for. Some employees are family oriented. They need work-life balance to support young children. Others have aging parents. Good leaders provide flexibility and support for their employees. It is a matter of integrity, doing the right thing when no one is looking. Supporting a healthy work-life balance fosters employee retention as well.

2.3 1:1s WITH REPORTS (JANUARY)

New year, we start fresh

Leaders should have a 1:1 meeting with each of their employees at the beginning of each year. It is a new year and we are starting fresh. Last year gone and forgotten from a business perspective, good, bad or indifferent. It is like a phoenix rising from the ashes. There is a nervous excitement at the beginning of the year. It is opportunity knocking. There is just so much ahead of us that we can do. Hopefully some of that comes across genuinely when you have those conversations.

Career goals moving forward

Ask each person about their career goals. That can be a very meaningful conversation if it is a new employee. For existing employees, it is a reset where we recap career goals from the last year and ask if the employee is still on that same path. Is that still what you want to do? It is healthy to have a refresh at the beginning of the year.

You have three options

Begin to focus career aspirations into actionable goals. Give each employee three career goal options at the start of the year:

- Stay in your current role
- Move laterally to another team
- Pursue leadership (no promises)

If the employee wants to stay in their current job for the next few years, we can focus on honing their skill set to be the best they can be in their current role. If they have a goal of transitioning laterally to another team, we will chart a path for that.

If the employee wants to pursue leadership, there are no promises. That is a challenging and difficult road. It takes a minimum of two to three years to be promoted from individual contributor to manager. It is necessary to be very good at your current job. That consistent performance lays the foundation. You also need to demonstrate leadership, which can be challenging as an individual contributor. Make your own opportunities by identifying the need for change and by leading projects. Deliver on projects that provide value, are challenging and demonstrate leadership. That is a big takeaway for those of you looking to prove themselves ready now for promotion.

Executives look for consistent high performance and leadership year-over-year as a prerequisite for promotion. They want new managers to thrive and excel in their new role. Executives care and will not promote an employee before they are ready.

Meet in a casual setting

It is a good practice to meet 1:1 with each employee at least very two weeks. Try to meet in a casual setting if you both work in the office or have a hybrid office/remote schedule. Employees have the option to meet in an office or conference room, especially if they want to screen share. Otherwise, suggest the option to go for a walk or to have a conversation in a coffee shop. Some employees will provide strong positive feedback on that approach, so think about work life and retention. Small things have an aggregate effect of having a good impact on a person's work life. Some people really love to go for a walk or to sit down and have a coffee.

Time waits for no one

Some organizations have a slow start to the year. There is a culture where everything is on hold until strategic goals are sent down from senior executives. In that environment managers are reluctant to start anything new until February. High level business goals have minimal impact on information security. We know our team members, our program, mission and vision. We focus on identifying and mitigating risk in the cyber domain. Therefore we should have program, performance and development plan goals in place at the start of the year. On January 2nd, begin to execute on those goals. If it is necessary to make minor course corrections when strategic goals are sent later, so be it. We can adapt and make use of those two months. This philosophy can be an advantage. Be discrete and execute toward your goals. Individual contributors take note.

Be advised that your performance plan does not cover 365 days in practice. While it may display January 1st through December 31st, performance ratings are assigned before that. Many organizations have the highest performance rating tied to a bonus structure. Human resources will only allow a small percentage of employees to be assigned that highest rating, such as ten percent. A performance calibration meeting is held with managers and executives to assign ratings as early as October. If you were to wait to start executing on your goals in March and you have until October, that is not much time, right? So make use of all of January and February. Remember that October is where executives snap the chalk line on performance ratings. Focusing on goal execution from January to October provides a better work-life balance as well. Adopting this philosophy is a competitive advantage. Do not leave opportunity on the table.

2.4 PERFORMANCE PLANS

Performance and development plans are something that your organization may take very seriously or they may go through the motions in a checkbox exercise. One of the core ways to drive your career forward is to set clear performance and professional development goals. Being a change agent, delivering results and developing new skills drives your career forward. Consistent high performance provides benefits such as performance bonus and promotion.

Plans of execution

An employee performance plan is a plan of execution. Performance goals should be designed to deliver meaningful results. Consider what you are going to do to identify and mitigate risk. Identify which actions are necessary to achieve the goal. Consider the outcome, the business value that will be delivered once the goal is achieved.

Above and beyond core duties

Performance plans are intended to go beyond minimum job requirements, beyond keeping the lights on. Here are high-level examples that are business focused:

- Create or significantly improve a process to generate revenue
- Increase efficiency to expand scope or reduce cost
- Establish new capabilities to identify or mitigate risk

That last example reflects the value-add of information security from an operational risk perspective.

Provide value: Answer the 'So what' question

When drafting your performance goals, consider what the value is from a business perspective. Senior executives think in terms of the 'So what' question. The tone of that question may seem a bit harsh at first but it is a good measure. Executives live in an unforgiving world. They must provide products and services that generate a significant profit. Each day they must make difficult decisions among competing priorities. Information security people, processes and technology cost money and have an effect on the bottom line. Therefore, it is very reasonable for executives to question the business value of any initiative that comes across their desk. What value is this providing? What kind of change are we driving here? So with that in mind, the 'So what' question seems practical and relevant now. Consider the view from the executive's side of the table when creating your performance goals.

Management by results

Management by results leaves optics and perception-based performance behind. For example, a manager may ask an employee why they were ten minutes late to work. If they were not late to a meeting and their performance is high, being ten minutes late is not worth questioning. In fact, that question can frustrate a hard working employee, having an impact on their job satisfaction.

Strong leaders evaluate employees based on their core duties and achievement of performance and development goals. Management by results is a great for remote workers. It does not matter if the message chat software light is yellow, indicating the employee is away. The measure is focused on whether they are doing their job, whether they are producing results.

Management by results supports employee work-life balance. Most employees gauge their supervisor and their company on the ability to work flexibly. They want the ability to care for their children when they are sick, to go to medical appointments and the other challenges that arise in everyone's personal life. A good, caring supervisor supports their employees as long as the work gets done. That is doing the right thing for your employees and it is also great for their work life and for retention.

2.5 PERFORMANCE GOALS

Take time each year to create purpose-driven performance goals. A performance plan fills your plate with initiatives that you want to work on. That plan also charts a path for accomplishments, which can result in a substantial bonus at the end of the year. Strong performance year-over-year may also lead to promotion and the benefits that come with it.

If you have direct reports, teach them how to create meaningful goals on their own. Identify three to five goals to make changes that provide value to the business. Provide metrics and targets so it is clear whether each goal was met or exceeded.

Creating goals

An employee may experience writer's block when working on performance goals. In that case, the supervisor should provide strategic goals to inspire them. Here are examples to consider:

• Improve visibility into cyber risk issues	• Research and analyze
• Mitigate cybersecurity and privacy issues	• Increase efficiency and capacity
• Mature processes and controls	• Improve communications

The employee should think about their team, about what they do day-to-day, areas where the team has challenges and opportunities for improvement. That focus and mindset will cause ideas to flow.

A new employee or recent college grad may not have experience with performance goals. The supervisor can define the goal, the problem it is intended to solve for. However, the employee should determine how to accomplish the goal. It is important for them to chart the path and develop that leadership skill.

Creating metrics and targets

Each performance goal must include a metric and a target. At the end of the year it must be clear whether the goal was met or exceeded. Here are examples with differing metric and target measurements:

Goal # 1: Influence Risk Mitigation

Security issues either need to be remediated within standards or documented with a Plan of Action and Milestones with executive sign-off.
Metric: 90% or higher
Target: 8 months in 2050

Goal # 2: Establish a Third Party Risk Management Program

Document a formal methodology. Author a procedures manual.
Metric: Identification of security issues
Target: Existence of third party assessments
Stretch Goal: Conduct a pilot and enter into production

Goal # 3: Increase Program Maturity

- Finalize high and mid-level processes; include control points
- Document communications and training plans

- Establish a program welcome packet
- Establish a quality assurance program

Metric: Completion of sub-goals
Target: 3 sub-goals

Goal # 4: Establish a Program Slide Deck

Establish a program 'walk-around' deck, intended to address any audience on short notice.
Metric: Enhanced representation of the <function> program, enabling orientation and process improvements
Target: Creation of a program slide deck in PowerPoint format
Stretch Goal: Presentation of the program to executive leadership, taking point for answering questions

So, we are going to have this person establish a program overview deck. The stretch goal is where this crosses into an area of professional development if the employee is a bit introverted.

Executives have keen insights and can ask thought-provoking questions. It can seem intense in the moment. Aspiring leaders need to account for a scenario where a senior leader asks them a question that requires a moment of thought or research, with an update to follow later. An individual contributor may need to develop those question-and-answer skills following a presentation. That is a foundational skill for promotion.

2.6 DEVELOPMENT PLANS

Focusing on your areas of professional development is a significant way to have a rewarding career and the benefits that come with that. Remember the three options from earlier in the chapter:

- Stay in your current role
- Move laterally to another team
- Pursue leadership (no promises)

The answer to those options at the beginning of the year define where that employee wants to go. An employee's career goal is the destination. The development plan helps chart a path to get them there. It may take years. It will take hard work. The development plan should have two to three professional development goals to accomplish in a year. Those are the skills and capabilities needed for the next role.

Here are high level questions to consider. How can I get better? How can I prove myself ready-now for my next role? Here are sample goals for individual contributors pursuing leadership:

Goal # 1: Demonstrate Cybersecurity Expertise

Objective: Develop information security management skills.
Action: Obtain the Certified Information Security Manager (CISM) certification

- Study from a CISM book and a collection of CISM exam prep questions
- Attend a CISM training course

This goal is all about what the employee learns. Pursuing a certification makes them find time to develop skills. If the employee wants to pursue cybersecurity leadership, obtaining the knowledge necessary to pass the CISM exam is a good start.

Funding is required for the cost of the exam, study materials and training. It is necessary to gather the costs and to receive funding approval before finalizing this goal as written.

Goal # 2: Demonstrate Financial Acumen

Objective: Develop an understanding of financial practices and requirements.
Action: Enhance financial acumen:

- Annual budget process
  - When initial budget requests are due
  - Elements of a budget request
  - Year-end use or lose (opportunity)
- How cybersecurity financials are managed
  - Tracking initiatives and burn rate
  - Forecasting, etc.
- Obtain a financial mentor

An individual contributor should know the annual budget process as a prerequisite to being promoted to a management role. Leaders understand the elements of a budget request and monitor for when they are due. They must manage their budget throughout the year. Leaders track burn rate to ensure that approved funding is consumed within budgetary constraints, month by month as expected.

The employee will need a financial mentor to complete this goal. Give them the name of the finance person that supports the information security team. When you are a manager people do not part the Red Sea for you, right? You have to chart your own path. That includes introducing yourself and talking to people that you do not know. Managers ask for help and admit they have something that needs to be improved. The employee needs to exercise those interpersonal skills. Leave it to them to ask for support.

Goal # 3: Communicates Through Public Speaking

Objective: Communicates information through presentations and slide decks. Able to present in a variety of formats (e.g. project progress update and educational presentation). Engages the audience. Exhibits confidence when presenting and encourages questions.
Action: Enhance public speaking skills:

- Provides a project update at a team meeting
- Presents cybersecurity at a new hire orientation
- <Presents on a cybersecurity topic in a webinar>
- <Joins Toastmasters and completes five speeches>
- <Presents at an in-person cybersecurity event (stretch goal)>
- <Obtains the Toastmasters Competent Communicator Award (stretch goal)>

Managers present in group meetings. Individual contributors that want to transition to leading a team should proactively develop that skill at a moderate pace. It is much easier to learn before promotion than to be called upon to present in a Town Hall with one week's notice. Fair warning…

2.7 MAINTAIN A CONNECTION

Maintaining a connection is something that really defines a leader. Teams function effectively and employee satisfaction is supported when communications routines are in-place.

It is a good practice to have weekly team meetings for 30 minutes, with a round-robin discussion. What's going on, what are you working on? Do you need help, do you need support? Those types interactions are very popular. People are encouraged to say, hey I'm having problems and receive the guidance and support they need. Team members need help with projects and funding. There may be capacity challenges, where people are working nights and weekends. When managers really engage, the team is productive and there can be a feeling of camaraderie and esprit de corps (Figure 2.1).

Now even though there is a weekly team meeting, employees need a half hour one-on-one at least every two weeks. That is an opportunity to have a conversation with the employee more privately. How are your performance and your development goals coming along? Any advice or support on escalation that you need from me? It is also a good practice to ask about the employee's job satisfaction every six months. If the supervisor is hesitant to ask, that is a sign of an underlying problem that may fester over time.

Most organizations have mid-year performance reviews. How this discussion is conducted is a measure of the supervisor. When the meeting begins some supervisors will mention they are busy and the employee is doing fine. They ask the employee to acknowledge the review

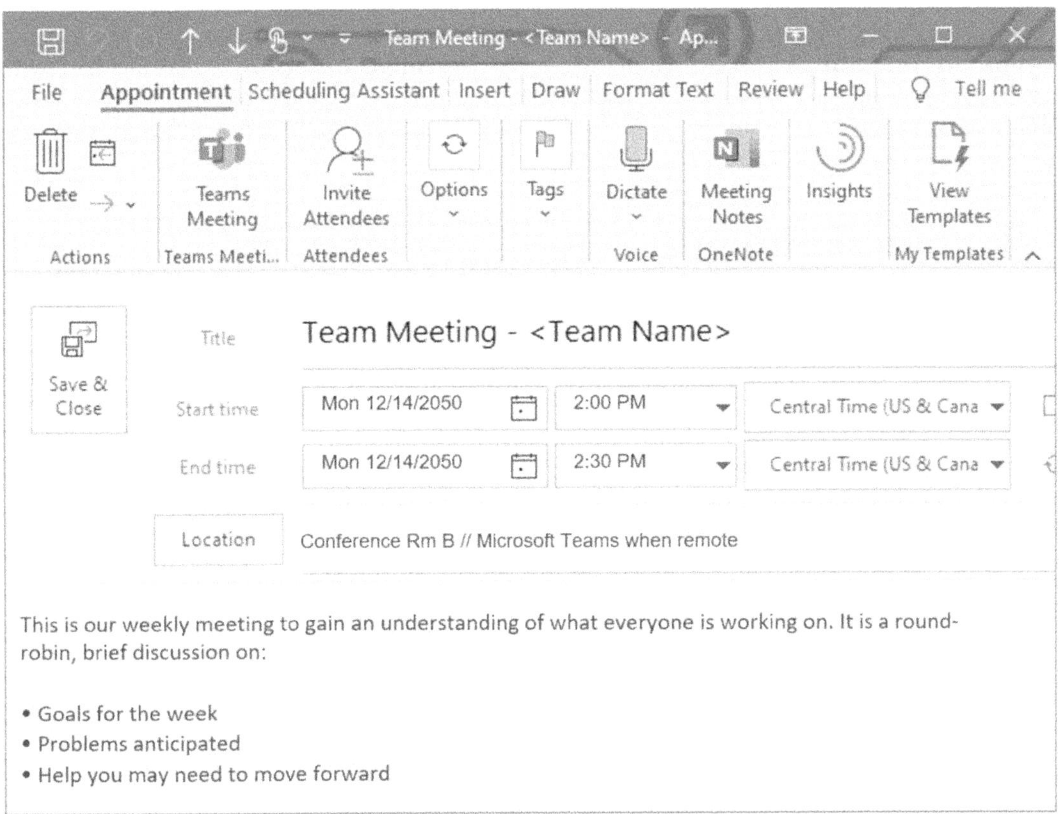

Figure 2.1 Team meeting.

in the human resources web application and conclude the call. That is a failed performance review, obviously.

Try this approach. Ask the employee to come to the meeting prepared to give a status of each of their performance and development plan goals, including current rating. The supervisor can agree or have a dissenting opinion. For example, that performance goal is not quite complete yet or I am not seeing you demonstrate those behaviors for that development goal. The conversation should quickly shift to next steps to make the employee successful before the end of the ratings period. That is a meaningful conversation in a mid-year performance review.

Team meetings and 1:1s help maintain engagement and team cohesion while working remote.

2.8 ANNUAL PLANNING (AUGUST)

Establish annual program goals

Setting annual goals is key to effective communication and provides a solid foundation to drive change forward. Begin planning well in advance of when annual goals are due to executive leadership. For example, if goals are due in early November, begin planning in August with an iterative approach (Figure 2.2).

The expression 'Plan the work, Work the plan' will serve you well. When a program has been initially established in the first year or two, the basic framework is in place. You need to determine how to drive this program forward to make good use of the company's resources, to mitigate risk and to provide value. Start by scheduling a meeting to brainstorm with your team. Use one of the team meetings to mention getting together to plan for next year's information security program goals. Provide six strategic goals that will be used to frame the conversation. Here are examples to consider:

• Improve visibility into cyber risk issues	• Research and analyze
• Mitigate cybersecurity and privacy issues	• Increase efficiency and capacity
• Mature processes and controls	• Improve communications

Increasing efficiency and capacity is a business-focused goal. We must be good stewards of the company's money, making every effort to spend it as if it were our own. Maturing processes and controls are a focus on continuous improvement. Identifying risk keeps pace with emerging threats and changes in technology. We can always improve on risk mitigation, influencing the necessary resources and funding. Deploying controls based on risk requires

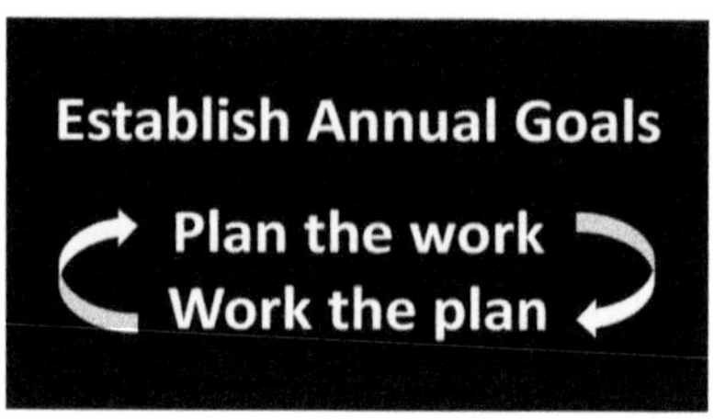

Figure 2.2 Plan the work, work the plan.

visibility into where data is present and keeping up with new features and functionality in our cybersecurity software. There is always an opportunity to improve program communications.

Here are questions to further develop information security program goals:

- What actions should be taken based on cybersecurity advisories?
- What are the trends within threat landscape reports?
- Which mitigations should be implemented from the MITRE ATT&CK Framework?
- What is our maturity level throughout domains and functions?
- Which new technologies may be disruptive?

Provide the six topics and questions a week or two in advance. Schedule an all-day meeting, in-person if possible. Get pizza for lunch and funding for dinner. Walk through the six topics, 45 minutes per topic. It is very important to have breaks so that people do not burn out. This approach provides great results because people realize that 'it's our team', 'it's our program'. There is a reason that the team is in place. They are bright professionals and we should be making use of their ideas. As they contribute goals, record it in a spreadsheet. There is no such thing as a bad goal, this is a brainstorming session. Document the person who submitted each goal. People should have ownership of their ideas, especially with initiatives that will significantly drive the program forward. Having names associated with program goals helps with performance calibration. The employee has an opportunity to achieve that goal or to lead a project to make it happen.

There will be many goals, in some cases too many to achieve next year. They can be used within a multi-generational plan, in years two or three. Once draft goals have been established within the team, discuss them in a touch base meeting with the program executive. 'Here's what I'm thinking of for goals next year. Do you see any significant issues?'

Next, discuss goals with support partners and leaders that may be impacted. They may add a shared goal to their plan or may need to include it in their budget request for next year. A good time to do this is three or four months in advance of when annual goals and budget requests are due. That leaves time to establish goals that are known and supported.

Establish employee performance plans

Distribute program goals throughout the team in performance plans. Assignment of goals helps grow employees from career and professional development perspectives. Achievement of goals provides accomplishments in consideration of performance ratings and bonuses. Project leadership helps prove individual contributors 'ready now' for promotion. If someone had an idea for a program goal, give them the opportunity to solve for it. Do you want this in your performance plan? Do you want to chase this alone or do you want to run a project? People enjoy turning their ideas into accomplishments, especially if they are recognized and rewarded.

Monitor, coach and represent

The team leader monitors program execution, projects and achievement of annual goals. Display an Initiatives Portfolio during weekly meetings and ask team members to provide a quick status. Monitor and coach team members 1:1. Throughout the year, act as a point of escalation, provide resources, represent and defend the program. Manage up, provide dissenting opinions on fire drills and unfunded mandates.

This three-tiered approach enables the team to accomplish goals throughout the year without the leader being in the critical path. Each team member owns their role, responsibilities and goals. Accordingly, they gain recognition and rewards for their efforts.

2.9 ON-SITE WORKING SESSIONS

On-site working sessions are a great way to collaborate and to drive your program forward as a team. Host on-site meetings on Tuesday, Wednesday and Thursday to leave time for remote travel within the work week. Schedule meetings to occur the same week as an executive routine such as a cybersecurity committee meeting. Schedule time for each team member to lead a session to be inclusive. Minimize reoccurring working sessions to keep things fresh. Have a tabletop exercise on-site at least once per year.

It can seem daunting to schedule three days of on-site meetings. The goal is to keep the information security program current. Focus on emerging threats, countermeasures and new technologies. Reputable practices can be used to identify and mitigate risk and to adapt to changes in the threat landscape. Here are inputs for on-site working sessions:

• NIST	• Regulations
• CISA	• Laws
• NSA	• Contractual Obligations
• IT vendors	• Benchmark reports
• Managed service providers	• Maturity models
• Universities	

Reference 'Goals and Working Sessions' in the appendix for a list of sample meeting topics.

Encourage meeting leaders to create a slide deck to frame the conversation and to provide an artifact for attendees to reference later. Each deck should include meeting minutes with action items to drive change.

Working sessions should produce service desk tickets for 'just do it' initiatives and research. Conduct a 60 minute out-brief meeting with the program executive(s) within a week of the on-site. This approach keeps everyone engaged and contributing to development of the program. It also lays the groundwork for the next committee meeting. Enter projects and annual goals into established processes and meeting routines.

2.10 TALENT REVIEW MEETING (OCTOBER)

Performance calibration

Only the highest performing employees will make the cut and receive a rating such as 'Exceptional'. Only five or ten percent of people can receive that performance rating and there are bonuses tied to it. When managers enter initial ratings for their teams, the number of combined submissions is too high. The group executive hosts a Performance Calibration Meeting to finalize which employees will receive Exceptional ratings within the threshold limit.

The meeting begins and managers present their candidates for Exceptional ratings around the room. Each employee's accomplishments are discussed versus their peers. The analogy is when a child plays a sport in the backyard and does well versus when they play with a group of children and perform worse than the others. Some candidates will not be approved for an Exceptional rating. There is not enough space in the threshold limit.

As a manager you need to be good at managing the expectations of employees that work for you. They may exceed their performance plan but not the performance of their peers across the group. If you believe one of your reports has Exceptional performance, bring a list of significant accomplishments to the Performance Calibration Meeting. Answer the 'so what' question. Do not provide opportunity for one of your peer managers or the executive to 'sink a Talon', like a bird of prey. If you present something weak, someone will point out that accomplishment out and say, I don't think that is significant. Most likely your employee will not receive an Exceptional rating due to competition among the peers and the rating threshold limit.

Another area of risk is if someone says they do not know who a candidate is. If an employee is demonstrating Exceptional performance, the managers and executives in the group should know who they are. The manager should mention the employee's accomplishments in meeting routines throughout the year. The employee should make themselves known as well.

Promotions

The executive will ask who is ready-now for promotion. There is a focus on the career and professional development of the employees. Retention risk is a consideration as well. Managers need to be prepared for that conversation in the meeting. Raise the topic of promotions in advance during a 1:1 meeting with the executive so you are already on the same page.

Succession planning

The executive will ask each manager who their successor is. It is important to groom a successor for continuity, for the career and professional development of that employee and if you want to transition internally to another role. If you do not have a successor immediately available, mention a member of your team that will be ready in a year or two or provide the name of an employee elsewhere within the organization that is ready-now (Figure 2.3).

The notion of this cartoon should be true, right? S/he gives their heart and soul to every annual performance review. So, if you think of the life of a manager, at the beginning of the year you are helping your reports write performance and development plans, you are having a meaningful mid-year conversations with them, you are talking and listening at team meetings, every two weeks you have a one-on-one conversation and then you are influencing on their behalf in performance calibration sessions.

Grooming employees for career and professional development takes significant effort. It can be stressful on the supervisor when combined with management routines. Please

Figure 2.3 Performance review.

appreciate that. This is what we should be doing and sometimes it is exhausting. This is who we should be as leaders.

2.11 RETENTION RISK

Retention risk represents the potential that an employee will leave the organization. There is a loss of institutional knowledge when that occurs. It takes significant time and effort to train a replacement. This section focuses on why an employee may leave for another organization and what supervisors can do to mitigate that risk.

Salary and bonuses

Employees typically two or three percent salary increase each year to keep pace with inflation. Human Resources rewards strong performance with annual bonuses. Employees fresh out of college and some individual contributors may not understand that incentive structure so it is important to communicate that with them. Supervisors may also reduce retention risk by effectively representing high performing employees in performance calibration meetings, which determine who will receive Exceptional ratings and higher-level bonuses.

Promotion

Promotions occur when an employee is ready-now (Chapter 1). Those seeking promotion must demonstrate consistent strong performance in their current role and two to three years of demonstrating leadership. A suitable leadership role must be available for them to transition into of course. Executives are conservative when promoting individual contributors into a management role. They want the employee to be successful and are protective of employees because they care. Communicate these concepts to hard charging employees to manage their expectations.

Work-life balance

Work-life balance is a key driver for most employees. They want the ability to work flexibly. Employees are required to fulfill responsibilities and operational activities within their role. Employees are also expected to complete their performance and development plan goals. Managers should empower them to work flexibility providing those requirements are met. Encourage employees to actively support their children. Provide flexibility to attend local chapter events and conferences. This approach drives employee satisfaction and reduces retention risk.

Recognition

Leaders have control over recognition. Recognize employees in team meetings and town halls. Submit recognition awards one month before performance calibration. Recognition awards have a cumulative effect that may help an employee receive a higher performance rating (and bonus). Recognize employees in other teams and departments as a matter of 'doing the right thing'.

Team cohesion

Being a member of a team with camaraderie and esprit de corps is a career highlight. Host weekly team meetings. Work together to establish program goals for next year. Encourage team members to partner on projects and to mentor each other. Host team dinners and events so that people get to see each other and spend time together. Go bowling or to a local baseball game. Foster an atmosphere where employees enjoy their work life.

Tools and training

Some employees are highly technical and want to remain that way. They need modern tools and training to identify and mitigate risk. Penetration testers are a great example. Threat actor tools and tactics continually change. Newly adopted technology must be secured. Every organization must invest in their information security program to provide protection in alignment with risk tolerance. It is necessary to fund tools and training for the program to remain effective. Highly skilled information security professionals are difficult to replace. Be mindful of their needs for tools and training.

'Corporate tax'

Corporate tax is the pain incurred by employees when working for a bureaucratic organization. Examples of corporate tax include:

- Unnecessary meetings
- Salary range restrictions by job code
- Transfer to a new role without option
- Mandatory training that is not applicable
- Multiple reviews required for
  - Presenting at conferences
  - Writing articles
- Freezes
  - Hiring
  - Travel
  - Training and conferences
- Expense policies
  - $75 and less should not require a receipt
  - Provide reasonable per diem

Leaders must be advocates for employee work life. That includes questioning the status quo. Job code salary ranges are often outdated. Give feedback to Human Resources. When an employee provides negative feedback, recognize that is a sign of retention risk and take action if appropriate. Be mindful of the view from the other side of the table and opportunities with other organizations.

Managing up

No one likes a manager that leaves the team exposed to the elements. Push back when there are fire drills due to another team. Push back when there are unfunded mandates. Push back when the team would need to work nights and weekends due to poor planning. Actively represent the interests of the program and the team.

2.12 SUCCESSION PLANNING

The ability for a team to function independently is a measure of a leader. The leader should be able to go on vacation without involvement and without impact. Their stand-in may become a successor when the leader transitions to a new role. Grooming a successor is necessary for continuity and benefits them from career and professional development perspectives. The act of establishing a successor may open career opportunities for the current leader as well.

2.13 ALTERNATE DUTIES LIST

Establish an Alternate Duties List to maintain operations when a team member is unavailable. The Primary contact is responsible for day-to-day tasks associated with their process/function. The Primary develops procedures, training materials and other relevant documentation. The Alternate contact is responsible for completing on-the-job training, critically evaluating documentation and being fully prepared to perform the Primary's role.

An Alternate Duties List can also be used to determine if the number of primary duties assigned to employees is reasonable, if workload should be further distributed and if additional staffing is warranted.

2.14 STAIR-STEP CAREER PATH

This methodology provides a defined career path for security employees. It increases retention of employees and organizational knowledge, conserving cost in the process. As employees resign or retire, the process fills openings organically (Figure 2.4).

2.15 PROGRAM ARCHITECTURE

Program architecture is necessary to design, implement and maintain an information security function. If an executive asks how you would build a program, you need to have an elevator pitch ready to go. Include in your response 'mission, vision, process, procedures, system of record, reporting and metrics'. Program architecture can be used to establish a wide variety of programs, including:

- Third party risk management
- Vulnerability management
- Identity and access control
- Security awareness
- Issue management
- Penetration testing
- Security operations center
- Incident management
- Application security
- Security architecture
- Insider threat
- Reporting and metrics
- Policy and standards
- PCI compliance
- Privacy management
- Fraud prevention

Mission/vision

Mission and vision statements are useful when pitching the idea of a new information security function to an executive. Mission can be loosely defined as the high-level goals of a team. A

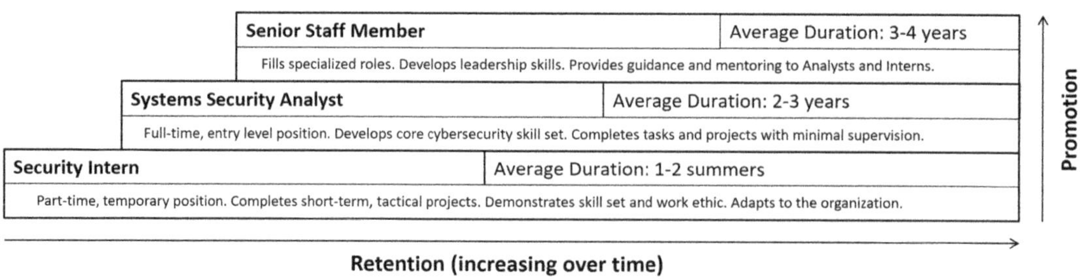

Figure 2.4 Stair step career path.

mission statement explains the purpose of the team from a business perspective. Vision can be defined as how the team accomplishes its mission. Create a Program Overview Slide with mission and vision statements and a bulleted list of priorities. If an executive expresses interest in creating that new function, offer to come back with a process diagram for additional detail.

Process

Process diagrams have utility for orientation, either a new team member or an executive in the leadership chain. FMEA process risk assessments require a diagram as an input. Process diagrams are approved by executive leadership. That can come in handy when someone in the organization resists working with your team. Process diagrams defend your program and team, helping answer the 'so what' question when a new executive is looking to cut costs. Process diagrams are a good program artifact when interfacing with an auditor.

Procedures

A procedures manual provides step-by-step instructions to ensure a consistent approach to day-to-day operations. It is a useful tool for training new team members. Procedures provide instructions for conducting program activities and reoccurring tasks. Team members should take an active role in maintaining the manual by providing feedback and by fleshing out and clarifying the procedures. The manual should include a change log, documenting annual reviews and content revisions.

System of record

A system of record is the official data repository for a program or function. A system of record aligns to the program and processes, providing increased efficiency. Information security teams often use Governance, Risk and Compliance applications, which have work flows, questionnaires and reporting built-in. GRC applications provide issue management functionality, with the ability to drill down from a high-risk pie slice in a report, to issue records and target dates. GRC applications also provide specialized modules such as incident response, vulnerability management and third party risk management. Reference '12.7 GRC System of Record' for additional details.

Reporting and metrics

Information security functions exist to identify and mitigate risk. Reporting and metrics provide risk transparency, enabling senior executives to make informed decisions. When operational risk exceeds risk tolerance, that can influence support and funding. Reference the 'Metrics, KPIs and KRIs' chapter for additional details.

Program overview

Create a 'walk-around' deck to represent your program. The deck should include content to address any audience on short notice, including a new executive, a new team member or an auditor. Here are topics that should be included:

• Program overview	• Projects and initiatives budget
• Process diagram(s)	• Communications plan
• Management routines	• Activity task scheduling
• Annual program goals	• Supporting policy
• Operating budget	• SWOT analysis

Topics within this section are good candidates for slides as well (e.g. reporting and metrics). Err on the side of having too many slides. The overview deck is intended to be a template. When there is a meeting request, make a copy of the deck and delete slides that are not needed.

Welcome packet

A Welcome Packet provides orientation to employees and contractors that participate in the program. It should include an executive summary, roles and responsibilities, a mid-level overview and resources to make employees and contractors successful. Here is a framework for an information security program welcome packet.

- **How to use this document**
- **All employees**
  - Security issues: Who to contact
  - Protect against social engineering (Phishing)
  - Methods to identify and mitigate risk
  - Information security resources
- **Technologists**
  - Roles and responsibilities
  - Remediation of security issues
  - Security by design
- **Management**
  - Program overview - Information security
  - Communications routines
  - Metrics and reporting
  - Risk register

Program overview documentation helps maintain continuity and is useful for training new personnel. It can also be used to represent the program when there is a change of leadership and in times of budgetary challenges.

Quality assurance

Processes fail due to inattention. Continuity may be lost during a team member transition. There is risk when a process crosses between two teams. Both teams may believe the other is taking action. Both teams may have limited visibility into what the other team is doing. A team member may make a mistake. There may be differing levels of experience between team members, with inconsistent results. These are just examples. It makes sense to critically evaluate process steps and determine where a failure may occur. In those instances, it can make sense to implement quality assurance with limited sampling. This is a way for the team to check and make sure things are functioning the way they should. We are watching our own backs. That is much better than having a customer or an auditor identify a significant issue.

Additional resources

If you are interested in learning more about Program Architecture, reference Chapter 6. It details how to design, implement and lead a Third Party Risk Management program.

Figure 2.5 Thank you!

2.16 END OF THE YEAR

In most organizations the momentum begins to slow down about mid-November. The Thanksgiving holiday is close and many people take off the last two weeks of December. This is a good time to focus on our people, how much we appreciate them and the importance of work-life balance (Figure 2.5).

Thank team members for their hard work throughout the year. Recap team accomplishments. Take time on a team call to thank the team and let them know how you feel about them.

When employees need to provide coverage during the holidays, tell them to focus on monitoring and response. Do not start anything new, do not stir up trouble. Avoid sending e-mail to people on vacation when it can wait until the new year.

Sometimes we have hard charging people that have difficulty slowing down for the holidays. Have 1:1 conversations with those individuals. Thank them for their hard work. Acknowledge it is difficult for them to reduce intensity during the holidays. Encourage them for the last couple of weeks of the year to rest, relax, enjoy time with family and friends. Sometimes that is not enough. Convince them by saying: Look, if you are well rested January 2nd, then you can really tear into the new year. They will appreciate your effort and may actually take some time to relax.

2.17 CALENDAR: MANAGEMENT ROUTINES

This time provides an overview of management routines driven by executives and human resources throughout the year. Specifics have been covered within this chapter. Take note of this high-level view. Plan and prepare for each of these events. You will be much more effective and less stressed out (Figure 2.6).

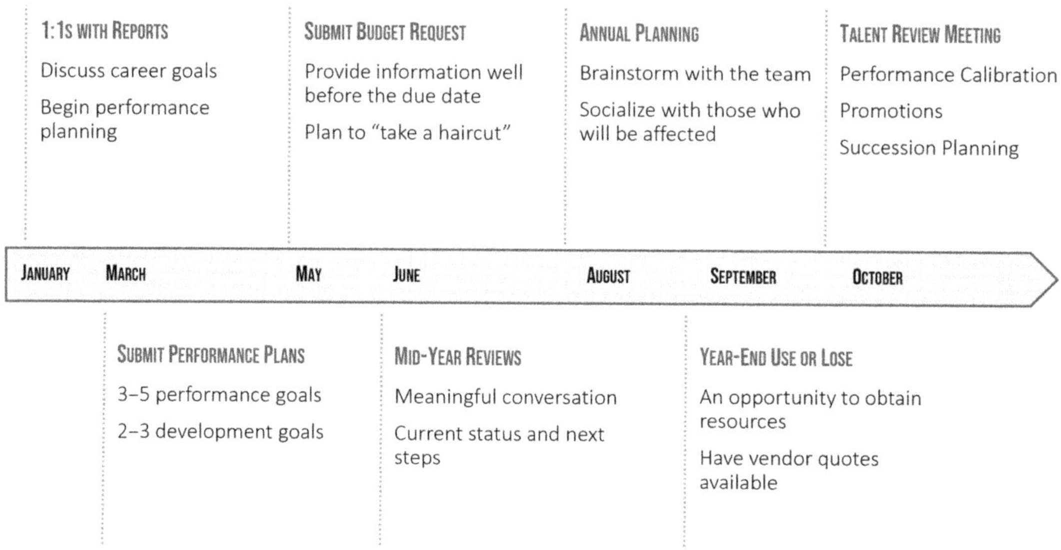

Figure 2.6 Calendar - Management routines.

Management routines

Establish and schedule management routines unique to your program and how you manage a team. Here are examples to inspire you (Figure 2.7).

2.18 FINAL THOUGHTS

Being a Leader is a significant responsibility. Management has entrusted you with process, delivery and its people. Employees spend more time at work than with family and friends. They depend on you, rely on you for their careers and professional development. Strive to improve your leadership skills year over year. Mentor, groom and raise up your employees. Maintain the balance of getting the work done and taking care of your people.

Activity	Description	Occurrence
Cybersecurity meetings	Discuss work efforts. Each team member has a change to speak. Discuss challenges and next steps.	Weekly
Cyber threat intelligence meetings	Discuss indicators of compromise, adversary tactics and mitigations. That feeds security work efforts.	Monthly
MITRE ATT&CK framework	Review MITRE ATT&CK top-to-bottom. Implement new controls to identify and mitigate risk.	Monthly
Cyber risk mitigation reviews	Discuss security service desk tickets, close out entries, add entries and stack rank in order of risk severity.	Monthly
Risk register meetings	Document risk acceptance and mitigation, which is communicated to the cybersecurity committee.	Every four months
Cybersecurity committee meetings	Provide risk transparency to the board through cybersecurity committee meetings.	Every four months
On-site working sessions	The cybersecurity team conducts three days of planning and brainstorming meetings.	Every four months
<Tier 1 vendor> briefings	<Tier 1 vendor> provides cybersecurity status updates within business review meetings.	Quarterly
Risk assessment	Conduct a cybersecurity risk assessment (e.g. Vendor web app, zero trust, threat landscape and controls).	Annually - <Month>
Cybersecurity assessment tool	Integrated into risk mitigation tickets. Highest risk addressed first. Risk register documents acceptance.	Annually - <Month>
Incident response exercise	IT and InfoSec participate in a cybersecurity incident exercise with executives and crisis management.	Annually - <Month>
Business impact analysis	The IT team reviews and updates Business Impact Analysis documentation with business units.	Annually - <Month>
Business continuity exercise	The IT team conducts a <tabletop/functional> Business Continuity Exercise with business units.	Annually
Disaster recovery exercise	The IT team conducts a <tabletop/functional> Disaster Recovery Exercise.	Annually
Vendor cybersecurity assessments	Suppliers with significant risk submit cybersecurity assessment reports from an independent firm.	Annually
Penetration test	The penetration tester uses hacking tools and techniques to attempt to gain access (external and internal).	Annually - <Month>
<Regulator> audit	The <Regulator> conducts an information technology audit.	Annually
Internal audit IT assessment	The Internal Audit team conducts an IT assessment.	Annually - <Month>
<Vendor> cybersecurity assessment	An external vendor conduct an Information Security Program assessment.	Every 3 years

Figure 2.7 Management routines - Information security.

Chapter 3

Program maturity

3.1 INTRODUCTION: FOUR MATURITY LEVELS

This chapter provides guidance to improve program maturity within four levels. Information security professionals must focus on maturity within cybersecurity and operational risk contexts. That starts with minimal compliance, pivots into common controls, then active risk management and finally strong risk management. This risk-prioritized approach can be used to influence funding. So that's part of the strategy, you need support and funding to mature the program over years.

Level one: Minimal compliance

Level one is minimal compliance and some organizations start there. Startup companies begin at minimal compliance because they are establishing the company, staffing, processes and technology all at once. Small companies may be at a lower level of maturity due to resource constraints. Minimal compliance can be viewed as adherence to foundational practices such as the NIST Cybersecurity Framework (CSF) or ISO 27001. Minimal compliance with laws, regulations and contractual obligations also fits into this tier.

Level two: Common controls

Common controls reside within level two. Control frameworks such as NIST CSF are not intended to be very specific or prescriptive. Therefore, it is necessary to use common controls to mitigate significant risk. Web application firewalls are commonly used to protect Internet-exposed websites that process sensitive information. Security architecture reviews are commonly embedded into project management, change management and third party risk management. While common controls may not be called out explicitly in the control framework, information security professionals expect to see them in place. We view them as necessary and common sense from an information security perspective.

Level three: Active risk management

Level 3 is active risk management, which is required in most of the control frameworks, laws and regulations. But may be skipped over in practice, so we'll get down a little deeper into what types of analysis, assessment and mitigation should be in place.

DOI: 10.1201/9781003543619-3

Level four: Strong risk management

Level 4 is strong risk management, typically for organizations that have a very low risk tolerance such as financial institutions, federal government and pharmaceutical companies.

3.2 MINIMAL COMPLIANCE: MATURITY LEVEL 1

Starting with minimal compliance maturity level one, most organizations will use either the NIST Cybersecurity Framework (CSF) or internationally they will use ISO 27001. The NIST Cybersecurity Framework is 100+ controls which provide a foundation, such as a requirement for encrypting data at rest. NIST CSF also provides a presentation layer for executives. So if we were to get into the elevator with an executive and they were to ask 'Tell me about our cybersecurity program'. You could say something like, 'first we look to identify risk to the organization and then we deploy protective controls to prevent cyber security issues, we detect suspicious activity and then we respond either with an incident response plan, disaster recovery and/or crisis communications, and finally, when we recover, we conduct root cause analysis to prevent reoccurrence'. That synopsis did not get deep into technical controls or some of the traditional domains of information security such as access control or physical security. That's for a good reason. If we're talking to a business leader who spent most of their professional life in accounting before becoming CEO, we start to leave them behind if we get too far in the weeds of cybersecurity.

At this minimal level of compliance, it's necessary to include requirements from laws, regulations and contractual obligations. Be mindful that regulatory bodies are biased toward their interests. For example, the payment card brands require adherence to the PCI Data Security Standard and only care about the security of their payment card numbers. If your organization has a disaster and cannot recover, that's not really a concern to them. Therefore it is necessary to focus on risk management within your organization rather than minimal compliance.

3.3 DATA GOVERNANCE (L–1)

Data governance is often overlooked or may not be done well. The first step to securing data is knowing where it is. That knowledge is necessary to begin to secure data. Start by establishing a high level view of what types of data we have and where it is stored (Figure 3.1).

Data Category	Data Custodian	Data Repository	Estimated Volume	Data Owner
Intellectual Property (R&D)	CTO / AWS	AWS	2,000 designs/formulas	Chief Innovation Officer
Business Strategy	CTO	Austin Data Center	Varies	CEO
Payment Card Numbers	Acme	Vendor IT environment	10 million records (# of customers)	eComm Executive Director
Bank Account Information	Acme	Vendor IT environment	10 million records (# of customers)	eComm Executive Director
Customer PII (SSN/DoB)	Acme	Vendor IT environment	10 million records (# of customers)	eComm Executive Director
Employee PII (SSN/DoB)	ADP	Vendor IT environment	5,000 records (# of employees)	Human Resources Director
Employee PHI (Health Info)	ADP	Vendor IT environment	5,000 records (# of employees)	Human Resources Director
E-mail	Microsoft O365	Vendor IT environment	Varies	Chief Information Officer
File Storage	Microsoft O365	Vendor IT environment	Varies	Chief Information Officer

Figure 3.1 Data inventory (High level).

The Data Owner is the person or the role that gives permission for data to be used in a certain manner. For example, they would give permission before data is moved from our on-premises IT environment to a vendor-hosted environment. The Data Custodian is the role that is responsible for protecting that information. Data management is a discipline, reference the Data Management Body of Knowledge for details.

3.4 IT SYSTEM OF RECORD (L–1)

An IT system of record provides more detail than a system or application inventories. Here are sample fields to consider:

• System Owner (Primary)	• Business Criticality (BIA)
• System Owner (Alternate)	• Internet Facing
• Data Owner (Primary)	• Vendor Hosted System
• Data Owner (Alternate)	• PII Data
• Management Contact	• PHI Data
• Tech Exec Contact	• Sensitive Data (etc.)
• Application Record	• Record Certified By
• Production Status	• Record Certified Date

It is necessary to have system contacts to coordinate maintenance windows and when responding to an incident. Management and Tech Exec contacts provide a point of escalation when there is difficulty getting a code fix created and tested. They also need access to reporting and metrics associated with their systems and applications. The 'Application Record' field in the table above is meant to be a link. An IT system of record provides functionality to transition between differing views. That enables an understanding of data, applications, infrastructure and associated contacts. The 'Record Certified By' field is used to ensure System Owners and Application Managers review each record once per year. They typically update contact fields due to staffing and organizational changes. Discovery software detects new systems automatically, including within cloud environments. It is also a good tool to detect sensitive data stored on PCs, laptops, servers, virtual machines, cloud environments, network file shares, SharePoint and in non-production environments. Take action to ensure sensitive data is protected by enhanced security controls, with access restricted by least privilege and separation of duties. Sensitive data stored in common use areas is at increased risk of disclosure and compromise.

3.5 COMMON CONTROLS: MATURITY LEVEL 2

Control frameworks such as NIST CSF or ISO 27001 provide mid-level guidance and are not meant to be prescriptive. That leaves gaps to fill in an organization's custom control framework. Common controls are safeguards and countermeasure that are necessary and common sense in a cybersecurity context. In this second level of maturity, expand beyond minimum compliance with a standardized control framework and begin to fill the gaps with common controls.

Examples of controls that are not mentioned in NIST CSF 2.0 include web application firewalls, privileged access management, web content filters and phishing test programs. They are not arcane. They are not unusual. We would, by and large, expect them to be in place in an environment that hosts sensitive data.

Use reputable practices to identify gaps in control frameworks such as the Critical Security Controls published by the Center for Internet Security. Start by adding controls that are already in-place to your organization's control framework. Next, use a risk-prioritized approach to implement controls in a three-year multi-generational plan for the information security program.

Every information security program must have a risk-based deployment of controls. Here is an example for web applications. Source code scanning will be conducted for all web applications throughout the organization. For applications that store process or transmit sensitive data, a second layer of dynamic application scanning will be added. Internet exposed web applications that host sensitive data will receive penetration testing as a third layer. Controls are layered on as the perceived risk grows.

This maturity level fills gaps in a standardized control framework. This activity is basic due diligence, nothing to be proud of. It is the second layer beyond the bare-bones foundational safeguards in a control framework.

3.6 ACTIVE RISK MANAGEMENT: MATURITY LEVEL 3

Active risk management is necessary to protect the interests of the organization, stakeholders, customers and employees. Control frameworks provide risk management guidance, which is a good place to start. Here are examples from NIST CSF 2.0:

- GV.RM-01: **Risk management objectives** are established and agreed to by organizational stakeholders
- GV.RM-02: **Risk appetite and risk tolerance statements** are established, communicated and maintained
- GV.RM-03: Cybersecurity management activities and outcomes are included in enterprise risk management processes
- GV.RM-04: Strategic direction that describes **appropriate risk response** options is established and communicated

It is also necessary to conduct risk analyses and risk assessments. Risk issues must be prioritized and communicated to managers and executives to enable them to make informed decisions.

From a risk management perspective, there are four options:

• Risk acceptance	• Risk mitigation
• Risk avoidance	• Risk transference

Risk can be accepted within a risk registry entry or within a Plan of Action and Milestone (POA&M), which is more common in the U.S. federal government. Risk registers and POA&Ms must exist in a formal process, where the appropriate management tier is required to sign-off on risk acceptance based on the severity of the issue. Management can also avoid risks, so there are times where a line of business or a business unit will decide the cost of compliance versus potential customer base is not worth conducting business in a given state or country. Risk mitigation is something that we are accustomed to in cybersecurity. We strive to remediate vulnerabilities within standards. Cybersecurity insurance is a good example of risk transference.

Some managers and executives are compliance-focused. Control frameworks, laws, regulations and contracts include risk management requirements. Use that narrative to influence change and to protect the organization.

3.7 RISK TOLERANCE STATEMENT (L–3)

Senior executives communicate 'tone from the top' within a Risk Tolerance Statement. This approach is validated within NIST CSF 2.0 (Figure 3.2).

Management has a low tolerance for data breaches and operational risk within this example.

They have a moderate tolerance for compliance and legal risk. The organization will not adhere to every compliance requirement. Management is willing to take some risk in that area. There is a desire to keep a balance between compliance control requirements and additional controls we will deploy on our own. That may result in compliance requirements that have been addressed with compensating controls.

If a risk tolerance statement is not in place, have conversations with executive management to establish one. The goal is to enable employees to make sound risk management decisions. The information security team can tie back to this 'tone from the top' when requesting funding or when we need to implement a new control.

3.8 RISK DEBATE (L–3)

Risk debate is a manner of constructive conversation that applies critical thinking. The debate focuses on risk to the organization, potential business impact and mitigations that align to risk tolerance. Direct questions and dissenting opinions are encouraged. Risk debate addresses the issue at hand, nothing personal is intended. It is best to start the conversation in private, escalating in partnership within a forum or committee.

Some roles organically foster risk rebate. Technology leaders are focused on features, functionality and frictionless service delivery. Information security leaders are focused on the threat landscape and controls to identify and mitigate risk. Make every effort to not be emotionally vested in the outcome of risk debate.

Data Breaches	Low Tolerance	Low: Management is risk-averse for data breaches that have significant impact; however, infrequent cybersecurity incidents with minimal damage will be tolerated.
Operational Risk	Low Tolerance	Low: Management has a low tolerance for the risk of operational disruption with potential for significant impact on Acme or our clients.
Compliance Risk	Moderate Tolerance	Moderate: Acme has a moderate tolerance for non-compliance with laws, regulations and contractual obligations.
Legal Risk	Moderate Tolerance	Moderate: Management has moderate tolerance for the risk that contracts or lawsuits will have financial or operational impact.

Figure 3.2 Risk tolerance statement [Example].

Issues of material risk should be mitigated or accepted within a risk register entry. If senior executives make an information decision to accept risk, information security has fulfilled our role. Shift focus to another exposure to the organization.

3.9 ZERO TRUST SECURITY MODEL (L–3)

Zero trust is a critical strategy to protect an organization. The goal of zero trust is to enable business-as-usual, while thoroughly restricting access to what is necessary. This approach significantly reduces the risk of data breaches and associated business impact (Figure 3.3).

Zero trust is a security model, not a product or solution. It requires analysis, design and deployment of controls. Zero trust takes into account:

- Business processes
- Where data is stored, processed and transmitted
- Who needs access to the data
- Existing networks, systems and applications

Zero trust is a journey, not a destination. It requires continued research and analysis, a multi-year approach.

The need for maintaining a mature, restrictive control environment increases with the advent of quantum computing and artificial general intelligence. Fair warning…

3.10 ATTACK-CENTRIC CONTROLS (L–3)

Attack centric controls mitigate how a threat actor gains access to an IT environment, finds sensitive data and exfiltrates it from the organization (Figure 3.4). The goal is to have controls in place to make that difficult or at the very least to detect that suspicious activity.

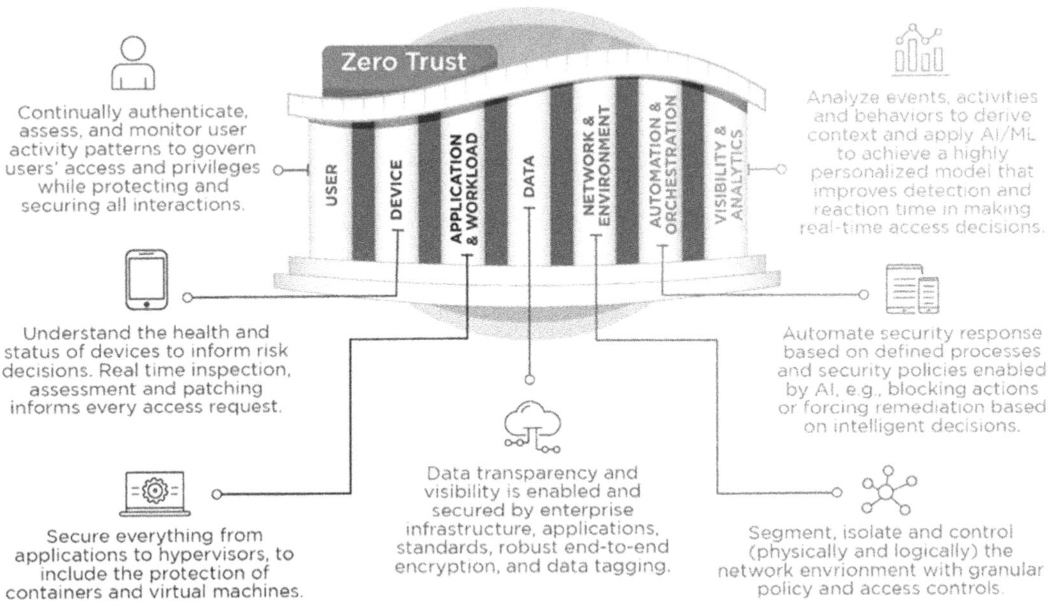

Figure 3.3 Description of the seven (7) pillars of zero trust. (NSA).

Threat Vectors Control Categories	Control Options	
Malware delivery	• **Phishing test messages** • Web content filtering • Advertisement blocking	• External message warning • E-mail authentication (DMARC, SPF and DKIM)
Gain system access	• Restrict workstation admin access from end users • **Known Exploited Vulnerabilities Catalog - CISA** • **Lock down PowerShell**	• Require Admins to leverage their end user account • Unique passwords for each server • **Allowlisting software** • **Multi-factor auth for servers**
Pivot and move laterally	• **Network segmentation** • **Jump box - Bastion host**	• Micro-segmentation
Data exfiltration	• **Granular source/destination firewall rules (network)** • Web application firewall • Resolve from internal DNS servers	• Monitor length of DNS queries and responses • **Research other forms of exfiltration and implement controls**
Detect	• **Suspicious command monitoring** • Threat hunting	• **Honeypots and honeytokens** • 24x7 SOC monitoring
Respond	• **Incident response plan** • Automated security response	• **Incident response exercises** • Crisis management team

Figure 3.4 Attack-centric controls.

3.11 EMERGING THREATS AND COUNTERMEASURES (L–3)

Information security programs must keep apprised of emerging threats and take action to implement countermeasures. Subscribe to security advisories to keep pace with new threat actor tactics, techniques and procedures (TTPs). Critically evaluate each advisory, considering whether it makes sense to:

- Implement a hardening security configuration as a preventive control
- Create a new security monitoring alert (looking forward)
- Create an analysis report when it is difficult to create an alert with low false positives/negatives
- Conduct threat hunting activity (looking backward)

Refer to the 'Cyber Threat Intelligence' chapter for more information.

3.12 RISK REGISTER ENTRIES (L–3)

Risk register entries can be used to influence mitigation of cybersecurity issues. Risk registers provide transparency to executives. Each register entry is assigned a risk severity rating such as high, moderate or low. High level technical details are acceptable but be mindful of the audience. Include potential for business impact in the conversation.

If an IT or business executive, says 'That's fine. We're not going to deal with this right now. We'll deal with it next year'. An Information Security professional can respond 'Sure, I understand. Let's fill out a risk register entry and we'll get that into the risk governance process'. That response implies the risk issue will be reviewed and decisioned by other executives. In some cases, mention of that process alone is enough to influence remediation with a sense of urgency. Otherwise, senior executives may make an informed decision to accept the risk. Typically that is a scenario of low risk and high cost. If the risk is considered material or significant, the issue owner may be required to create a risk-mitigate register entry. It is a good practice to establish four or five milestones, which are logical steps that support a target remediation date at the end.

Figure 3.5 is an example of a Risk Register Slide used to communicate risk to executives. Risk register entries are also documented within a system of record, typically a Governance, Risk and Compliance (GRC) application.

3.13 REPORTING STRUCTURE (L–3)

The information security leader should have independence from the Information Technology organization. There is a conflict of interest when cybersecurity reports into a technology executive such as a Chief Information Officer (CIO). The role of a technology executive is to provide features and functionality, while a Chief Information Security Officer (CISO) is focused on risk mitigation. When those roles exist independently there is a healthy risk debate that occurs between the CISO and the CIO that helps maintain a balance of productivity and risk mitigation. If the CISO reports into technology, that can have a chilling effect on the entire InfoSec team, where they are hesitant to speak up in areas where the CIO has expressed a dissenting opinion. That can impact the effectiveness of the information security program such as minimizing risk transparency to the Chief Executive Officer (CEO) and the board of directors.

The Board of Directors does not receive adequate risk transparency if:

- An intermediary such as the CIO provides information security updates
- Information security updates are infrequent such as every six months or annually
- Minimal time is allotted for updates such as 10–15 minutes
- The board is not briefed on results of assessments, penetration tests and tabletop exercises
- The board does not receive copies of metrics, benchmark reports and risk register entries

The cybersecurity leader should report into a risk focused executive such as the Chief Risk Officer (CRO) or the Chief Operating Officer (COO). In some organizations the CISO reports into the General Counsel or the CEO.

3.14 STRONG RISK MANAGEMENT: MATURITY L–4

Strong risk management is used by organizations that have a very low risk tolerance. That includes financial institutions, government entities and pharmaceutical companies.

Transparency

Information security metrics, Key Performance Indicators (KPIs) and Key Risk Indicators (KRIs) should feed into an Enterprise Risk Management (ERM) program. An ERM program and supporting processes help ensure information security risk is elevated to the appropriate tier of leadership, business-as-usual. ERM engagement helps influence risk mitigation and necessary funding.

Risk Register

Risk ID : <Insert risk register issue number>
Subject : <Risk issue name>
Scenario : <Brief description of the risk issue>
<second line of the description>

Risk Issue Details

- <Provide mid-level detail that sizes the issue from a risk perspective such as calling out low probability.>
- <Include details so the core elements of the issue are presented.>

Impact

- <Describe how the risk issue could cause impact to Acme and our customers. If there is space, include mention of compensating controls that help reduce impact.>
- <Consider impact to productivity, replacement, response, reputation, competitive advantage and judgments. Consider whether the risk issue would be noted as preventable in the aftermath of a loss event.>

Recommendations

1. <Include two or three recommendations to mitigate the risk issue.>
2. <Provide remediation time frames that will be perceived as reasonable.>

Risk Mitigation

- <Explain the benefits of remediation from a business perspective.>

RISK INDICATORS

Severity	<1-5>
Occurrence	<1-5>
Detection	<1-5>

This space can be used for supplemental information such as a chart or table.
It can also be used for narrative (e.g. if something is out of scope).

Risk Register Benefits:

- **Risk communications improve**
- Reduce skeletons in the closet
- Each issue is either mitigated or accepted
- Risk transparency to appropriate levels of the organization
- Risk acceptance sign-off requirements rise with severity level
- Internal audit and risk partners are aware of the process
- **An opportunity to learn about risk management and keep that skill sharp**

Review this slide with a sounding board for feedback and potential revision before presenting to senior leadership. If remediation effects a specific business unit or team, review with the process owner in advance.

Figure 3.5 Risk register slide.

It is necessary for the CISO to provide updates to the Board of Directors or a similar oversight function such as a Risk Committee. C-level executives and Board members ask questions as part of their decisioning process. They need access to the information security leader to foster a balanced risk debate.

Business focus

The information security program must extend beyond an enterprise technology focus to business processes. It is necessary to maintain controls specific to products, services and assets. Start by embedding information security professionals into business operations meetings and project planning. Determine what the critical business processes are. Help establish process diagrams if necessary. Act as a partner to determine if appropriate information security and fraud prevention controls are in place. Have a plan to get to that next level to prevent business impact. Establishing process diagrams can be year one. Year two can be process risk assessment using Failure Mode and Effects Analysis (FMEA - Figure 1.4). Establish a process management program, to include policy, an inventory and FMEA.

Program intersections

The cybersecurity program should have reoccurring meetings with risk functions throughout the organization, such as privacy management, data governance and fraud prevention. There is significant overlap between cybersecurity and privacy control frameworks. Fraud prevention and cybersecurity can partner to be more effective such as supporting fraud monitoring within Security Operations Center processes. When InfoSec identifies unstructured data and a business unit conducting their own reporting, data analytics can fulfill that need and legacy access to sensitive data can be rescinded. Those are just examples.

3.15 INSIDER RISK MANAGEMENT PROGRAM (L–4)

Be mindful that a subset of employees and contractors may seek to steal, commit fraud or otherwise cause harm to the organization. These are authorized personnel with access to systems and facilities. It is necessary to have specifically designed processes in place to mitigate that risk. Refer to the 'Insider Risk Monitoring and Response' chapter for details.

3.16 THREAT HUNTING (L–4)

Automated security monitoring may fail to detect a threat actor, with significant business impact as a result. Threat hunting is a process to actively search for adversaries and malicious software within an IT environment. Hunts may be conducted based on a hypothesis. So an example, we know that sooner or later there will be an employee that is seeking to export data to take it to their next employer. What would they do? How would we detect that activity?

Cybersecurity advisories are also used as input for threat hunts. Hunts may be sourced from the MITRE ATT&CK Framework, which provides details of threat actor tactics, techniques and procedures. Threat hunting feeds security monitoring requirements, which adds even more value from an operational risk management perspective.

3.17 NECESSARY CYBERSECURITY (L-4)

When an organization has a low tolerance for cybersecurity incidents and data breaches, that calls for a strong focus on identifying and mitigating risk in the cyber domain. This visualization provides an overview of what that entails (Figure 3.6).

3.18 HIGH SECURITY (L-4)

High security is necessary when an organization has high value assets and a formidable adversary is actively targeting them. Research and development information such as pipeline drug formulas, semiconductor chip designs and source code must be kept highly secure. Threat actors include hostile nation states, criminal enterprises and competitors depending on the type of intellectual property.

Common controls and zero trust are foundational to high security. Additional rigor is necessary to fend off persistent, well-funded, sophisticated adversaries. Layer on controls to match management's low risk tolerance. An air-gap between the computer room network and any external connection mitigates risk significantly. That will cause threat actors to follow the path of least resistance, with a focus on authorized insiders, physical security and complacency.

Focus on preventing data exfiltration. Issue accesses based on a person's need-to-know, in performance of their duties. Disable write access to USB ports. Implement data loss prevention software. Encrypt hard drives. Terminal servers can be used to provide access to data and systems while preventing file downloads. Disable printing in high security environments. Otherwise, it will be used to exfiltrate sensitive data.

Restrict administrative 'super user' access with Privileged Access Management (PAM). Design physical security controls with resistance to breaching tools. Restrict access to the computer room with two-person controls. Replicate system and physical access control logs to security monitoring software. If a storage device is brought into the facility, it must be confiscated and destroyed. That includes but is not limited to, mobile phones, laptops and portable storage devices with no exceptions. Design security controls to support off-site storage and disaster recovery.

Take the human factor into account. Authorized personnel are an insider threat when high value assets are in-scope. Repeat personnel background checks annually. Assign an Information Security Officer (ISO) to monitor for suspicious activity. Cleaning crew personnel must not have access to the computer room. Be wary of maintenance and repair personnel. An ISO should escort and closely monitor all visitors.

There must be separation of duties between ISOs, system administrators and R&D personnel. No one should fulfill more than one of those roles. Prevent conflicts of interest. ISOs must have a separate reporting structure from operations. Each ISO must be empowered to resist undue influence from an individual leader, when that instruction conflicts with security of the computer room or information housed within.

Conduct annual operations security briefings to ensure all personnel are aware of threats to intellectual property. Authorized personnel may be comprised in a variety of ways, including bribes, romance, infidelity and threats to family members. If an attractive person approaches at a bar, that could be an issue. Foreign nationals may be a threat to security.

Conduct annual risk assessments and penetration tests. Confirm controls remain in-place and account for changes in the threat landscape. Be mindful of how controls can be circumvented. Stuxnet malware infected an air-gapped network by a repair person. Edward

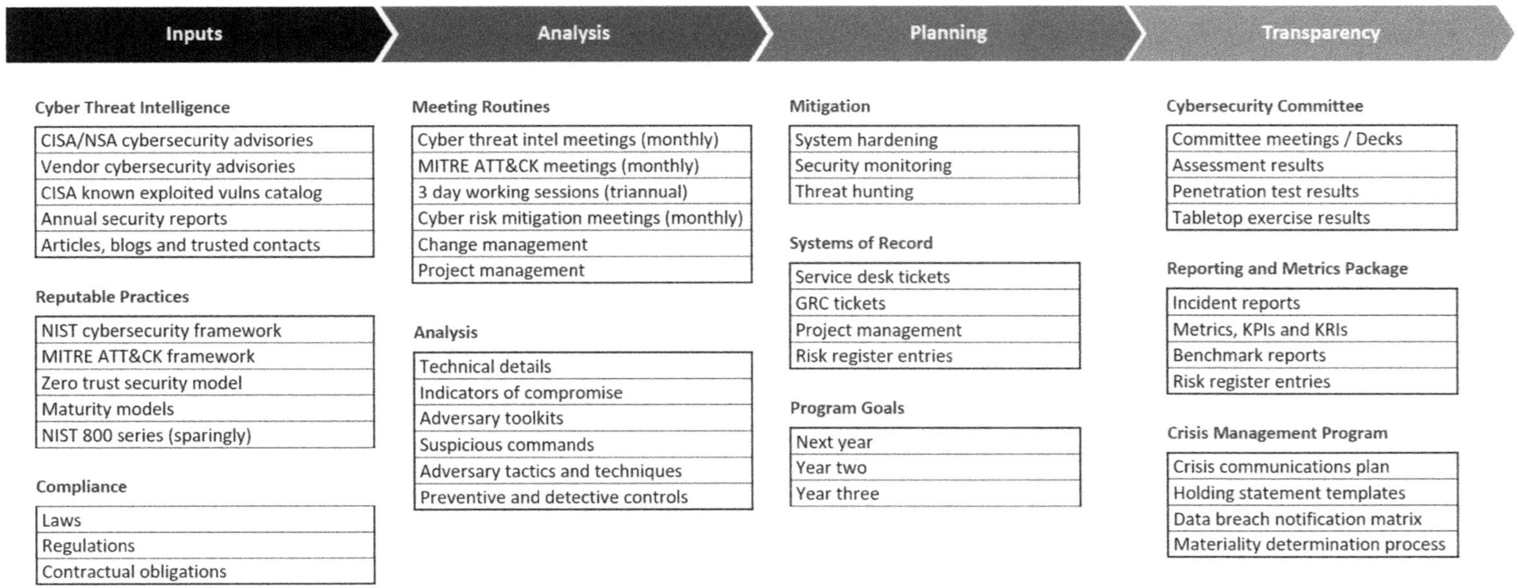

Figure 3.6 Necessary cybersecurity.

Snowden had system administration privileges and stole classified information with a USB drive.

This section provides an overview of a high security control environment. When protecting high value assets and intellectual property, start with a cybersecurity control framework, leverage the zero trust security model and design and implement controls to further mitigate risk.

3.19 CONCLUSION

If an organization has significant assets, someone will come for them. Do not rely on a few controls. Defense in depth layers have been eclipsed by the zero trust security model for good reason. A persistent threat actor will find a way. It is necessary to detect and eradicate them early, before an incident evolves into a data breach.

Control effectiveness will determine the extent of business impact. Having a sense of program maturity helps to chart a path forward, to align information security capabilities with management's risk tolerance. Maintain a three-year multi-generational plan for that purpose.

Chapter 4

Influence support and funding

4.1 INTRODUCTION

Influencing change with business and IT executives is a learned skill. This chapter begins with five areas of focus to influence support and funding. The concept of 'bring friends' solicits the support of other operational risk functions. Management routines are provided as effective ways to mitigate risk, including a risk register process, a cybersecurity committee, tabletop exercises and a cybersecurity risk management framework. Three risk analysis methodologies are provided as practical advice to communicate security risk. Tips to develop financial acumen include two budget slide examples. The chapter concludes with emphasis on the need to be a change agent and to close on projects, initiatives and risk mitigation.

4.2 INFLUENCE FUNDING

To gain support and funding, start by considering which industry your organization exists in, what types of risk matter to your executives and how to establish trust. If you understand the view from the executives' side of the table, it is much easier to be relevant to them. Influence, support and funding will follow.

Compliance

Organizations such as financial institutions, government and pharmaceutical companies are required to comply with regulations. If you can align a security or risk issue to a regulatory requirement that is an easier path toward getting support and funding. The business driver is active monitoring by regulators. Include operational risk and the potential for business impact within the discussion.

Contractual obligations may also be an effective way to communicate the need for risk mitigation. Retailers, merchants and service providers that store, process or transmit credit or debit card numbers are required to adhere to the PCI Data Security Standard. If your organization falls within that scope, it is necessary to be PCI compliant from compliance and operational risk perspectives. That perspective can be an effective way to influence closure on a security or risk issue.

Every organization is subjected laws that must be accounted for. Privacy and healthcare laws provide requirements. It is also important to protect consumer and patient information from an integrity perspective (doing the right thing when no one is looking).

Raise security issues within the business context of laws, regulations and contractual obligations. That applies a risk lens beyond information security. Partners that may support you at the executive table include the General Counsel and the Compliance Officer.

DOI: 10.1201/9781003543619-4

Operational risk

When discussing a topic of exposure with executives, try referring to it as a 'risk issue' versus mentioning security. Executives bristle a bit when we talk about security because security is binary. Something is either secure or it is not. Executives live in a world of risk management, which has shades of grey. They may choose to accept, mitigate, avoid or transfer risk. We can be more effective in our communications and our ability to influence by using terminology that resonates with executives.

Influence support and funding through metrics. For example, consider a metric that tracks critical vulnerabilities in Internet facing systems that process sensitive data. If that metric has passed the threshold into Red status, that will definitely get an executive's attention.

Assessments can be an effective way to influence support and funding. An assessment report is a non-repudiation control. There are times when an executive may say I do not remember that conversation. I do not remember that e-mail. I never saw it. It is difficult for an executive to say I never saw that assessment report. I was not in the meeting when the high risk findings were discussed. Assessments also have 'the stranger effect', where senior executives decide to take action based on the advice of an independent third party firm.

Tabletop exercises are an effective way to test incident response capabilities. Gather representatives from information technology, information security, senior executives, line of business leaders, legal, crisis management and critical suppliers. A tabletop provides a simulation of a cybersecurity incident based on the threat landscape and real-world events. Tabletop participants act as a team following incident response and crisis communications plans. The exercise also evaluates the experience and tools available to the organization. The exercise may begin with an adversary discovered in the IT environment. How do we respond initially? What are our next steps? How effective are we in containing the damage and eradicating the threat actor from the IT environment? While this is a fictitious incident now, executives will experience challenges and the potential for business impact. They do not want to experience those stresses in real life. Therefore, executives will be receptive to recommendations for risk mitigation and change coming out of the exercise.

Capacity

Be careful when trying to gain support and funding due to capacity challenges. It is common for leaders to believe they do not have enough staff. However, there can be times in your career where your team is significantly understaffed and it is difficult to complete necessary security operations activities. If you need to influence based on capacity, the need must be compelling. You will need data and rationale to support your position. If a team has 10 primary and alternate duties for each member, it may not be reasonable to expect they can execute on mission critical activities. Tracking common tasks and activities within service desk tickets quantifies work volume, which can be used to determine whether additional staffing is necessary. A staffing capacity slide is included in Figure 4.8.

Planning

Planning comes down to your strategy and ability to deliver. Establish annual program goals within a three-year multi generational plan. Request support, resources and funding. Prove through closure and completion that you and your program are a good investment from a risk management perspective. A track record of delivery builds trust and confidence with executives. That can be another bit of influence that you have and more momentum toward getting approved.

Communications routines

Communications routines are a foundational path to influence support and funding. Leaders need to know throughout the year how the security program is progressing and its value-add from a risk management perspective. Provide program and project updates in existing meeting routines. Have one-on-one meetings where it makes sense. Executives need time and information to make a decision. Communicate in advance when the outcome is critically important, such as program goals, budget and performance ratings or promotion. Do not approach an executive for the first time in a meeting, where you have 5 or 10 minutes to convince them. Good communications routines make a difference because the executives are already familiar with your program and why you are asking for support.

Financial acumen

It is very important to develop financial acumen as you move forward in your career from individual contributor, to manager and executive. Many of us begin our careers in information technology and transition into information security. From there we are promoted and suddenly have a budget. It is necessary to anticipate that change and develop an understanding of the budgetary process in advance.

Start by understanding the annual financial schedule within your organization. For example, the schedule may align with the calendar year, with budget requests submitted in November. There may be a tollgate review in January and then a second in March. Everyone may be asked to reduce their budget by 10%. One or two line items may be declined. It is important to understand that no budget request will make it through that process unscathed. Just knowing that can help you prepare and be more effective at securing the funds necessary for your program.

Managers and executives have year-end use or lose money which you may be able to access. Throughout the year executives are executing toward their budget and are focused on their monthly burn rate. As they come up on the end of the year, that behavior changes. If executives have surplus funds in the last two months of the budgetary cycle, it is in their best interests to spend it in an ethical way. Otherwise, in the first tollgate next year they will immediately lose same percentage from their new budget submission and they know that. So executives are inclined to spend that money so they consume their budget and have value for the company out of that money. So what this means to you is right around October 1st have a 1:1 meeting with your supervisor bring three quotes with you for products or services needed for your program and team. You may be surprised on how quickly they are approved.

A summary of options to influence funding is included below in Figure 4.1.

4.3 BRING FRIENDS - INTERSECTIONS

Information security has intersections with other programs and disciplines within your organization. Establish partnerships and communications routines with other leaders to prevent duplication of effort and conflicts between programs.

Information security

Consider the motivations and priorities of your partners. At a high-level, information security programs are focused on where sensitive data is stored, processed and transmitted. That enables more effective deployment of controls.

- **Compliance**
  - Regulations (finance, gov't, pharma, etc.)
  - Contractual obligations (client, PCI)
  - Laws (privacy, HIPAA)
- **Operational Risk**
  - Risk tolerance statement
  - Metrics, KPIs and KRIs
  - Assessments (non-repudiation)
  - Tabletop exercises (executive involvement)
- **Capacity**
  - Alternate duties list
  - Ticket volume/hours
- **Planning**
  - Annual goals and delivery
  - Multi-generational plan
- **Communications Routines**
  - Program updates
  - 1:1 meetings
- **Financial Acumen**
  - Annual budget process
  - Submission and tollgate dates
  - Year-end use or lose

Figure 4.1 Influence funding.

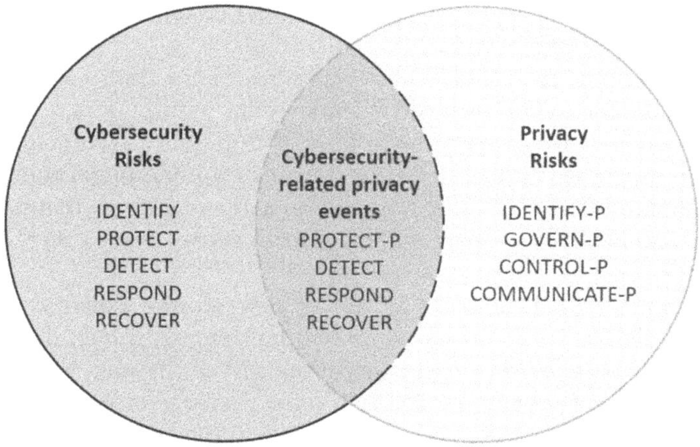

Figure 4.2 Cybersecurity and privacy intersections.

NIST Privacy Framework v1.0

Privacy management

Privacy leaders have a mantra that consumers should never be surprised by how their data is used. There is a significant overlap between privacy and information security. Privacy also focuses on data minimization and data spillage (Figure 4.2).

IT operations

IT leaders provide features and functionality to enable business operations. IT operations also focuses on availability, change management, system hardening and monitoring controls.

Data governance

Data analytics transforms data into actionable insights for business leaders. That enables executives to make informed decisions, which can generate more revenue.

Fraud prevention

Fraud prevention leaders strive to reduce the occurrence of fraud and related consequences. They use link analysis to discover hidden relationships and risky behaviors.

Have an introduction meeting with each program leader. Discuss the mission of your respective programs. Include where you have shared priorities and intersections between programs. Identify opportunities to work together. Discuss annual program goals. It is also a good practice to partner and 'bring friends' when presenting a budget request to executives. Schedule reoccurring meetings to keep your programs aligned.

4.4 RISK TOLERANCE STATEMENT

It is important for every organization to have a Risk Tolerance Statement, where senior leadership publishes a document that describes levels of risk they are willing to accept. Executive communications influence risk management and related funding. A Risk Tolerance Statement is a 'tone from the top' message from executives. As an example, some organizations realize there will be some cybersecurity incidents and will tolerate limited damages. They have very low tolerance for privacy breaches, where customers' personally identifiable information is disclosed. Some organizations may have a moderate tolerance for compliance and legal risk issues.

A Risk Tolerance Statement has utility when discussing cybersecurity issues with managers and executives. Meet in partnership and determine where the issue falls within senior executives' risk tolerance. Start a conversation and listen to each other's perspectives. That can lead to finding common ground and a path forward. Reference Figure 3.2 for an example of a Risk Tolerance Statement.

4.5 RISK MANAGEMENT – CYBERSECURITY

Cybersecurity risk management can be thought of in terms of fire. We stoke the fire and make it grow by identifying risk (Figure 4.3). When we mitigate risk, it tamps down the flames and the fire dims. This is a continuous process.

Information security professionals identify risk by conducting assessments, scans, penetration tests and exercises. Tabletop exercises identify opportunities to improve incident response capabilities, preventing business impact from playing out in real life.

We detect suspicious activity via security monitoring software and a Security Operations Center. We analyze cyber threat intelligence and configure our security log and event correlation software with threat actor Tactics, Techniques and Procedures (TTPs). Our goal is to maintain suspicious activity monitoring that is current within the threat landscape. The Security Operations Center monitors and responds 24/7/365. Many threat actors are on the other side of the world, their day is our night.

We conduct threat hunting, where qualified information security professionals actively search for threat actors within an IT environment. Threat hunts are necessary because our adversaries may not be detected by security software. An active approach is warranted.

We remediate security vulnerabilities with a sense of urgency. Risk exists when vulnerabilities remain in-place. Metrics help influence the right behavior.

We establish controls for emerging threats and new technologies. Generative and Agentic AI require governance. Systems must be hardened to protect against AI attacks that operate at machine speed. Design and implement preventive, detective and corrective controls. AI

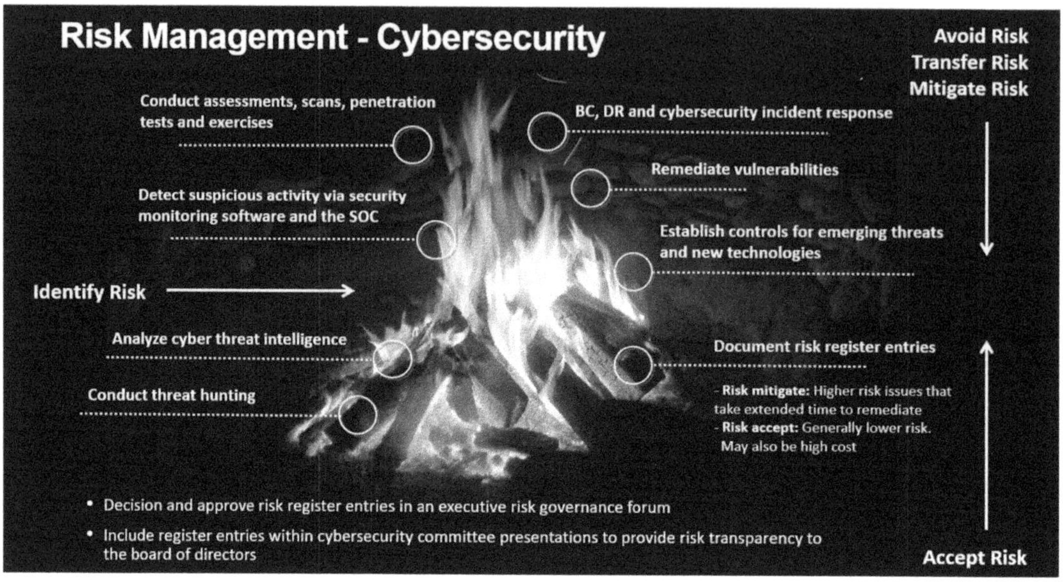

Figure 4.3 Risk management – cybersecurity.

capabilities will become more formidable as quantum computing and artificial general intelligence come online in the future. Technology will continue to evolve. Information security programs must keep pace and adapt to protect the organization.

We raise risk issues by severity for review by the appropriate management tier. Issues are documented within a risk register, subjected to a formal process. Transparency helps senior executives and the board make informed decisions. Metrics and reporting also have utility in risk management processes.

Avoid risk

Leaders have risk management options to choose from. A line of business may determine that General Data Protection Regulation (GDPR) is very prescriptive and fines can be substantial. There are few customers in Europe. Therefore a decision is made to avoid risk and cost, by not conducting business in Europe.

Transfer risk

Cybersecurity insurance is used to transfer risk to the insurance company. It is still necessary to have a strong information security program. Cybersecurity insurance has utility in the gravest extreme, when there is a significant incident or data breach. Coverage should include funds to help mitigate business impact and supporting services such as data breach response and crisis communications. Each insurance policy should be analyzed by an attorney for coverage effectiveness, paying close attention to policy limits, exclusions and insurance term definitions.

Mitigate risk

Information security professionals are accustomed to mitigating risk. The goal is to reduce risk to an acceptable level, aligned to the organization's risk tolerance. When a vulnerability is identified, installation of a patch or security configuration should mitigate that risk issue. It is necessary to expand focus beyond technology to mitigate risk within business processes as well.

Accept risk

Accepting risk should only occur within a risk register process. A manager cannot accept significant risk for the whole organization. In some cases an executive cannot either. Some risk issues need to be reviewed by C-level executives and the board of directors. Sign off must be conducted at an appropriate management tier, based on risk severity. If senior leadership makes an informed decision to accept risk, the risk register process is functioning effectively.

4.6 RISK REGISTER PROCESS

If you do not have a risk register process in your organization, this is an effective method for you to influence support and funding. A risk register process provides transparency to senior executives and the board of directors. If an executive resists mitigating a risk issue, information security should offer to introduce a risk-accept entry into the Risk Governance Committee. Do that in a spirit of partnership. Sometimes just having that conversation may cause that leader to reconsider. We can save a lot of time that way and without saying 'no' or by being passive aggressive.

It is necessary to document the end-to-end process of how a risk register entry is created, decisioned, monitored and eventually closed out. The Information Security team and the Process Owner work together to draft a risk register entry. Each register entry is either categorized as risk mitigate or risk accept. The Process Owner and Information Security present each register entry to a Risk Governance Committee comprised of executives. Executive leadership may initially reject a register entry, asking the Process Owner to conduct more research to revise the entry and come back in the next meeting. When they approve a risk-accept entry, it must be presented and reviewed again in one year. When the committee approves a risk-mitigate entry, the Process Owner tracks completion of milestones, Information Security confirms planned activities have been completed and sends notification that the registry entry has been closed. Figure 4.4 below documents that process.

A risk register communicates risk to the appropriate leadership tier. If they are making informed decisions to mitigate and accept risk, the process is working as it should. Risk registers help prevent skeletons in the closet and associated impact to the organization.

An organization has two choices, fund necessary controls or accept the risk of material business impact. Do not be emotionally vested if executives sign off on a risk register entry. Shift focus to risk issues within your span of control.

4.7 CYBERSECURITY COMMITTEE

The purpose of a board of directors is to ensure that an organization operates effectively. Therefore, it is appropriate to have a board-level cybersecurity committee with at least one board director that is security savvy. Other board members will join as well. The presentations and discussions occur at a mid-level from a technical perspective, in consideration of

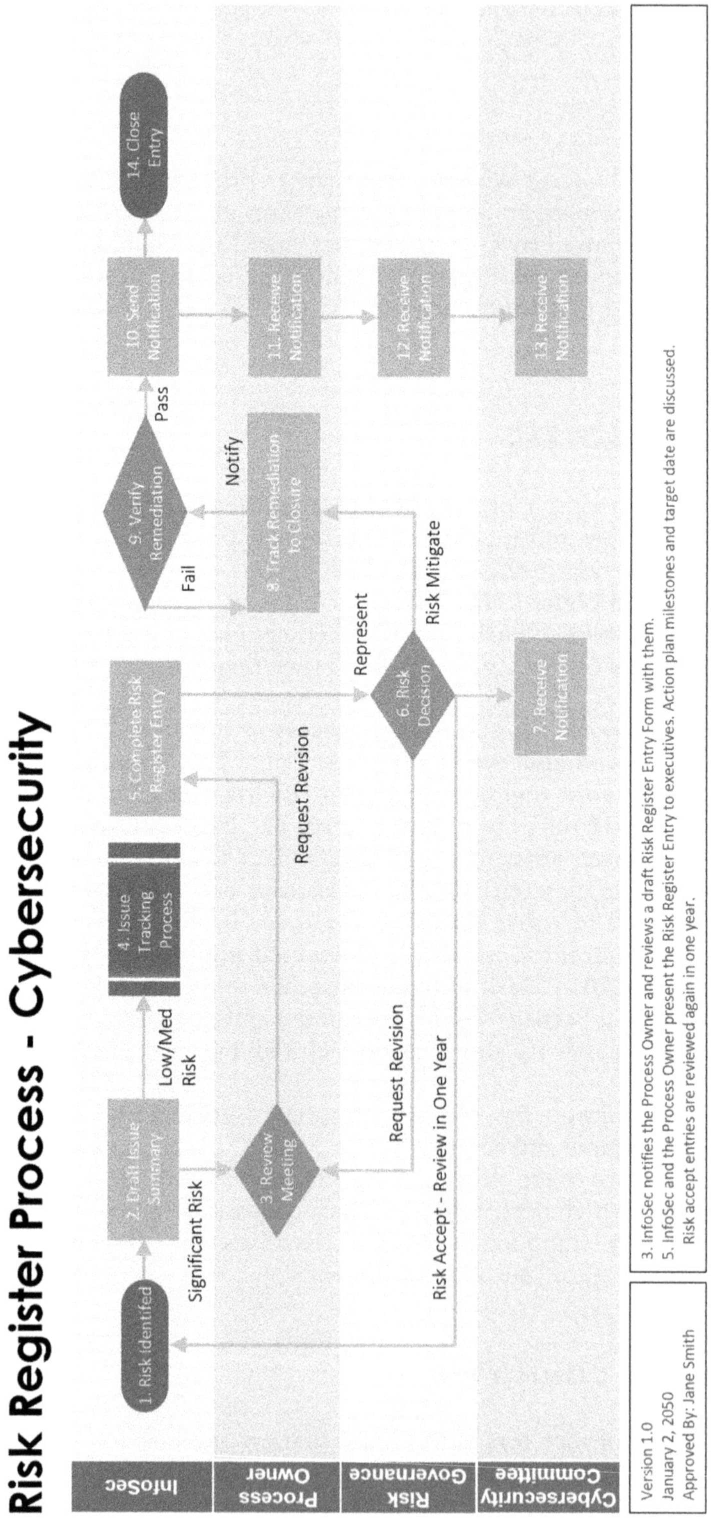

Figure 4.4 **Risk register process – cybersecurity.**

the committee. When there is a question, it is acceptable to go deeper and a bit more technical to provide the information requested.

The committee will be compromised of board members and C-level executives because we are discussing operational risk. Committee members may include:

• Board Director with cybersecurity experience	• Chief Information Officer
• Chief Information Security Officer	• Chief Operating Officer
• Chief Risk Officer	• Chief Privacy Officer
• Chief Counsel	• Chief Executive Officer

It is a good practice leverage a flexible framework when preparing for the next committee meeting. Here is an example to start with:

• Cybersecurity incidents	• Project discussions
• Threat landscape	• Reporting and metrics
• Emerging laws and regulations	• Risk register entries
• Control frameworks and reputable practices	• Annual program goals

If there was a cybersecurity incident since the last meeting, that is a natural first topic to discuss. Keep the board apprised of changes to the threat landscape by discussing emerging threats and countermeasures. Mitigate compliance risk by reviewing draft laws and regulations. If there are worthwhile controls, plan to adopt them in advance from an operational risk perspective. Control frameworks and reputable practices fall within that same mindset, identify and mitigate risk. Do what makes sense for the organization. Opportunities for improvement fall into tickets (just do it) and projects. Give the committee visibility and transparency into those work efforts. Reporting, metrics, KPIs and KRIs are provided within the committee reporting package. Discuss metrics and reporting that require attention and provide a high-level go-to-green plan. New risk register entries of material risk should be included within the reporting package and the committee slide deck. Discuss those register entries, the rationale for risk-accept or risk-mitigate. That transparency and risk debate are a core purpose of the committee. We are duty-bound to have open and fact-based conversations with our executives and the board. Once per year we can discuss SWOT analysis, annual program goals and accomplishments closing out the year. Recognize employees and leaders for their hard work.

Carefully consider how many times per year the committee should meet. Publicly traded companies meet quarterly to align with reporting requirements. That cadence can be challenging due to the need to preview reporting and deck content before each meeting. If you can avoid that, consider having three meetings a year such as February, June and October. That schedule avoids the holiday season. Three meetings are plenty, if the board is provided with risk transparency.

Establish reoccurring themes with the board. Cybersecurity must extend beyond compliance and foundational controls. Risk management is necessary to adapt to emerging threats and changes in technology. We need to detect adversaries quickly, preventing a cybersecurity incident from becoming a data breach.

4.8 TABLETOP EXERCISES - CYBERSECURITY

Two teams are about to play the first football game of the season. One team has not practiced at all. The other team has been going to regular practices before the season. Odds are the team that has practiced is going to ride roughshod over the other team and win no problem. So we would not do that in football, right? It is necessary to test your company's incident response capabilities.

Level 1: Awareness tabletops

If your company has not conducted a tabletop exercise recently, consider starting with an awareness tabletop. This format provides an introduction to tabletop exercises. Each scenario includes a significant event such as a data breach. There is an awareness and training component where a scenario is presented and participants select the best answer from four options (A, B, C and D). Cover nine scenarios in 90 minutes. Conduct this exercise with the IT and security teams as a starting point.

With each scenario the team has a discussion to determine the best option to respond. The next slide reveals the best response and why some of the other options are less appropriate. The exercise concludes with a 'hot wash', a discussion of where the team performed well and opportunities for improvement. The effectiveness of the exercise can be measured by action items, what we do differently after the exercise. That is similar to root cause analysis and lessons learned from a real-world incident.

Most teams will become accustomed to awareness tabletops after one or two occurrences. At that point it makes sense to increase the difficulty and exercise in a real-world scenario.

Level 2: Tactical tabletops

This second level of difficulty introduces a degree of stress, which tests the effectiveness of response capabilities and Incident Response Plan design. A real-world cybersecurity incident scenario is presented followed by 'injects', updates on how the adversary has adapted and other events. Options of A, B, C, D are not provided. The response team discusses how to respond and next steps. The next slide is displayed and the adversary has done something different. That is the inject. Participants have to respond. There may be 10 or 15 injects in a tabletop. The facilitator leads a hot wash at the end of the tabletop, while the events are still fresh in everyone's mind. What did we do really well? Where could we improve? What did we learn? What should we research? So if you have not been through tabletop exercises, there is a lot of value there.

Conduct two 90 minute sessions over two days. Focus on technical incident response in the first session, which will engage IT and cybersecurity with other roles providing guidance and support. Focus on crisis management in the second session, exercising the Crisis Communications Plan and holding statement templates. This approach exercises the incident response and crisis management teams, inclusive of senior executives. We are testing the effectiveness of our plans, the experience of our team and the tools and technology we have available.

Tabletop exercises are a must if your senior executives have a low tolerance for cybersecurity incidents. Reference Figure 4.5 below for a sample list of tabletop participants.

4.9 CYBERSECURITY RISK MANAGEMENT FRAMEWORK

Establish a cybersecurity risk management framework to identify and mitigate risk. Assign RACI designations to help keep them that way (Responsible, Accountable, Consulted and Informed). Apply an iterative approach to develop the framework over time. Add controls to adapt to emerging threats and new technologies. Increase maturity over time to align with senior executives' risk tolerance. When senior executives adopt a control framework

Tabletop Exercise Participants - Cybersecurity

	InfoSec			Crisis Mgt		Privacy		IT		TPRM		Fraud		HR		Compliance		Execs
Name	Primary	Alt	Staff	Primary	Alt	Primary	Alt	Primary	Alt	Primary	Alt	Primary	Alt	Primary	Alt	Primary	Alt	
Jane Smith	X																	X
		X																
			X															
				X														
					X													
						X												
							X											
								X										X
									X									
										X								
											X							
												X						
													X					
														X				X
															X			
																X		
																	X	
(CEO)																		X
(COO)																		X
(LOB)																		X
(LOB)																		X

Figure 4.5 Tabletop exercise participants – cybersecurity.

that is tacit approval for support and funding. Reference Section 12.5 'Cybersecurity Risk Management Framework' for more information.

4.10 ZERO TRUST SECURITY MODEL: YEAR ONE

Move past the basics of zero trust guiding principles and design concepts. Conduct a zero trust controls analysis leveraging 'Advancing Zero Trust Maturity' documents from the National Security Agency (NSA). There are seven documents, one for each zero trust pillar.

Fair warning, it will take significant time to conduct that analysis. Start each Friday morning with a stiff cup of coffee or divide the seven documents among the team and meet to review together. Consider what actions should be taken within each of the documents. Determine which of the recommendations can be implemented within existing software and services. That may require further research, which is fine. Consider what makes sense from project and annual goals perspectives. Use a slide deck to document observations and next steps. Track 'just do it' initiates to closure in service desk tickets.

4.11 THREAT LANDSCAPE AND CONTROLS ANALYSIS: YEAR TWO

Threat landscape and controls analysis starts from the executive's side of the table and spends a significant time on business risk. It transitions to technology and cyber risk at the end.

- **Inherent Risk**
  - Company Profile
  - Assets
  - Potential Adversaries
- **An Adversary's Perspective**
  - Techniques for Compromising Data
  - Cybercrime Ecosystem
- **Potential Impact**
- **Risk Tolerance**
- **Risk Mitigation**
  - Protection Boundaries
  - Control Framework
  - Risk Assessments
- **Residual Risk**

Reference 'Chapter 9: Threat Landscape and Controls Analysis' for additional details.

4.12 FAILURE MODE AND EFFECTS ANALYSIS (FMEA): YEAR THREE

FMEA is a great way to identify and remediate potential failure modes before they cause business impact. It is a tool that resonates with executives. Reference Section 1.11 for additional information.

4.13 CONTROL DEPLOYMENT VERSUS RISK RATINGS

Control deployment versus risk ratings are an effective way to influence support and funding. Start by creating a simple risk scoring methodology that executives buy into. Next, stack-rank using that risk score, with high risk applications at the top. Finally add controls that should be in place for high risk applications. Reference Figure 4.6 as an example below.

This table provides a visualization of how applications are evaluated by an Application Risk Score, with gaps in control deployment highlighted in black. This approach relies on a

Risk Score	Application	Control # 1	Control # 2	Control # 3	Control # 4	Control # 5
104.3	Application - K		X	X		X
101.7	Application - F	X	X		X	
98.6	Application - V	X		X		X
93.8	Application - U	X	X		X	
89.5	Application - N					
82.6	Application - O					
77.3	Application - T					
66.7	Application - G					
65.9	Application - A					
61.8	Application - R					
59.9	Application - I					
57.1	Application - C					
54.4	Application - S					

Figure 4.6 Control deployment versus risk ratings.

preceding slide that details the risk model in simple terms. Funding can be raised using this technique.

4.14 DECEPTION TECHNOLOGY

Niccolò Machiavelli is known for having said "It's a double pleasure to deceive the deceiver". In this example, we are trying to secure funding for deception technology. Honeypots are decoy systems that send an alert when someone interacts with it. Honeytokens are decoy files or fictitious account credentials that trigger an alert when used (Figure 4.7).

Deception technology takes advantage of an adversary's tactics, how they conduct their business. If we understand how they work, we can detect their presence. It can be difficult for

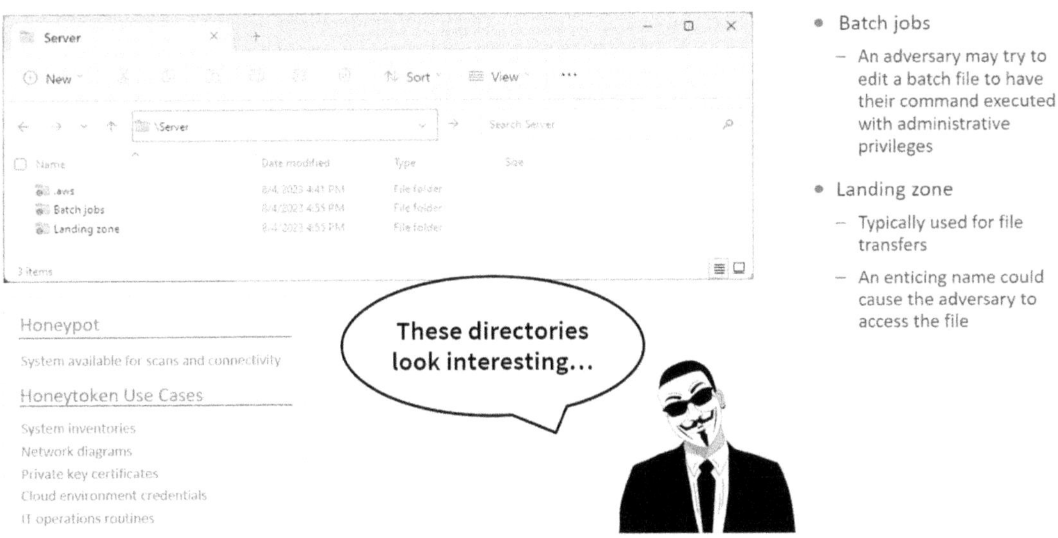

Figure 4.7 An adversary's perspective – honeytokens.

an adversary to search for sensitive data without tripping a honeypot or a honeytoken. Try implementing this technology in demo mode, just before a penetration test. It is likely that the pen testers (ethical hackers), will set off deception technology, sending alerts to your Security Operations Center. That can make a compelling case for purchasing licenses.

4.15 STAFFING CAPACITY: CYBERSECURITY

Be cautious when mentioning your team does not have enough staff. Many leaders in the organization have the same opinion. If your team is significantly understaffed, consider Figure 4.8 to represent capacity challenges.

This visualization provides an overview of security operations activities. It provides a view into activities, daily, weekly, monthly and annually. It lists the audits, assessments and analysis the team must support. Management routines are also included. Compare these operational requirements to what is reasonable for the current number of employees to perform. If there is a significant gap, this technique can be effective to gain funding for new team members.

4.16 INTERNAL CUSTOMER SURVEY

Operational functions and lines of business may feel like captive customers of the information security team. There must be a balance between deploying controls and enforcing policy, while been mindful of introducing friction and productivity impact to our business partners. It makes sense to solicit their feedback.

Distribution of the survey will vary based upon scope. Send a survey to all employees to gain feedback on the information security program. If your team focuses on a domain such as application security, it may be more productive and thoughtful to gather feedback through a series of meetings. For example, if your team shares processes or has governance over two or three teams, have individual meetings with each team (Figure 4.9).

Review survey results with the program executive. Identify themes and which areas of improvement it makes sense to solve for. Host a single meeting with all survey respondents.

- Start the presentation with a program or team overview
  - Include mission, vision, priorities and scope
- Quickly display the survey questions to refresh everyone's memory
- For each question display a slide with feedback from the respondents
  - Highlight in bold the feedback we intend to solve for
  - Displaying negative feedback is professional courage
  - It also demonstrates we are listening
- Display action items arising from the feedback
  - Provide timeframes to manage expectations
  - Mention if a funding request is being submitted
- In the final slide, thank everyone for their feedback

When a budget request arises from employee feedback and risk management, that can have a positive impact on support and funding.

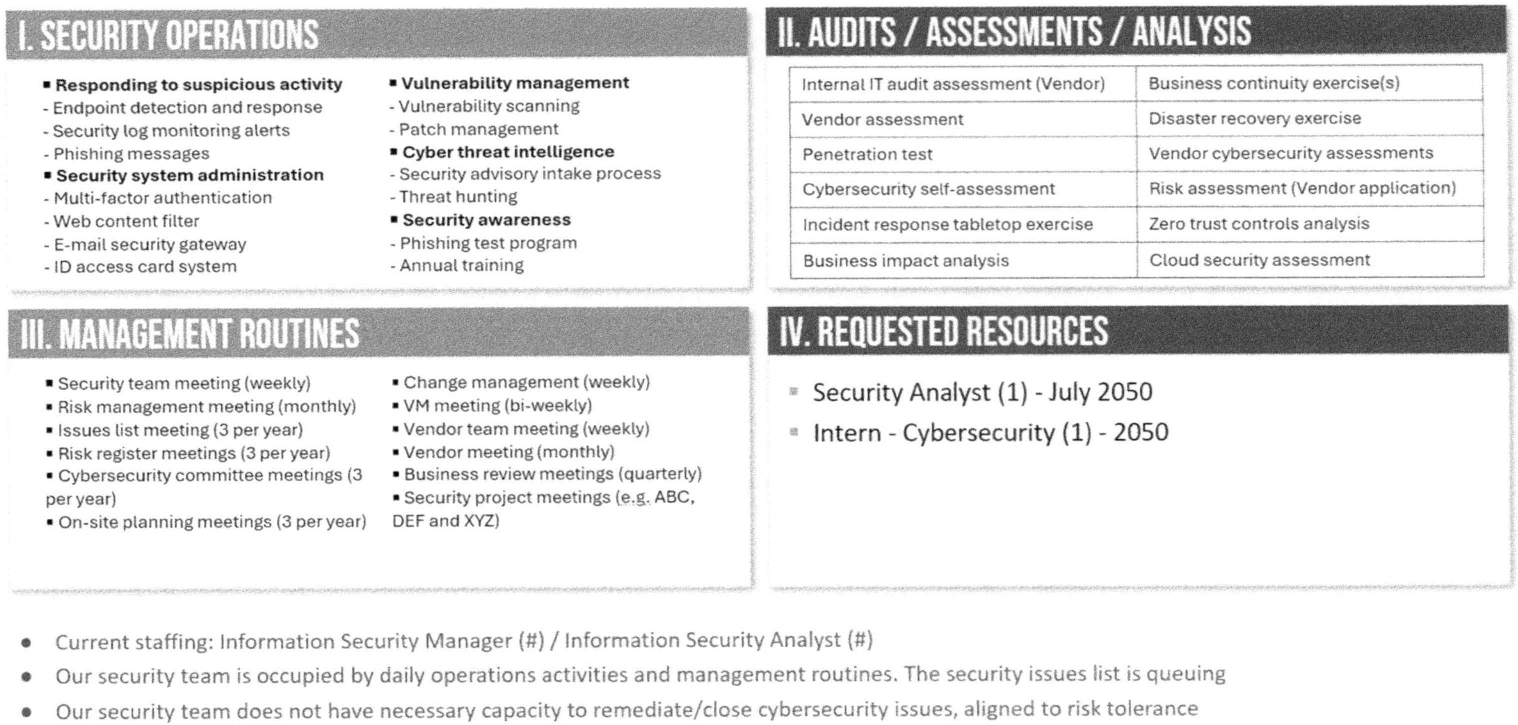

Figure 4.8 Staffing capacity – cybersecurity.

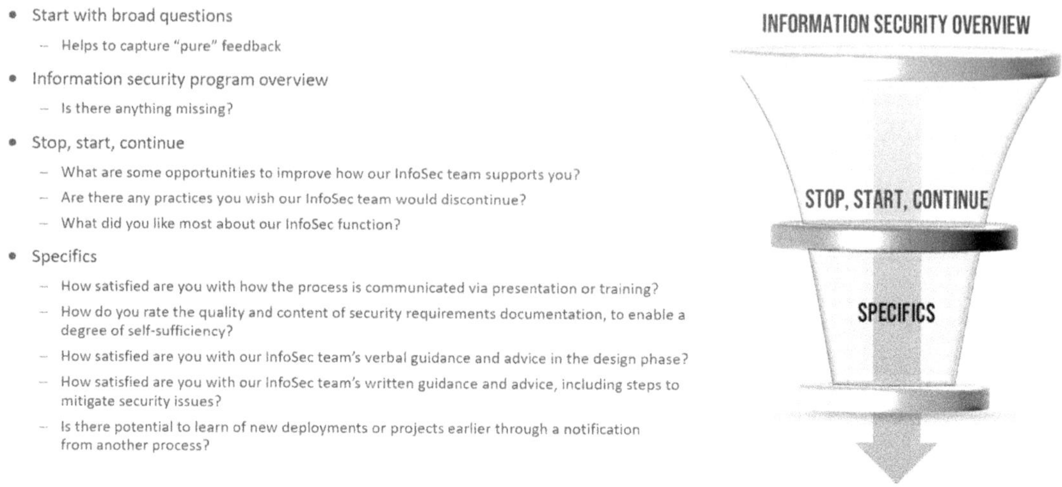

Figure 4.9 Internal customer survey.

4.17 PLAN TO DRIVE THE PROGRAM FORWARD

Establish annual goals to drive your program forward. Develop goals for your team well in advance of when they are due. If team goals are due in October, begin working on goals in August.

Brainstorm with the team

Schedule an all-day meeting to brainstorm with the team. Meet in-person if possible. Provide goals in advance, such as:

• Improve visibility into cyber risk issues	• Research and analyze
• Mitigate cybersecurity and privacy issues	• Increase efficiency and capacity
• Mature processes and controls	• Improve communications

Leverage the high-level goals to frame conversations with 45 minutes per topic. Facilitate a discussion where each team member presents their ideas. This is a brainstorming session so participants are encouraged to be comfortable. There are no bad ideas in a brainstorming session. If a person provides a goal, they have the option to own it and establish a project to drive it to completion. That gives them the opportunity to demonstrate leadership, which may result in a performance bonus. As people call out ideas, screen share a spreadsheet and capture each goal with the name of the person that submitted it. Have lunch catered and take the team out to dinner at the end of the day. This approach is inclusive and can result in team cohesion.

Select goals from the spreadsheet that make sense from cybersecurity, risk management and business perspectives. Be mindful of team capacity and the need to request funding. Discuss proposed goals with your program executive and ask for any significant issues. Socialize draft goals with support and business partners. If they will be impacted, discuss the potential for a shared goal. Unfunded mandates are doomed to fail. This approach gives partners time to submit a budget request if needed. These new goals will have been evaluated by leadership and affected parties. When an e-mail arrives requesting team goals for the next year, a simple copy-and-paste is all that is needed.

4.18 OPERATING BUDGET

An operating budget provides funding to support security operations throughout the year. Establish a precedence for training and conference within your operating budget. Information security team members must keep current with emerging threats and new technology. Training and conferences also have utility when implementing new controls and risk management processes (Figure 4.10).

4.19 PROJECTS AND INITIATIVES BUDGET

There must be sound rationale for each project and initiative request. Provide details of how new technology will identify and mitigate risk. Answer the 'so what' question from a business perspective.

Be prepared to 'take a haircut' when submitting a budget request. There are typically one or two tollgates or budget reviews. Your budget may be reduced by an arbitrary number such as 10%. Otherwise, one or two line items may not be approved as a result of that process.

Budget reviews and tollgates typically decline requests for training. Be proactive and explain why training is required such as: 'This is a new, complex technology and our team will not be able to install and configure it without training. The cost of having it implemented by a service provider is substantially higher'.

There is an aggregate impact of new technology and governance processes. Two or three projects may exceed the capacity of your team when those tools/functions enter into production. If it is necessary to onboard a new team member, provide supporting data in your budget request (Figure 4.11).

4.20 PROGRAM UPDATES

Communicating program updates is a tried-and-true method to influence support and funding. Look for an opportunity to join an existing meeting routine with managers and

Expenditure	Q1	Q2	Q3	Q4	Comments
Staffing					
Manager	Leave blank				
Individual Contributor	Leave blank				
Staff Training					
Threat hunting training			$XX,000		
Security conference & travel		$XX,000			
Software, Hardware and Support					
Vulnerability scanning	$XX,000				
Penetration testing				$XX,000	
Quarterly Totals	$XX,000	$XX,000	$XX,000	$XX,000	
Operating Budget Total	$1,275,000				

- Team training is included as an annual business-as-usual expense
- Be prepared to "take a haircut"

Figure 4.10 Operating budget 2050 - Team name.

Expenditure	Q1	Q2	Q3	Q4	Comments
Insider Threat Program					
Behavioral analysis software				$XX,000	
Insider threat training			$XX,000		
Software Composition Analysis					
SCA software and support			$XX,000		
SCA software training		$XX,000			
Deception Technology					
Software and support		$XX,000			
Technical training	$XX,000				
Quarterly Totals	$XX,000	$XX,000	$XX,000	$XX,000	
Projects and Initiatives Budget Total	$252,500				

- [Does a project drive a need for headcount for operational support of a new technology or function?]
- [Are we depending on another team that needs to submit a budgetary request to support our project?]

Figure 4.11 Projects and initiatives budget 2050 - Team name.

executives. Determine if there is a standard template for providing updates. If not, ask for meeting materials from the last two sessions to understand what leadership is used to seeing.

Provide program progress updates, which are veiled accomplishments. That content can be reused if your executive asks for team accomplishments at the end of the year. Discuss issues and challenges. If you raise a problem, provide a solution or give the executive options to select from. Discuss program next steps over the next three months to complete the update.

Report progress and accomplishments within status meetings and a month before the performance calibration meeting at the end of the year. Providing updates within management routines orients leadership to you and your program. That can be an advantage.

4.21 THE HOOK

Sales techniques are time-tested ways to influence support and funding. Consider 'The Hook' in Figure 4.12 below.

The hook is a compelling message that closes the sale. Here are examples in an information security context:

- **Reduce dwell time, prevent an incident from becoming a data breach.** (Security information and event management (SIEM), threat hunting, etc.)
- Incident response at machine speed. Prevent business impact. (Security orchestration, automation and response (SOAR))
- **Control which files are allowed to execute. Prevent ransomware from shutting down business operations.** (Allowlisting)
- The dog that didn't bark. UEBA (User and entity behavior analytics) is needed to detect adversaries. (Behavioral monitoring)
- This approach detects when adversaries conduct their work, their tactics, techniques and procedures. (Deception technology)
- DRM is a good way to rescind access when a file with sensitive data leaves the company. (Digital rights management)
- **We're doing what's necessary from an operational risk perspective.**

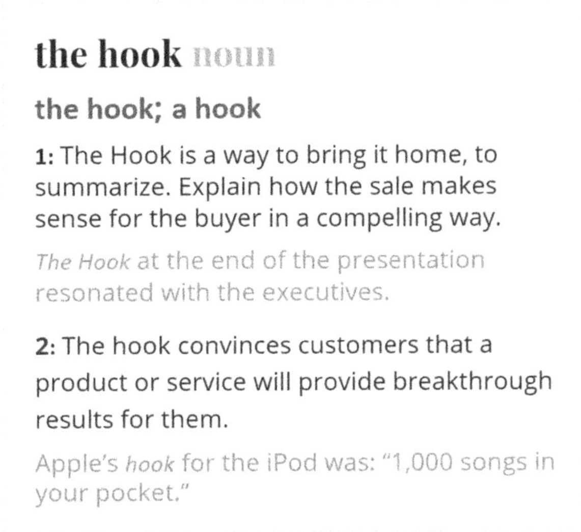

the hook noun

the hook; a hook

1: The Hook is a way to bring it home, to summarize. Explain how the sale makes sense for the buyer in a compelling way.

The Hook at the end of the presentation resonated with the executives.

2: The hook convinces customers that a product or service will provide breakthrough results for them.

Apple's *hook* for the iPod was: "1,000 songs in your pocket."

Figure 4.12 The hook.

4.22 ALWAYS BE CLOSING

There's a sales expression that also applies to cybersecurity, 'Always be closing!'. So if we have a risk issue, get it closed. If we have a project, get it closed. When we have annual goals, get them closed. Always be closing is a powerful mantra. Develop a track record for delivery. That reputation will help influence support and funding.

4.23 IN SUMMARY

Know your audience. Consider the view from the executives' side of the table. They do not want to hear about security. Something is either secure or it is not. Executives operate in a world of risk management, which gives them more options. Focus on cybersecurity with a business lens:

- How can we identify risk?
- How can we mitigate risk?
- How can we increase efficiency and capacity?

Influence support and funding by communicating effectively. Be genuine. Be ethical. It is the right thing to do, right? Your word is your bond. That provides benefits in terms of support and funding.

Always be closing!!!

Chapter 5

Cyber threat intelligence

5.1 INTRODUCTION

A Cyber Threat Intelligence (CTI) Program drives change to adapt to emerging threats and new technology. That change reduces incident occurrence, with a goal of preventing an incident from becoming a data breach. An information security program cannot be allowed to remain static. Take action against new threat actor tools and tactics to protect assets such as payments, sensitive data and intellectual property (Figure 5.1).

5.2 SOURCES - INPUTS

CTI provides visibility into the threat landscape. The CTI program requires many sources of input to be effective. CTI team members must actively monitor emerging threats and vulnerabilities to protect the organization.

Advisory subscriptions

Cybersecurity advisory subscriptions are quality sources of CTI. They have been thoroughly vetted by government and/or vendors. It is a good practice to subscribe to these reputable distributions:

- Cybersecurity and Infrastructure Security Agency (CISA) Updates
  - Known Exploited Vulnerabilities Catalog
  - Cybersecurity Advisories
  - Vulnerability Bulletins
- Vendor Cybersecurity Advisories
  - For installed hardware devices and software
- InfraGard (Only available to US citizens)

CTI feeds

Integrate CTI data feeds into security software such as endpoint protection. It is common practice to integrate multiple feeds into SIEM log monitoring and event correlation software, beyond the vendor feed. Conduct research and ask your 'friends with dark circles' what they are using in their organization. Determine if the SIEM receives quality CTI feeds. Ask a member of the SOC to screen share which feeds are integrated into the SIEM.

DOI: 10.1201/9781003543619-5

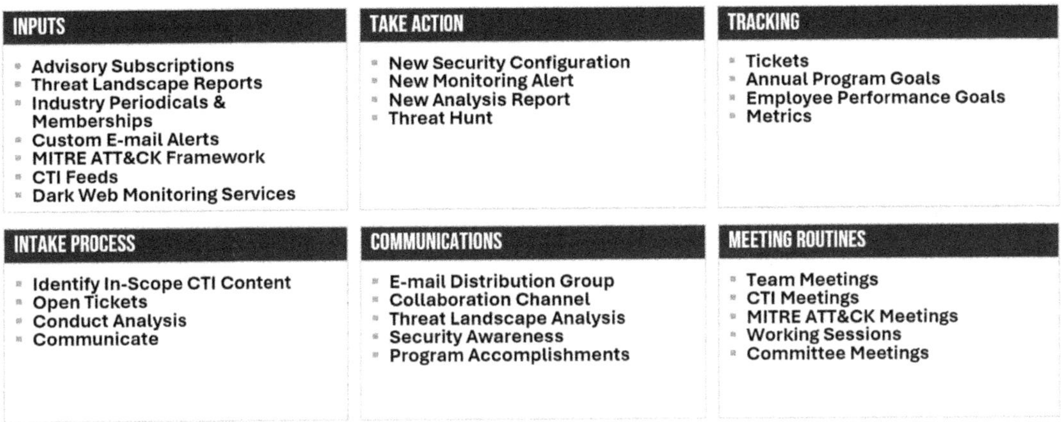

Figure 5.1 Cyber threat intelligence program.

Industry periodicals and memberships

Expand CTI scope beyond enterprise security to include your organization's industry. For example, if you are within a financial institution consider these resources:

- BankInfoSecurity - www.bankinfosecurity.com
- American Banker - www.americanbanker.com
- Financial Services Information Sharing and Analysis Center (FS-ISAC)
- American Bankers Association

There are 20+ ISACs across private sector critical infrastructures. ISAC membership provides services beyond CTI, including tabletop exercises. Some resources cover an industry as a whole, with cybersecurity and operational risk as sub-topics. It is worthwhile to consume that content as well to develop business acumen and to understand how the industry is evolving and changing moving forward.

Threat landscape reports

Threat landscape reports provide real world trending of threat actor activities. There are many reports to choose from. Consider reviewing these on an annual basis:

- Data Breach Investigations Report - Verizon
- M-Trends Report - Mandiant
- Cost of a Data Breach Report - IBM and Ponemon Institute
- X-Force Threat Intelligence Index - IBM Security
- Threat Detection Report - Red Canary

When a reputable cybersecurity report is published, conduct a critical review that answers the 'so what' question. Distill the report into consumable content with sections and bullets to frame a conversation. Focus on answering 'which of our practices and plans align with this' and 'which new controls should be established'. Pull risk mitigation recommendations from the report and discuss them with the team. Make recommendations to adapt to the threat landscape using tickets, projects and annual goals. Some initiatives may need to wait until next year based on team capacity and funding.

Custom E-mail alerts

Create a Google e-mail alert with a boolean search such as 'Compromised OR breached OR hacked' to keep apprised of recent data breaches. Adding the operator 'AND' with a vendor name can be useful for the Third Party Risk Management program.

E-mail distribution group

Establish an e-mail distribution group so each team member receives alerts and advisories (e.g. cyber-threat-intel-dg@acme.com). Recipients can configure a mail processing rule to save inbound messages to a folder.

Dark web monitoring services

Leverage a service that searches for suspicious or malicious activity related to your organization. For example, you would want to know if someone posted login credentials or company data for sale. The service should also include CTI specific to your organization and industry in a broader context.

5.3 INTAKE PROCESS

Receiving advisories is only the first step. Each team member may think someone else is addressing an advisory or alert. Therefore, it is necessary to have an intake process to ensure each message is addressed. Here are options:

- When an advisory is received, assign a team member to process it
- Have a periodic meeting to analyze threat intelligence
- Enter each advisory into a service desk ticket to ensure it is processed

Identify advisories that must be analyzed, researched and actioned as appropriate. Establish procedures and tracking to ensure in-scope advisories are subjected to that end-to-end process.

5.4 PROCESSING AN ADVISORY

Critically evaluate each advisory, considering whether it makes sense to:

- Implement a hardening security configuration as a preventive control
- Create a new security monitoring alert
- Create an analysis report when it is difficult to create an alert with low false positives
- Conduct threat hunting activity
- Conduct research to determine if action is necessary

Create a service desk ticket to track each new task or work effort to closure. Assign ticket categories to ensure employees and the team receive credit for their work. It's also good to have data when requesting additional headcount and to defend the value-add of the CTI program.

5.5 HIGH RISK SECURITY ADVISORIES

When a high risk security advisory is received, it must be evaluated with a sense of urgency. CISA Known Exploited Vulnerabilities fall into this category. Upon receipt of a high risk security advisory:

- Determine if it applies to installed operating systems or software
- Open a ticket with an appropriate risk rating
  - Consider in-place compensating controls that reduce the risk
- Track and facilitate remediation in accordance with standards

5.6 TAKE ACTION!

Leverage cyber threat intelligence to combat emerging threats. Be mindful that risk exists when controls are not deployed. Stack rank security issues in order of risk priority. Move with a purpose when it comes to closing them out. Measure performance of the CTI Program with quality assurance and metrics.

The CTI Program must influence risk mitigation identified by cyber threat intelligence. It is not enough to assign a ticket to another team. If high risk CTI tickets are not addressed with a sense of urgency, determine whether existing metrics provide risk transparency to senior executives. For example, most organizations have metrics to track patch implementation. However, the need for a security configuration to be implemented may not be tracked. The CTI leader needs to influence creation of a new metric in that event. Creating a high risk CTI mitigation metric is another option.

5.7 CTI MEETINGS

Assemble the team to discuss cyber threat intelligence from a variety of sources.

- Have an informal round robin discussion where each team member shares threat intelligence (e.g. advisories, articles, blog entries, etc.)
- With each topic consider whether it makes sense to:
  - Implement a hardening security configuration as a preventive control
  - Create a new security monitoring alert
  - Create an analysis report when it is difficult to create an alert with low false positives
  - Conduct threat hunting activity
- Team members should volunteer to take point
  - Open a service desk ticket to track to closure
  - You will get credit for your initiative

Establish a practice of 'take one', meaning that each person leaves the meeting opening at least one ticket to address cyber threat intelligence. That prevents the meeting from being a coffee break, where attendees admire the problem. Instead, everyone leaves taking action to identify or mitigate risk.

CTI meetings are a quality assurance measure. CTI is a continuous operational process. Team members should review CTI content throughout the week and take action without waiting for the next meeting.

5.8 SECURITY MONITORING ALERTS

Leverage the knowledge gained from cyber threat intelligence to create security monitoring alerts. The goal is to reduce dwell time, from when a threat actor gains access to the IT environment to the time they are detected. Detecting a threat actor quickly provides time to eradicate them from the IT environment, preventing an incident from evolving into a data breach.

Living off the land

Threat actors are reluctant to bring malicious software into a target environment because it increases the risk of discovery and alert by security monitoring software. A common tactic is to 'live off the land' by using software already present in the IT environment. Create monitoring alerts for suspicious commands, attempts to disable logging and use of administrative tools such as PowerShell.

Adversary toolkits

Create monitoring alerts based on commercial, freeware and open-source software that is not used by your organization. For example, if your organization has purchased WinZip for file compression, then monitor and alert on 7-Zip because that may be an adversary trying to avoid detection. Use this same technique to create alerts for alternative file transfer tools and remote desktop management software that is not in use. Monitor for penetration testing tools as well.

5.9 THREAT HUNTING PROGRAM

Threat hunting is a process to actively search for adversaries and malicious software within an IT environment. It is a proactive approach to security that assumes breach. The goal is to detect suspicious activity early to prevent a security incident from progressing to a data breach (Figure 5.2).

A Threat Hunting Program should monitor for emerging threats, Indicators of Compromise (IOCs) and adversary Tactics, Techniques and Procedures (TTPs). Threat intelligence should feed implementation of security monitoring (looking forward) and threat hunting (looking backward). Hunting activity may result in incident response, creation of monitoring alerts and new analysis reports.

A threat hunt may be initiated upon review of a security advisory or as an outcome from a cyber threat intelligence meeting. It is a good practice to conduct monthly threat hunts at a minimum.

5.10 THREAT HUNTING ACTIVITIES

Security events

Research available security logging events for operating systems and commercial software. Search logging for events such as a username does not exist. Search for threat actor activity detailed in CTI advisories. In the aftermath of security incidents and data breaches, details of suspicious activity are often found in logs. It makes sense to actively search for that.

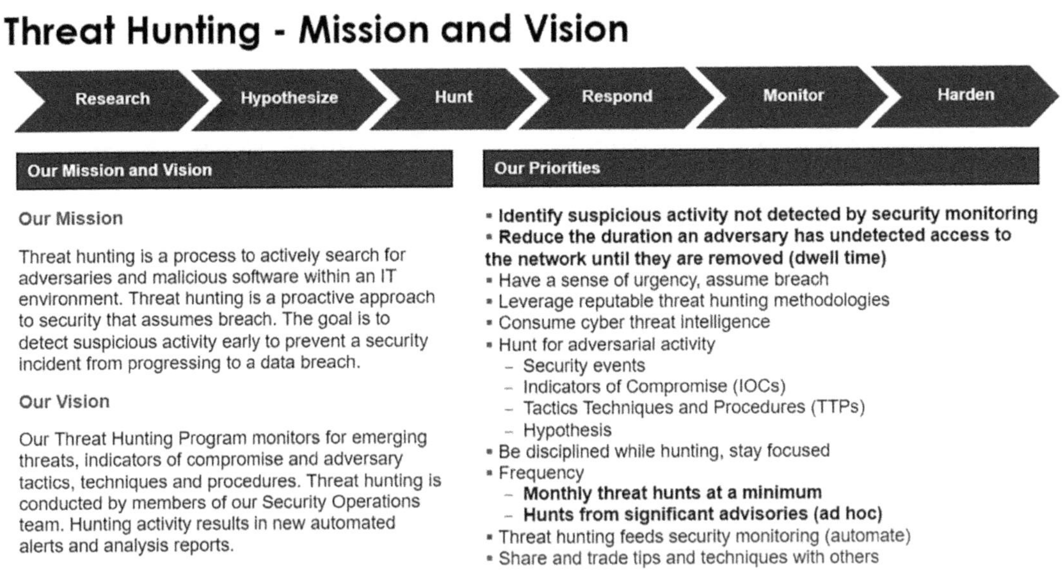

Figure 5.2 Threat hunting - Mission and vision.

Indicators of compromise (IOCs)

CTI advisories provide evidence of past instructions such as IP addresses, domain names and file hashes. It is typical for threat actors to change IOCs to evade detection moving forward. However, log and event data contain historical IOC data, which can be used to identify threat actor activity. All that remains is to search for it. Keep in mind that threat actors may persist in an IT environment for months.

Tactics techniques and procedures (TTPs)

Search for lateral movement. When an adversary gains access, they move from system to system searching for sensitive data. Search for that change in behavior, such as two systems that communicated for the first time in six months. Search for use of a privileged account late in the night and failed attempts to export data.

Hypothesis

Hypothesis is a core component to threat hunting. Here are examples:

- An adversary has gained access to the IT environment and is searching for sensitive data
- An employee seeks to export data and take it to their next employer
- An employee is committing fraud without being detected

Documentation

When conducting a threat hunt, document mid-level details within a ticket or a report.

- Reference the source material such as a CISA security advisory
- Include the IOCs and/or TTPs

- Document how the threat hunt was conducted (e.g. using the SIEM or by logging into a server)
- Include details of the search criteria (based on the IOCs/TTPs)

If suspicious activity is detected, initiate your organization's Incident Response process immediately.

5.11 THREAT HUNTING BUSINESS CASE

Threat hunting is a modern practice to detect threat actors before they cause business impact. Here are talking points for a conversation with executives:

- Endpoint protection and security monitoring alone are not sufficient
- When an adversary slips by, threat hunting is necessary to detect them
- Threat hunting is an active search for adversaries within the IT environment
- Need to detect adversaries quickly (dwell time and mean time to detect)
- Early detection can mean the difference between an incident and a data breach
- Threat hunting feeds security monitoring requirements

5.12 ADVERSARIAL TACTICS

Past is prologue. History repeats itself. All information security professionals should familiarize themselves with adversarial tactics such as the MITRE ATT&CK Framework and Sun Tzu.

If you have not already, read Sun Tzu's The Art of War and internalize that way of adversarial thinking:

- "To fight and conquer in all your battles is not supreme excellence; supreme excellence consists in breaking the enemy's resistance without fighting."
- "If you know your enemy and know yourself, you need not fear the result of a hundred battles."

In their book Unrestricted Warfare, two Chinese generals discuss warfare. They mention the United States' dependence on systems and describe eight "beyond limits" warfare principles:

- **Omnidirectionality:** There are no boundaries to the battlefield, including technological space. Ordinary people and experts may be targeted.
- **Synchrony:** Attack to completion, in different locations, at the same time. "With modern, high-tech measures, this process may take the blink of an eye."
- **Limited objectives:** "When setting objectives, give full consideration to the feasibility of accomplishing them. Do not pursue objectives which are unrestricted in time and space."
- **Unlimited measures:** Rules of engagement do not apply when pursuing a combat objective. The burning of the south in the U.S. Civil War is an example.
- **Asymmetry:** Do not confront the enemy head-to-head. Instead, be unpredictable and use the tactics of guerrilla warfare, terrorism and network war. Strike where your adversary does not expect to be hit and exploit their soft spots. This use of force will result in a huge psychological shock.

- **Minimal consumption:** "Combine the superiorities of several kinds of combat resources in several kinds of areas to form up a completely new form of combat, accomplishing the objective while at the same time minimizing consumption."
- **Multidimensional coordination:** This principle refers to cooperation between different forces in different spheres in order to accomplish a combat objective. Non-military and non-war factors are included in the sphere of war.
- **Adjustment and control of the entire process:** "Modern, high-tech measures may make the entire course of a war extremely short, and incidentally make adjusting and controlling it much more difficult."

The generals' words are sobering. Since foreign entities consider cyberspace a soft target and commercial industry to be fair game, these are principles worth considering when formulating defensive strategies.

Clear your head and put yourself in a ruthless mindset when conducting analysis. Identify gaps and design controls against a hostile nation state and artificial intelligence. They are capable of no courtesy, no warning, no honor and no mercy.

5.13 CTI PROGRAM INDICATORS

A CTI Program is critical to protecting an organization against modern threats. It must be monitored to remain an effective control. Here are CTI Program Indicators for your consideration:

- Each team member sends several submissions per month as an indication of consistent cyber threat intelligence monitoring
  - There are submissions throughout the month, versus a pattern of prepping one week before the cyber threat intel meeting
- Subscriptions from common cyber threat intelligence sources are processed by the program, including CISA and vendor advisories
  - Team members submit cyber threat intel from reputable sources beyond the basics, such as articles and blog entries
- Evidence of program execution
  - Messages to the cyber threat intel e-mail distribution group
  - Minutes from the monthly cyber threat intel meeting
  - CTI service desk tickets to conduct research or to take action, such as implement mitigations, create new monitoring alerts or to conduct a threat hunt

For additional guidance, reference Chapter 9: Threat Landscape and Controls Analysis.

Chapter 6

Third party risk management

6.1 INTRODUCTION

This chapter describes designing a Third Party Risk Management (TPRM) program. It details the end-to-end process: identify, risk rank, assess, risk treatment, monitor, oversight, escalations and decommissioning. A framework is provided as a program outline, with decision points to select from. Options presented will help mitigate third party risk, whether you have an existing TPRM program or if you need to establish one. This chapter is also an example of program architecture in practice. These concepts can be used to design, implement and lead other risk management programs. The goal of this chapter and this book is to provide you with practical advice you can use upon return to work.

6.2 THIRD PARTY RISK

A third party is an external entity that your organization does business with. Third parties include vendors, service providers and partners. Third party risk can be significant. Vendor and service provider security posture varies. A large organization may have significant issues within their security posture. Conversely, a medium-sized organization may have strong risk management and a mature control environment in place. Therefore, the size of an organization cannot be used to determine security posture.

There is limited visibility into vendor and service provider control environments. Think about it. We are giving an external organization access to our sensitive data. They have their own technology platform and their own people and processes. That is a lot of trust. Our organization is still responsible for that information and the business impact of a data breach. A TPRM program must validate the security posture of third parties and mitigate that risk.

Threat actors follow the path of least resistance, compromising vendors and service providers. Data breaches can have a significant impact on the clients. For these reasons third party risk has been elevated to a board-level concern.

6.3 THIRD PARTY RISK MANAGEMENT PROGRAM

A TPRM program begins by identifying third parties to ensure they are evaluated and managed. Next, risk rate and stack-rank them in order of risk priority. The highest risk third parties are subjected to the most thorough evaluation. The assessment process includes an

DOI: 10.1201/9781003543619-6

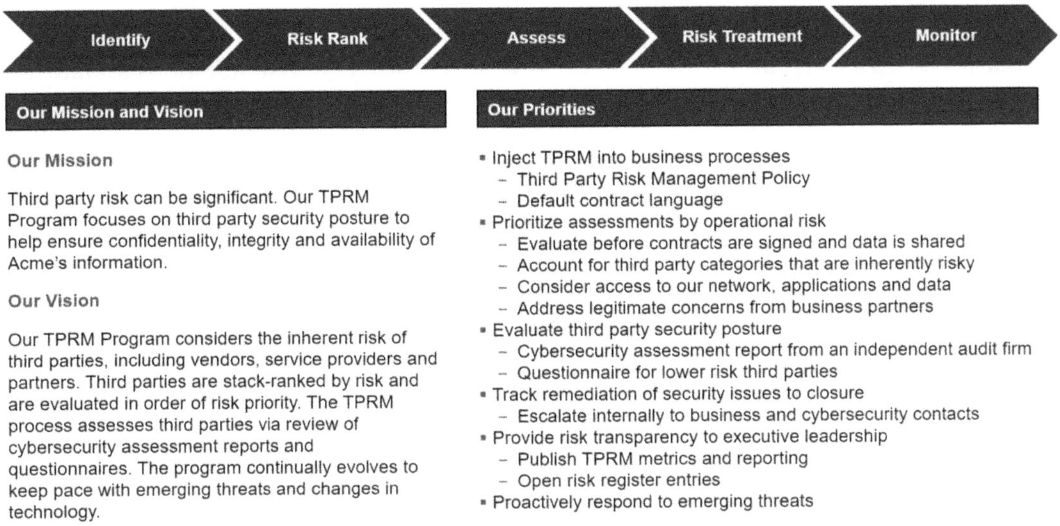

Figure 6.1 Mission and vision – TPRM.

on-site assessment or a self-assessment questionnaire, based on the risk of the vendor or service provider. Next is risk treatment, to identify security issues and influence risk mitigation. When vendors or service providers refuse to work within the program, it is necessary to escalate and enter into risk governance such as a risk register entry. The TPRM program monitors vendors and service providers year-over-year. This process repeats and must evolve to adapt to the threat landscape and newly adopted technology (Figure 6.1).

6.4 IDENTIFY THIRD PARTIES

The first step in the TPRM framework is to identify third parties. Start with program scope, which types of third parties are in-scope and out-of-scope for TPRM processes. A sample program scope could include vendors and service providers as in-scope, with partners, subsidiaries and affiliates as out-of-scope. Document third parties in an inventory to enable program processes.

New/prospective third parties

Notification of new and prospective third parties should be sent by sourcing, procurement and/or supply chain management. IT, lines of business and business units should provide notice in the initial stages of planning. The TPRM program needs to be included early-on in those due diligence processes to leave time for a thorough risk assessment of each new or prospective third party. The TPRM assessment process must conclude before a contract with a new third party is signed. Any deviation from that policy should require a risk register entry approved by senior executives.

6.5 RISK RANK

The next step in the TPRM framework is to stack-rank third parties in order of risk priority.

Vendor profile questionnaire

Send a survey to Third Party Business Process Owners each year. Ask questions about their vendor or service provider. Be mindful that service subscriptions can change year-to-year. Perhaps one year a service provider does not have access to sensitive data and next year, they do. Ask each year, 'does this third party store, process or transmit our sensitive data' as a catch all question that is difficult to avoid. Follow up with a separate question of what types of data are shared, with options and definitions such as PII, Personal Health Information (PHI), payment account numbers, etc. Include a catch-all category of 'Other' to capture all types of sensitive data.

Ask if the third party has internal network or system access. System administration and remote support access are a significant security exposure. Determine if the third party conducts software development or if they provide a business critical service. Each of these trigger questions should result in the third party being rated at a higher risk tier.

Risk score

A risk score can account for cybersecurity, privacy, finance and other processes to identify and mitigate third party risk. It is a proprietary approach customized to the organization.

6.6 ASSESSMENT OPTIONS

How third parties will be assessed depends on the risk tolerance of the organization, staffing and funding (Figure 6.2).

Option I

Option 1 above includes on-site assessments conducted by the TPRM program. In this model assessment work papers are created based on your organization's control framework, inclusive of information security and privacy requirements. Assessment of the third party service is conducted. The results are a thorough assessment that identifies risk where sensitive data is stored, processed and transmitted. The downsides of this approach are third parties may refuse on-site assessment due to operational impact and there is an incurred cost of on-site assessment employees and travel expenses. Option 1 is the most expensive, with the lowest residual risk.

Option	Restricted	Confidential	Internal	Resource Consumption	Residual Risk
1	On-Site Assessment	On-Site Assessment	Questionnaire w/Artifact Review	High	Low
2	SOC 2 Type II Report	SOC 2 Type II Report	Questionnaire w/Artifact Review	Medium	Medium
3	SOC 2 Type II Report	Questionnaire	Questionnaire	Low	High

Definitions:

On-Site Assessment: An information security professional is sent to the service provider's facility to evaluate if required controls are in place to protect data confidentiality and ensure data is available in accordance with service level agreements.

Questionnaire and Artifact Review: The vendor or service provider answers a list of security questions. Artifacts are requested for a percentage of controls. Artifacts include screen shots and excerpts from process and procedures documents.

Questionnaire: Only a questionnaire is requested from the vendor or service provider. This results in the highest residual risk due to reliance on an attestation without any validation of controls.

Figure 6.2 Assessment options – TPRM.

Option 2

Option 2 applies to many TPRM programs. SOC 2 Type II assessment reports are evaluated for information security issues. Lower risk third parties are required to complete a questionnaire. Some TPRM programs also request artifacts such as vulnerability scan summary reports. Option 2 is moderately expensive, with moderate residual risk due to reliance on SOC 2 assessments. Reference 'SOC Report Reviews' later in this chapter for more information.

Option 3

Option 3 is a passive approach. The TPRM program conducts cursory reviews of SOC assessment reports and questionnaires, searching for controls that are not in place. No artifact reviews are conducted. Some organizations operate in this model. It is a sign of a compliance driven organization. Option 3 is least expensive, with high residual risk.

Each of the three options above rely on contract language that provides an annual right of assessment.

Questionnaires

Questionnaires are typically used for lower risk third parties. Questionnaires are an attestation, meaning a statement versus the result of an independent test. Questionnaires are a self-assessment. Therefore the accuracy of responses will vary. A person that fills out a questionnaire may provide responses without making informed decisions. They may not know whether a control is in place or not. Some questions may not be answered truthfully. Other answers may be forward-looking statements, with plans for that control to be in place in the future. For these reasons, questionnaires should not be relied upon for third parties where sensitive data is shared or for those that provide a mission-critical service. Artifact reviews can be used to mitigate risk, such as reviewing a penetration test summary or the results of disaster recovery testing.

TPRM assessment scope

Remember to document assessment activities that are out-of-scope for the TPRM program. For example:

- On-site assessments
- Non-cybersecurity assessments
  - Legal and financial
  - Privacy assessments
  - Business continuity assessments
- Fourth parties

The TPRM program should not be solely driven by information security. In many cases it is owned by sourcing and procurement or supply chain management. In that scenario, information security is a part of that process. Fourth parties are out of scope for most organizations due to resource constraints and lack of a direct contractual agreement.

Data volume

Determine with senior executives how data volume will affect the TPRM program. Most organizations accept the risk of sharing a small amount of sensitive data with a third party. If the number of records falls beneath that threshold, an assessment will not be conducted that year. Update TPRM policy and procedures to match management's directive.

6.7 QUESTIONNAIRE CONTENT

Most TPRM programs have third parties that are evaluated by questionnaire. Here are three options for paths you can pursue:

1. Map to an internal control framework
   Create a custom questionnaire. Map to your organization's internal control framework. That typically includes reputable practices such as the NIST Cybersecurity Framework, requirements from laws, regulations and contractual obligations and controls to mitigate emerging threats. Be conservative with the number of questions. Otherwise, third parties may be on solid ground when they refuse to fill it out.
2. Purchase a question set
   Commercial TPRM questionnaires are peer reviewed and are kept current. Some questionnaires are mapped to service categories, which provides a more targeted evaluation of controls. This may be a good use of resources depending on price, versus creating and maintaining a custom question set. Third parties may appreciate this approach because the same questions are submitted by other customers.
3. Leverage a service provider
   Consider leveraging a service provider to take point for questionnaires. The process is straight forward. Introduce the service provider to your third party. The service provider takes it from there, sending a link to a question set, following up to have it filled out or to chase down artifacts. That is significant time and energy. They review the questionnaire and the artifacts. At the end, they generate a report. The downside to this approach is some service providers will not allow customers to use a custom question set. A benefit of this approach is vendors and service providers fill out the questionnaire once per year. When a customer submits a request, a completed questionnaire may be already available. That can speed up your TPRM process.

6.8 TPRM PROCESSES

Create process diagrams to flesh out the design of your TPRM program. This sample diagram represents the questionnaire component of a TPRM program. It includes references to the 'TPRM Initiation Process' at the beginning and the 'TPRM Risk Treatment Process' at the end (Figure 6.3).

Process diagrams are a core component to program architecture, a way to design and implement operational risk programs. There are several uses for process diagrams:

- **Building a new TPRM program:** Establish diagrams for process design sessions with executive leadership. Once a process is approved, the team is cleared to make the necessary changes.

- **TPRM team members:** Include process diagrams in the TPRM procedures manual. Provide it to new team members on day one and have a conversation.
- **Business process owners:** Include process diagrams in the TPRM program welcome packet. When a new process owner is onboarded, host an orientation meeting with them.
- **Process risk assessment:** Leverage Failure Mode and Effects Analysis (FMEA) to determine where the process may break down. Reference Section 1.11 for more information.
- **Defending the program:** Process diagrams should be used to represent the TPRM program when a new executive in the chain-of-command is onboarded. They will want to understand the value add of the program at a mid-level. Process diagrams are also a good way to partner with auditors and regulators.

6.9 SOC REPORT REVIEWS

Service providers that submit a SOC 2 Type II report may have control deficiencies that are not identified during the exam. This is due to reliance on the Trust Services Criteria (TSC) versus a more detailed list of requirements such as 100+ controls and 300+ implementation examples within the NIST Cybersecurity Framework.

Some organizations conduct a passive review of SOC 2 reports. The high-level approach is to check for an 'unqualified' or clean opinion from the Auditor.

It is necessary to conduct an active review of SOC 2 reports to conduct proper due diligence. The focus should be controls that are not detailed within the TSC. The basic approach is to:

1. Start with a list of expected cybersecurity controls
2. Review the SOC 2 report from top to bottom, crossing off controls from the list as you go
3. Send an e-mail to the service provider asking about controls that are not included in the report
4. Request artifacts for a subset of controls to verify whether they are in place

6.10 ANNUAL ASSESSMENT CADENCE

TPRM programs run on an annual cycle (Figure 6.4). Document assessment priorities to foster a risk-based conversation with executives. Agree upon an annual assessment capacity to manage expectations. That provides context when an operational function or a line of business makes a request that exceeds TPRM program scope. They may want a new population of third parties evaluated. Mergers and acquisitions can also exceed TPRM program scope. When annual assessment capacity is documented in advance, a request for additional assessments should include funding. This is a fundamental way of managing up and defending the program.

6.11 RISK TREATMENT

Risk treatment is a process for mitigating risk to an acceptable level. That begins with assigning a risk rating and remediation timeframes to each control. When an assessment concludes, the TPRM program sends notification of security issues to the third party. That includes a request for target remediation dates within standards. The Business Process

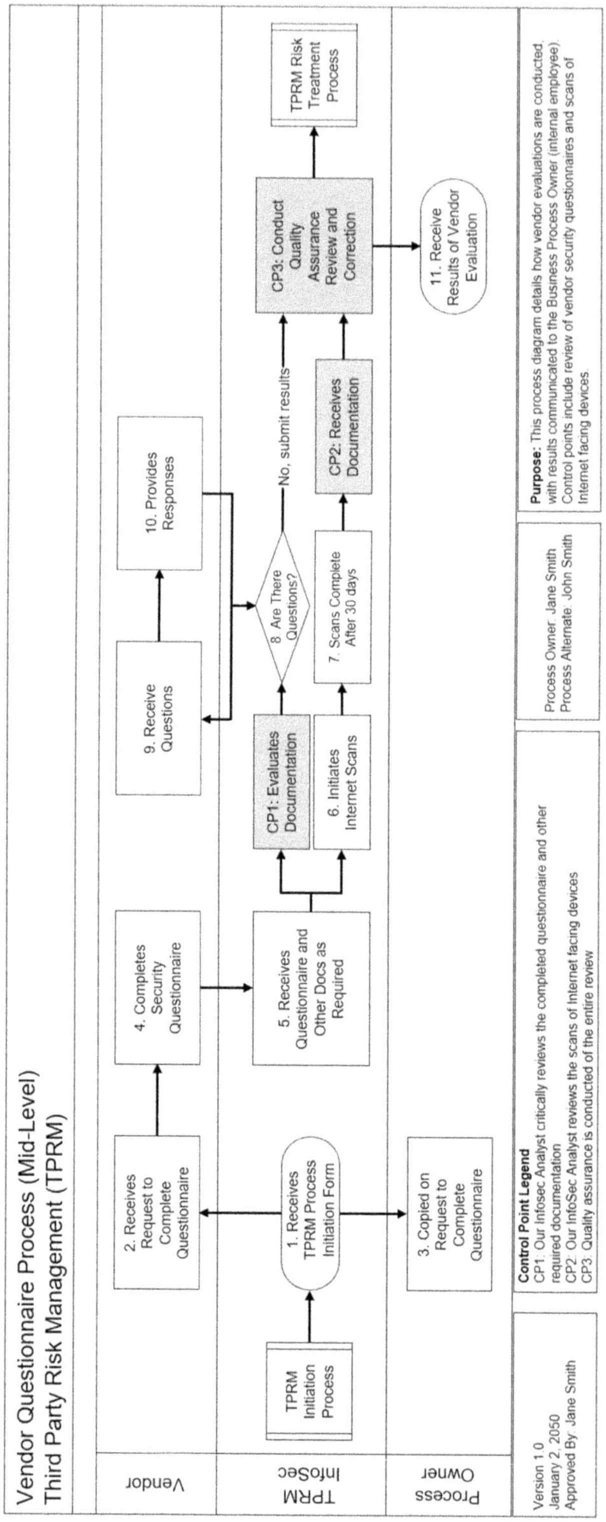

Figure 6.3 TPRM processes.

Priority	Scope	Rationale	Capacity
1	New (prospective) third parties	Determine third party security posture prior to signing a contract and initiating service (i.e. before sharing data).	*100* assessments (example)
2	Legitimate concerns from risk partners	Risk-based requests for assessments from corporate, lines of business or business units.	
3	Existing third parties	Leverage a list provided by sourcing and procurement. The TPRM Manager selects third parties from the list once it has been stack-ranked by risk.	
4	Documentation reviews	When a large company refuses to participate in the TPRM process, alternative documentation may be used to validate their security controls (e.g. SOC 2 Type II, ISO 27001 or government certifications).	

Figure 6.4 Annual assessment cadence.

Owner is included on related communications. The TPRM program follows up periodically and tracks remediation to closure. If the third party will not remediate a significant control deficiency, TPRM escalates to the Business Process Owner. Third parties consider the Business Process Owner as their customer, so this is an important step. Reference to contract terms may be a way to influence remediation. Otherwise, it is necessary to file a risk register entry to ensure executive leadership has information to make informed decisions. Risk register entries must be mitigated or accepted within a risk governance process. The TPRM program will have fulfilled its role of providing risk transparency in that scenario. If the risk is significant, executives may decide to avoid doing business with this third party and transition to another company.

6.12 WHEN A THIRD PARTY REFUSES

When a third party refuses to participate in the TPRM program or to move forward with a process step, reach out to the Business Process Owner for support. Sometimes a call from the customer contact to their account representative is all that is needed to move things forward. If a third party refuses to answer the TPRM questionnaire, ask if there are other options available such as an assessment report or a program certification. If a third party refuses to provide vulnerability scans, ask if they will sanitize an existing report or if they will provide summary pages that include the number of high and moderate risk findings. Think in terms of how can we verify the security posture of the third party to a level of quality that meets the needs of our TPRM program. When sending the TPRM assessment closeout message, mention the third party provided limited risk transparency. Include compensating controls and which information/documents were excluded. Determine whether it is appropriate to file a risk register entry.

6.13 TPRM CONTRACT ADDENDUM

Include information security requirements within third party contracts. A TPRM Contract Addendum is used for that purpose. The addendum is incorporated into to an existing contract, especially if we are using the third party's contract template. That contract template is biased toward the third party organization, so we need to add security requirements with our TPRM addendum.

- Compliance with reputable information security practices such as the NIST Cybersecurity Framework or ISO 27001
- Data protection
- Vulnerability management
- Access control
- Detective controls
- Incident response planning and exercises
- Data backup
- Disaster recovery
- Multi-Factor Authentication
- Third party risk management
- Privacy management
- Information security assessment
- Security awareness training
- Security incident and breach notification
- Return and destruction of data

The information security assessment section should include requirements for the third party to participate within the TPRM program. This is a partial listing of addendum section headers. Collaborate with an attorney to ensure appropriate legal narrative is included.

Redline process

Third parties will want to redline or modify security contract language. Establish a process with legal to engage someone with a cybersecurity background, such as TPRM or the information security team. If a service provider says we would like to strike this control that does not apply to the services we are providing, that may be reasonable. It is necessary to ensure they are not removing controls that need to be in place to protect your organization. The redline process should require an information security professional to review contracts pertaining to IT services. This is especially important when the contract is written by the service provider. We need to take our default security language and enter it as an addendum or have one of our security professionals negotiate inserting the same requirements throughout the contract. Qualified information security professionals should participate in the redline process.

6.14 DECOMMISSION

Third parties must be securely decommissioned when service is terminated. Ensure removal of company/client data and any access to company systems or network, if applicable.

Meet internally with the Business Process Owner and our Information Security Manager to determine which data is in scope and timing for decommissioning activities.

Discuss these areas of focus and take action as appropriate:

- Return of client data: Submit a written request to the third party requesting a copy of client data in a mutually acceptable format. Confirm with the business unit or operational function that the data export appears to be complete.

- Destruction of client data: Submit a written request to the third party asking them to erase, destroy and/or render unrecoverable all client data.
- Rescind accesses: Submit a written request to the third party asking them to rescind all accesses to their service, including network, system and application accounts. Confirm with our IT department that any company internal hosted accounts or network connections with the third party have been terminated.

The third party should certify in writing that these actions have been completed within seven days. Where practical and technically feasible, confirm that decommissioning activities have been completed.

6.15 QUALITY ASSURANCE

So at this point the TPRM program is performing well right? To be determined. If a TPRM program does not have a mature intake process, third parties are unaccounted for and there can be significant operational risk issues. Quality assurance is necessary to ensure the program is functioning as intended.

Definition of third parties

If your TPRM program has an intake process fed by sourcing, procurement and/or supply chain management, review their policy documentation. Understand their definition of third parties. If there are any business categories out-of-scope such as law firms, that same criteria omits those third parties from the TPRM program. So watch for that. If you are depending on a business process to feed your cybersecurity program, keep in mind that process may not be entirely cyber focused, so you need to take a hard look at the data that is being submitted and the processes that provide that data.

Shadow IT

There are times when a business unit or an individual leader will directly engage a service provider. When this occurs outside of IT and TPRM processes, then obviously we are not going to know that sensitive data is exposed and if the control environment is weak. It is necessary to monitor for business units using cloud computing environments on their own. The cost of service is relatively inexpensive and an employee may use their corporate card to fund it.

Systems of record

Request access to systems of record within sourcing and procurement and export a list of third parties. Compare the list to the TPRM system of record. Gain access to financial systems. Verify the company names on invoices and within corporate credit card transactions match what is expected within the TPRM system of record.

Business category

Here are examples of service providers that most likely have access to sensitive data:

• **IT Services** – Cloud hosting services – SaaS applications – Infrastructure support – Data analytics • **Healthcare** – Health insurance – Dental insurance – Pharmacy benefits card – Health savings accounts – Life insurance – Medical labs	• **Finance** – Payroll – Financial services – Expense – Travel – Corporate credit card • **HR Services** – Performance planning – Job applications – Document signing – Background checks • **Law Firms**

Business categories are a useful risk lens. When a third party has access to the internal network or hands-on system administration access, that is something to be concerned about. Human resources services have access to performance planning, performance evaluations, salary data and employee Personally Identifiable Information (PII). Be mindful of healthcare third parties. They expand beyond the primary insurance provider to a litany of third parties such as dental, pharmacy benefits card, health savings accounts and life insurance providers.

Business categories can be used as a final quality assurance measure beyond best effort identification with vendor profile questionnaires and risk scoring. Conduct your own analysis:

1. Gather a comprehensive listing of third parties
2. Assign a business category to each organization
3. Determine which third parties obviously have access to sensitive data
4. Assign a risk tier to each entity without regard for existing process
5. Compare your analysis to a listing of how those third parties are tiered by risk today

Quality assurance is an internal control where a team looks out for its members. It is better for the team to identify an issue and correct the root cause, then for a client or auditor to bring it to our attention. Identification and resolution of legitimate issues should be encouraged and recognized as accomplishments. To do otherwise encourages skeletons in the closet and related business impact.

TPRM program metrics

Metrics are a core component of program architecture. Key Performance Indicators measure how a control performs by process design. Key Risk Indicators measure current posture versus the organization's risk tolerance. Reference TPRM program metrics within the 'Reporting and Metrics' chapter.

6.16 WELCOME PACKET

A Welcome Packet is an orientation document for anyone that is subjected to the TPRM program. It is a courtesy to explain their role and what is expected of them. Here is a framework for a TPRM Welcome Packet.

- **Program overview**
- **Threat landscape**
- **Roles and responsibilities**
  - Business Process Owner
  - Third party risk management
  - Third parties
  - Sourcing and procurement
  - Legal
  - Information security
- **Required documentation**
- **Initiating the TPRM process**
- **Timeframe for the review**
- **Questions and comments**
- **Complementary processes**
- **Communications routines**
- **Metrics and reporting**
- **Process diagram**
- **References**

A Welcome Packet also helps manage expectations. It includes the TPRM process, timeframes, metrics and reporting. If there is a line of business or an executive asking for something beyond that, there is program documentation to maintain boundaries.

6.17 SHARED RESPONSIBILITY MATRICES

Risk is incurred when a process transitions between a service provider and their client.

Both parties may think the other is taking action. A Shared Responsibilities Matrix documents who is responsible for a list of security tasks. The matrix divides responsibilities between service providers and clients. As an example, cloud hosting providers are responsible for **security of the cloud**, the hardware, software, networking and data centers. The client is responsible for **security in the cloud**, their applications, virtual systems and data stored in the cloud. There is a shared security model where both service provider and client have security tasks.

Service providers communicate shared responsibilities within SOC 2 Type II reports and/or within guidance documentation. The client is responsible for a list of security tasks. Business users are focused on having the service up and running. The TPRM program should conduct a review to ensure client responsibilities are addressed by internal personnel.

Host a meeting with the business unit or operational function. Discuss a Shared Responsibilities Matrix containing client security tasks listed by the service provider. Consider whether additional controls are required. Service providers communicate client responsibilities with a focus on liability. Controls within internal processes may be necessary to mitigate operational risk. Ensure primary and alternate personnel are designated and trained for each security task. Confirm that necessary procedures are in place for continuity. Repeat the review process annually.

A sample Shared Responsibilities Matrix is included in Figure 6.5 below.

#	Control Description	Responsible (Primary)	Responsible (Alternate)	Accountable	Consulted	Informed
1	Customers add and delete user accounts within the application.	Jane Smith	John Smith	Alice Smith	Bob Smith	Jill Smith
2	Customers assign access roles within user segregation of duty principles and workflow requirements.	Jill Smith	Jane Smith	John Smith	Alice Smith	Bob Smith
3	Customers are responsible for maintaining their own data retention.	Bob Smith	Jill Smith	Jane Smith	John Smith	Alice Smith
4	Customers must assign someone to perform security administration.	Alice Smith	Bob Smith	Jill Smith	Jane Smith	John Smith
5	Customers are responsible for reviewing access rights on a periodic basis.	Jane Smith	John Smith	Alice Smith	Bob Smith	Jill Smith
6	Customers are responsible for staying informed of new functionality and for updating any internal controls or processes as appropriate.	Jill Smith	Jane Smith	John Smith	Alice Smith	Bob Smith
7	Customers are responsible for ensuring they are running the latest version of the application or for accepting the risk.	Bob Smith	Jill Smith	Jane Smith	John Smith	Alice Smith
8	Customers configure password settings or integrate their own SSO.	Alice Smith	Bob Smith	Jill Smith	Jane Smith	John Smith

Figure 6.5 Shared responsibility matrix.

6.18 POLICY - THIRD PARTY RISK MANAGEMENT

By now it is clear there is significant complexity in a TPRM program and what is required by the organization as a whole. Companies run on internal policies. Employees are required to sign-off on them and may be held accountable for significant violations. Leverage the weight executive directives by publishing a TPRM Policy. Here is a list of topics for inspiration:

- Program scope
- Roles and responsibilities
- Identify third parties
- Risk tiering
- Minimum number of records
- Assessment scope
- Assessment capacity
- Out-of-scope assessments
- Risk treatment
- Contract addendum
- Redline process
- Decommission

6.19 ROADMAP/MULTI-GENERATIONAL PLAN

Establish and maintain a multi-generational plan with three years of annual program goals. The first generation are goals to mature the program this year. We have committed to these goals. They must be accomplished by the end of the year. The second generation are tentative goals for next year. Some of them may change. The third generation are aspirational goals for two years out. We are applying foresight, predicting what will be needed in the future. The third generation are visionary goals, subject to change.

Lead change thoughtfully and deliberately. Be sensitive to the cues around you. People are more receptive to change in phases over two years than all at once. If you slow your pace, leadership may appreciate that more and you end up having a better work-life balance.

Goals presented to executive leadership are similar to a bond written in blood. Be conservative when committing to goals for the coming year. Unforeseen organizational changes may erode your ability to execute. Maintain a hidden portfolio of skunkworks goals to be safe and to demonstrate exceptional performance.

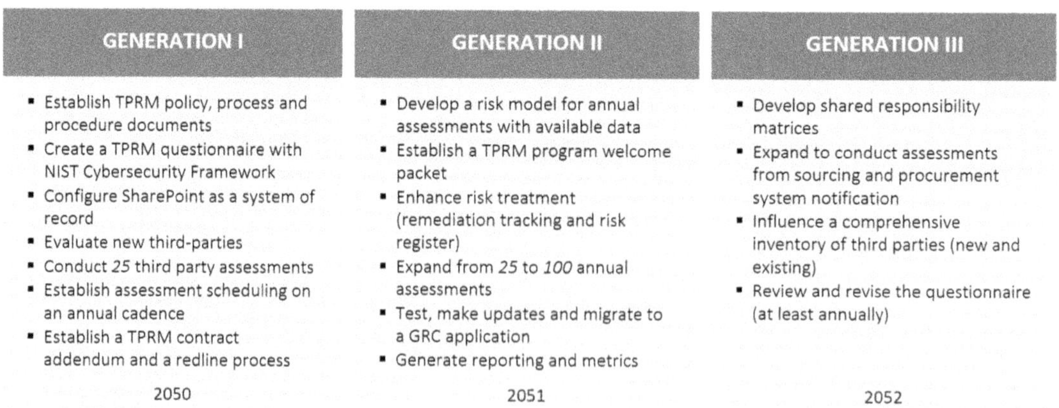

Figure 6.6 Roadmap/multi-generational plan.

6.20 COMMUNICATIONS

Be thoughtful and deliberate with program communications. When a new TPRM program executive is assigned, you need to introduce and defend the program. Plan for that first one-on-one meeting with your new executive. Be prepared to discuss a program overview and plans to drive the program forward. Have program documentation available to tell the story such as mission/vision statements (Figure 6.2), a process diagram (Figure 6.4) and a multi-generational plan (Figure 6.6). Send an e-mail after the meeting to summarize current state and future plans. Include a TPRM program overview deck, with links to supporting documentation. That enables your new executive to come up to speed quickly. The goal is for them to believe the TPRM program is functioning effectively and efficiently.

Look for opportunities to speak with lines of business and business units in established forums. Have a thoughtful and deliberate approach. Consider other stakeholders to speak with such as sourcing, procurement, supply chain management and information security. Join existing meeting routines to speak with your target audience where they gather. Present a few slides like a process diagram and a welcome packet if you are making changes to the TPRM program. Offer to have one-on-one meetings to answer questions or concerns from the leaders. Create and maintain a Communications Plan such as the one in Section 1.7.

6.21 PROGRAM ARCHITECTURE

TPRM is a challenging discipline. Focus on program maturity through program architecture.

- TPRM policy
- Mission/vision statements
- Process diagrams
- Procedures manual
- System of record
- Reporting
- Metrics, KPIs and KRIs
- Risk register
- Quality assurance
- Multi-generational plan
- Program overview deck
- Welcome packet
- Communications plan

That listing provides a path to implement a TPRM program and to identify opportunities for improvement. Consider to what extent each program element is in place. Is it in use? Is it comprehensive, high quality? Has it been reviewed recently? Is it current?

Section 2.14 contains more details on program architecture. Be mindful that you can apply program architecture techniques to other programs such as PCI compliance, application security, vulnerability management and insider threat. A Program Architect is a change agent. With those skills and experience you can build or significantly change programs, stabilize, transition and move on to the next adventure. It is possible to do that within one organization. You do not need to leave.

6.22 CALL TO ACTION

Establish or enhance your TPRM program. You can also identify a program within information security that is missing within your organization. Raise your hand in a one-on-one meeting with your manager. Broach the subject the program you want to establish or significantly change. Offer to lead a project. In the next one-on-one meeting, bring a mission/vision slide and a process diagram. Establish a project from there. You are empowered to drive change. Have professional courage and step outside of your comfort zone.

Chapter 7

Metrics and reporting

7.1 INTRODUCTION

This chapter provides practical advice to establish information security metrics, Key Performance Indicators (KPIs) and Key Risk Indicators (KRIs). It begins with an explanation of the differences between them and why each is necessary. Mid-level details of the end-to-end process are provided, from creating a metric to entering it into production. Examples of how to design metrics, KPIs and KRIs are provided. Areas of focus include information security measurements for all organizations, for a new process or function and in alignment with a control framework. The end game is to measure if processes and controls are functioning as designed. This chapter includes metrics and reporting readers can leverage upon returning to work. That saves time and helps influence risk mitigation.

7.2 METRICS, KPIs AND KRIs

Metrics are a path to an information security program under control. They provide opportunities to identify and mitigate risk. Metrics spark meaningful conversations.

Metric: A measurement of a process or technology objective by specific criteria.
KPI (Key Performance Indicator): A core program metric that measures how a process or technology is executing based on design criteria.
KRI (Key Risk Indicator): A core program metric that monitors conditions to predict an outcome that may exceed risk tolerance.

7.3 DESIGN COMPONENTS

Metrics are an effective way to monitor information security and operational risk. Leverage metric components as 'tools in a toolbox', to produce a quick initial design.

Metric Name: What are we concerned about? What condition are we monitoring?
Description: Which elements make up the metric? Does it answer the 'so what' question?
Measure: How is the metric calculated?
Thresholds: When the metric outputs a measurement, where does that fall? Executives tend to like green, yellow and red statuses, so it makes sense to go with that.

The basics have been covered above. Here is an initial metric draft using that framework (Figure 7.1):

DOI: 10.1201/9781003543619-7

#	Metric	Description	Measure	Thresholds
1	**Past Due Critical Vulnerabilities**	Systems with one or more past due critical vulnerabilities versus the total number of systems.	Systems with at least one or more past due critical vulnerabilities / Total number of systems	**Yellow:** <= 5% and > 10% **Red:** <= 10%

Figure 7.1 Metric draft v1.0 (Design View).

#	Metric	Description	Measure	Thresholds
1	**Past Due Critical Vulnerabilities - Internet-Exposed Systems**	Internet-exposed systems with one or more past due critical vulnerabilities.	Internet-exposed systems with one or more past due critical vulnerabilities / Total number of Internet-exposed systems	**Yellow:** <= 5% and > 10% **Red:** <= 10%

Figure 7.2 Metric draft v1.1.

This first iteration is a good start. However, that metric draft will raise questions in practice. Add details to better articulate the risk. Be more specific about which populations are being reported.

<u>Exposure:</u> What is the risk exposure of this process or technology? Is it internal or externally exposed?
<u>Scope:</u> Which control, system or group is in scope?
<u>Occurrence:</u> How often will the metric be generated? Does the time period make sense? Consider monthly occurrence for trending and to enable corrective action before an executive meeting routine that is less frequent. Monthly reporting can provide early warning when a metric starts to come out of threshold. Then we know and can course correct before two or three months goes by.
<u>Risk Transparency:</u> Who will have visibility into the metric (e.g. a manager, an executive, C-level executives and/or Board Members)? Into which communications and meeting routines will be metric be available? (Figure 7.2)

This second iteration of the metric is more specific and will draw less questions. These are Internet-exposed systems. A risk-focused executive will be concerned if this metric outputs a yellow or red status. It is clear that action is required.

If your organization does not have an information security metrics program, start with 3-5 metrics across critical cybersecurity functions such as vulnerability management, third party risk management and identity and access management. Identify activities that indicate whether the program is operating effectively and whether material risk exists. Start with just those relative few to avoid overwhelming control owners or executive leadership.

7.4 VULNERABILITY MANAGEMENT

The fire pyramid consists of fuel, oxygen and heat. Take one away and the fire is extinguished. Threats exploit vulnerabilities to compromise assets. Reduce vulnerabilities and mitigate risk of assets being stolen (Figure 7.3).

Past due vulnerability metrics

Past due in this context refers to a vulnerability management standard where remediation must occur within a certain timeframe. Vulnerabilities are categorized by risk severity such as critical, high, etc. Infrastructure vulnerability scans provide external, internal and authenticated coverage of systems such as servers, endpoints and network devices. Application

Figure 7.3 Fire versus compromise pyramids.

vulnerability scans include static code and dynamic web application coverage. Infrastructure and application penetration testing are also necessary. All infrastructure and application vulnerabilities should be represented in some form of this metric.

Unsupported technology metrics

If an organization is running an operating system or commercial software that is not supported, then the vendor no longer provides patches for it. When vulnerabilities are discovered for an unsupported technology, the system remains exposed to compromise.

7.5 THIRD PARTY RISK MANAGEMENT (TPRM)

Sensitive data is shared with service providers and vendors without much visibility into their control environment and security posture. That is what makes TPRM so important from an operational risk perspective.

Third-party security reports received

Third-party security assessment reports must be submitted every 365 days. It is necessary to have access to those reports to evaluate the security posture of third parties with access to sensitive data.

TPRM security reviews completed within SLA

Third-party security reviews that complete greater than two weeks from receiving required documentation and/or responses to security questions. This is a key performance indicator to monitor if TPRM Analysts are completing reviews as expected. If this metric measures out of threshold, it may be due to an increase in our population of third-parties or perhaps TPRM Analysts have resigned and a hiring freeze is in place. Attention is required when there is a change in performance execution of the program.

Annual TPRM security review volume

Third-party security reviews that have been completed this year, compared to annual volume requirement divided by monthly increments. If there is a goal of evaluating 120 third-parties, then it is expected to be roughly halfway through that population mid-way through the year. It is a good practice to track this metric monthly. Most organizations slow down mid-November through the end of the year due to holidays. For that reason, red, yellow and green thresholds should account for January through October. Metrics require a thoughtful and deliberate approach, accounting for the nuances of what is being measured.

Security requirements within third party contracts

Percentage of vendor and service provider contracts that do not include Acme security requirements. Redline edits approved by the information security or TPRM teams do not count against this metric. Risk register entries for significant security requirements missing from a contract are in-scope.

Assessments closed within timeframe

Percentage of open assessments with 'Date Started' field greater than six weeks. The assessment process includes having received all available documentation from the third party and a call to discuss remediation plans and target dates with them. That activity is expected to complete within a six week timeframe.

It is necessary to track how well our TPRM program is executing and the risk of service providers and vendors to our organization, especially when sensitive data is shared.

7.6 IDENTITY AND ACCESS MANAGEMENT (IAM)

Access control is one of the most significant domains in information security. Access should be only be granted for those that need them for their role. Check over time to determine whether they still need those accesses. As their role changes, rescind legacy accesses. When someone leaves the organization, systematically remove their accesses. Maintain metrics that track and measure that end-to-end process.

Access control reviews – employees

Employees with access control reviews completed within six months, divided by the total number of employees. Does that employee still need all the accesses they have and is their supervisor willing to attest to that? This metric should be generated by the time period required by policy.

Terminated user access

The number of user accounts that remain available for login after the user is no longer employed, divided by the total number of end users. This metric's threshold should be set at a very low percentage. As soon as someone leaves the organization, all of their accesses should be systematically rescinded. To allow otherwise opens the organization to significant risk, such as an outage or data loss due to a disgruntled former employee.

User local admin access

The number of end users with administrative access to their company-issued desktop or laptop, divided by the total number of end users. There needs to be oversight to ensure only endpoint administrators have administrative access to company issued workstations.

Otherwise, end users have access to install unauthorized software and to disable security software. If someone is logged in as administrator and malware is introduced, it is much easier for it to install.

Application MFA - Sensitive data

The percentage of web applications hosting sensitive data without multi factor authentication (MFA) in place, divided by the total number of in-scope applications. In this case, there is a policy that requires MFA to provide additional security where there is sensitive data within an application.

Single sign-on integration

The percentage of applications without SSO in place, divided by the total number of in-scope applications. More and more frequently, IT is using software as a service and vendor hosted applications that store sensitive data outside of our span of control. It is necessary to implement simple sign-on authentication where technologically feasible to mitigate that risk. In that scenario, when someone resigns or is terminated, their account access is disabled within an organization's directory service and SSO rescinds access to the externally-hosted application as well.

Privileged access management integration

The percentage of servers and virtual machines with PAM in place, divided by the total number of in-scope systems. Privileged access management software is installed in servers and virtual machines to restrict administrative (super user) access by role. As an example, if there is a backup administrator that works night shift, they are only granted administrative access to restart backups. PAM enables the backup administrator to do their work without the exposure of full administrative access.

7.7 INCIDENT RESPONSE

Mean Time to Detect (MTTD)

The average time it takes to discover malware or adversarial activity. If an adversary or malware gets into our IT environment, we need to detect it very quickly. That enables us to respond and eradicate either that adversary or that malware. If we can get them out quickly, that may prevent an incident from becoming a data breach. To find data to populate this metric, go back through the logs and events to determine the first time the adversary entered the IT environment or the first time malware was introduced. Then compare that time when the incident was first detected. Measure by adding totals of times incidents started and were detected by the number of incidents.

Mean Time to Respond (MTTR)

The average time it takes to initially respond to an incident. Measure by adding the time between when incidents started and when the team began response efforts. Divide by the number of incidents. This is similar to MTTD above. Once we have detected the adversary or the malware, how long before we took action?

7.8 PROGRAM METRICS

Here are additional metrics that have utility within an information security program.

Phishing

We know as security professionals that threat actors send phishing e-mail, which are social engineering messages. Their goal to convince employees or contractors to click on a malicious link or a malicious file to introduce malware or ransomware. A phishing click may give that adversary a foothold in our IT environment. Beyond training, it is necessary to test people's knowledge in practice with simulated phishing messages. Measure the percentage of users that click. It should be low. That metric evaluates the effectiveness of our phishing test program. By and large, our employees and our contractors should not be clicking on our test messages and obviously we need to make those test messages more sophisticated over time.

There are repeat clickers, people in our organization that click on multiple test messages. They are hidden in that first metric. We need to identify those that keep clicking and provide them with additional training. If repeat click behavior persists, get their manager involved and perhaps human resources over time. Create a metric that measures the percentage of repeat clickers to determine the effectiveness of remedial training and escalation procedures.

Measure the percentage phishing test messages that are reported by employees and contractors. Many organizations embed a phishing report button in e-mail clients and acknowledge those that report a significant volume of phishing messages.

Endpoint protection

Measure to evaluate to what extent endpoint protection software is installed and operational. Measure software and scanning engines to determine if they are on current versions.

Encryption

Encryption is a foundation control to protect sensitive data. Combine that with laptops that may be stolen while off-site. Measure for encryption at rest at a minimum.

Change management

In order for change management to be effective, emergency changes should be few and far between. Measure the emergency changes versus change requests that follow the standard process. Changes should be critically evaluated for the implementation plan. Measure the percentage of changes that required failback in the past year.

System backups

System backups are a critical recovery mechanism in the event of hardware failure, ransomware and data corruption. Measure the number of systems with two or more days of failed backup.

Application security

If your organization develops software code, establish metrics to track past due critical and high application vulnerabilities. Measure the percentage of software builds that receive security testing before release to production. Measure how penetration tests are conducted in accordance with policy. Measure the percentage of Developers with secure code training completed in the last year.

Business continuity

Large organizations have lines of business or agencies the size of companies. In that scenario, one Business Continuity Plan for the entire organization is not effective. Measure for individual entities with a business continuity plan updated annually.

Crisis response exercises

Require annual crisis response exercises by policy, including business continuity exercises, disaster recovery exercises and cybersecurity tabletop exercises (TTX). TTXs should also exercise the crisis communications plan. Measure adherence by this metric.

Self-identified issues

Extend your awareness program and risk culture beyond training and phishing test messages. Require business units and operational functions to report a specific number of self-identified operational risk issues each year by policy. Measure adherence by this metric.

Issue management

Percentage of issue records with 'Last Follow-Up Date' field less than 30 days. Analysts are expected to follow up every 30 days on open security issues. Here is the rationale for tracking this metric. When an issue's target remediation date is three months out, it is unlikely to be completed in that time. It is a good practice to ask for three to five milestones or steps that result in a target date. If the Analyst follows up every 30 days, asking which milestones have been completed, that continued contact can influence remediation within the agreed upon timeframe. This metric has utility for any function that tracks security issues to closure.

Unresolved risk register entries

A risk register provides transparency by documenting decisions to mitigate or accept risk. A risk governance process allows for requests for more information and to update milestones and target dates. In rare cases, executive leadership may not want to accept risk or to truly participate in the process. In that scenario, executives 'spin' register entries by repeatedly asking for revision and the process is dysfunctional. Design a metric that measures risk register entries that have not been designated as risk mitigate or risk accept within six months. It is also a good practice to measure risk mitigate entries that are older than one year. If the risk governance process is not functioning effectively, those metrics will turn yellow or red.

7.9 FIRST SET OF METRICS

When you begin to establish a first set of metrics, meet with a process or control owner. Mention our organization is launching a metrics program. Discuss the rationale and the need for metrics from an operational risk perspective. Explain the benefits of how metrics enable us to focus on day-to-day operations and how they let us know when risk is increasing. It is a good approach to give them a sampling of metrics to choose from. Solicit feedback on the metric, how it would be calculated and the thresholds for green, yellow and red. So rather than dictating metrics to them, let them participate in the process.

Metrics risk culture

Speak with senior leadership when initially launching a metrics program. Encourage them to be thoughtful and deliberate when a metric turns yellow or red. That is necessary to foster a culture of risk transparency. The focus should be the root cause of the issue, the plan to bring the metric back into threshold and how to prevent reoccurrence. If there is negligence or dishonesty, that is a different conversation.

The metric owner may need support or risk acceptance from senior leadership, such as loss of personnel on a small team during a hiring freeze. If team capacity is exceeded in that scenario, the options are an exception to the hiring freeze or acceptance of the performance or risk issue reported by the metric.

In the end all that matters is processes and technology are functioning effectively and issues are being identified and mitigated within the risk tolerance threshold. If we make it a really negative experience every time a metric turns yellow or red, then process and control owners are going to be less transparent about risk and certainly reluctant to support new metrics.

7.10 METRICS STATUSES

Metrics have a lifecycle, that transitions from draft, to grey, to production and decommissioned. Closely monitor and control metrics as they pass through those stages of development.

Draft metrics

A metric in 'Draft' status is in the design phase, under consideration. No mention of draft metrics should be included with production reporting. Draft metrics should not be introduced to management yet. They are untested, in an early stage of development. We need access to data to evaluate the metric calculation and green, yellow and red thresholds. Leave new metrics in draft status until they have been tested and approved.

Grey metrics

A 'Grey' metric has been designed, approved and data is being generated. Data has been applied to the metric calculation and thresholds have been evaluated and approved. New metrics may appear in production reporting with a metric name and definition, however the threshold should be displayed in a grey status, versus green, yellow or red ratings.

A metric may appear out of threshold in yellow or red status when first generated. The process or control owner needs time to make changes to bring the metric into threshold. Each new metric should be introduced in grey status for that reason. The rationale is we should not meet with process owners to establish a metric and then almost immediately bring them in front of executives with a yellow or red status. If that is the case, that person is not going to want to work with us on future metrics. Give process and control owners courtesy, with three months in grey status when a metric is first introduced.

Production metrics

A production metric has been fully approved and appears within reporting with green, yellow or red status. Process owners and executives are accustomed to seeing production metrics.

Decommissioned metrics

The utility of some metrics diminishes over time. There is a limit to how many metrics can be maintained and how many the audience will review (TL;DR, too long did not read). Some metrics may lose purpose due to automation, monitoring or quality assurance. It is healthy to include a periodic 'stop, start, continue' analysis within your metrics program.

7.11 QUALITY ASSURANCE

Be mindful of 'conference room risk', where a group of people get together and create something. In the 'Metrics Components' section above, a metric draft was created in version 1.0 and refined in version 1.1. At that point it may seem like a good metric to report to management.

The initial phase of using metric components to draft a metric is a good approach. It is necessary to apply quality assurance from there.

Relevance

Does this metric answer the 'so what' question? If it turns red, does that mean there is a significant issue within process execution or a significant operational risk exists? Is there a monitoring or quality assurance process that already covers this metric? Is this an existing metric that is no longer necessary?

Calculation

Does the metric calculation accurately measure what is written in the description?

Thresholds

Does the metric output range specified for each green, yellow, red metric status reflect whether the process is performing effectively (KPI) or whether the status accurately aligns to the risk tolerance of the organization (KRI)?

Coverage

Are the areas of performance and risk appropriately covered? If a metric has a narrow scope, there may be a broader population that is not monitored. For example, 'Past Due Critical Vulnerabilities - Internet-Exposed Systems With Sensitive Data' provides a tight risk lens. However, it does not account for other Internet-exposed systems or internal systems with past due critical vulnerabilities. Are additional metrics needed or should the coverage scope be increased?

Data source

How will the data for this metric be gathered? Is it consistently available from the system of record? For example, if someone has the idea of tracking a metric with a specific vendor, the first step is to determine if the vendor is willing to provide the data on a consistent basis. It many cases they are not. Unless the vendor is contractually obligated to provide the requisite data, that metric cannot be generated.

Separation of duties

Will the metric be sourced, calculated and published by a function that is independent from the Metric Owner?

Organization

Large organizations have lines of business or agencies the size of companies. Maintain accountability by reporting metrics at that level.

Automation

Can the metric be automated for accuracy and to conserve resources?

Inventory

Maintain a Metrics Inventory. Here is a listing of fields for inspiration:

• # (metric number)	• Metric Owner
• Metric Name	• Go Live Date
• Description	• Comments
• Measure	• Category
• Yellow	• Control Alignment
• Red	• Distribution
• Status	• Audience
• System of Record	

7.12 SUPPORTING METRICS OWNERS

Consider the metrics program from a process or control owner's point of view. They may see little return from the metrics program. Either the metric is green and all is quiet or the metric is yellow or red and they are required to present to executives.

Provide support for Metrics Owners. Be an advocate for them. Speak up when they need more resources. Walk them through the design of a new metric. Be inclusive. Work together with them to establish the calculation and thresholds.

Introducing a new metric

Be protective of metric owners when a metric is introduced in grey status. If someone wants to know whether the metric is actually green, yellow or red, answer it is still in grey status. That is the consideration and courtesy that is provided to process and control owners when a new metric is introduced. Politely hold the line.

Go-to-green plan

It is common practice for the Metric Owner to provide an update to executive leadership when a metric comes out of threshold. We can provide support by working on a go-to-green slide with the Metric Owner. Executives want to know:

- What caused the metric to output yellow or red status?
- What are the implications from a process execution or risk perspective?
- What are the plans to bring the metric back into green status?
- What is being done to prevent recurrence?

The trend chart in Figure 7.4 below displays a historical view of metric performance. There are cases of compliance jitter, meaning one month there was a blip, an issue that occurred once and has been resolved. In other cases, the metric was trending toward yellow or red over time. There is a systemic issue that needs to be resolved. Leadership will want those details. Displaying a trending chart helps frame that conversation.

Provide support to the Metric Owner based on their professional development. That may include creating the slide, role playing with questions executives tend to ask and chiming in to support the Metric Owner as they speak with executives. Do not leave Metrics Owners exposed to the elements. Do your best to help them.

Watch items notification

Process and control owners may feel victimized when metrics have very tight timeframes such as seven days to remediate a critical vulnerability. In that case, the vulnerability management team should send automated notification when a critical vulnerability issue record is opened. That gives Issue Respondents the maximum amount of time to remediate before the metric threshold is exceeded.

Metric	Measure	Thresholds	Status
Past Due Critical Vulnerabilities - Internet-Exposed Systems	Internet-exposed systems with one or more past due critical vulnerabilities / Total number of Internet-exposed systems	Yellow: <= 5% and > 10% Red: <= 10%	Reference the chart below

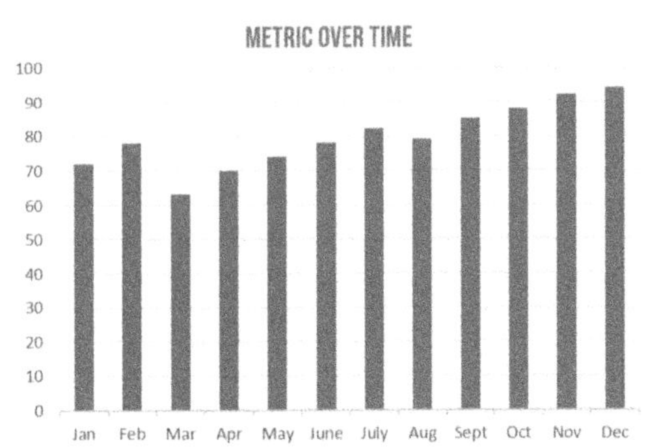

- <Insert commentary that speaks to the current state of the metric and a go-to-green plan.>
- <Insert commentary that speaks to trending and history of the metric.>

Include this metric within a reporting package quarterly.

Generate the metric monthly to provide history and context in the event the metric changes from green to yellow or red.

Data current as of January 2, 2050

Figure 7.4 Go-to-green plan.

Watch items notification can also include:

- Issues older than two weeks with no target remediation date
- Issues with target remediation dates that occur in the past
- Issues that are past due or have a target date that exceeds the remediation standard, with no risk registry entry in place

Send a 'heads up' message to Issue Respondents on Week # 1. Let them know there are watch items in their space and the executives will have visibility the following week.

On Week # 2, send the current list of Watch Items to executives. Repeat the process bi-weekly to keep the portfolio of issues under control.

Embed Watch Items into established communications routines such as staff meetings. Notification is critical to driving executive awareness and accelerating remediation in practice.

Staffing impact

There must be a balance of how risk management resources are distributed across the information security program. The need for metrics must be balanced against competing priorities to identify and mitigate risk. When an organization has two or three people within the information security team, that amounts to a bare-bones metrics program. Unless... If there is a data analytics or reporting function, ask them for support generating metrics. Automation can reduce staffing impact further. Information security professionals come at a significant cost. It makes good business sense to focus them on their core duties. That helps with employee retention as well.

Staffing impact depends on the number of metrics and the complexity of the metrics program. Consider the current scope and plans for expansion. Most information security metrics programs begin with a focus on IT and cybersecurity. Privacy metrics typically follow. Meeting routines have an impact on the need for staffing. If metrics are generated and reported out quarterly, that will require less resources than hosting monthly metrics meetings and reporting out to a board-level committee. Make a listing of the activities and their occurrence and estimate the number of hours. That is a reasonable method to estimate staffing impact. Some organizations lift metrics out of operational functions into a governance, risk and compliance team.

7.13 PHASED IMPLEMENTATION

A metrics program measures critical control points within performance execution and operational risk. Be thoughtful and deliberate when establishing or enhancing your metrics program. If you are standing up a program, resist the urge to start off with 50 metrics. Start with something like three in each information security domain and gently move forward. Consider the impact to stakeholders such as process owners and senior executives. Move at a moderate pace. They will appreciate it if you conduct quality assurance, communicate grey metrics and introduce new metrics in phases. Think in terms of a three year multi-generational plan. In the first year, roll out a basic set of cybersecurity metrics, similar to what has been outlined in this chapter. In year two, leverage industry resources to fill gaps in metrics coverage. Peer-reviewed metrics from cybersecurity organizations are reputable and take less time to implement then creating metrics from scratch. In year three, analyze your organization's internal control framework to develop an opinion of which controls should be measured with KPIs and KRIs. Depending on risk culture and feedback from executives, that three year period may expand to four or five years.

7.14 REPORTING VERSUS METRICS

Tactical remediation

There are times where existing metrics fail to detect significant risk. Figure 7.5 below depicts an example of when vulnerabilities are remediated in an IT environment and then have a pattern of reoccurring.

In this scenario each team is busy and believes the vulnerability management process is functioning effectively. The issue is the same vulnerabilities keep popping up. That leaves the IT environment and the organization exposed.

Apply a different risk lens

Within each information security domain and function, it makes sense to consider what are our top 10 reoccurring issues? (Figure 7.6).

Address the root cause of these reoccurring vulnerabilities. Why do they occur? What can be done to prevent them? Are security configurations and patching automated within the install process? Some vulnerabilities are bound to repeat within software development. Are developers required to take secure code training? Do they have templated security code such as a filter that prevents a vulnerability from being exploited? In that case the vulnerability exists, but the filter makes it not exploitable. If a vulnerability continues to occur despite our best efforts, what compensating controls can be implemented to mitigate the risk? That provides coverage until the vulnerability is identified and remediated. These are examples of a thought process, a culture of active risk management. It is healthy to have a top ten list of reoccurring findings and to always be working to address the root cause.

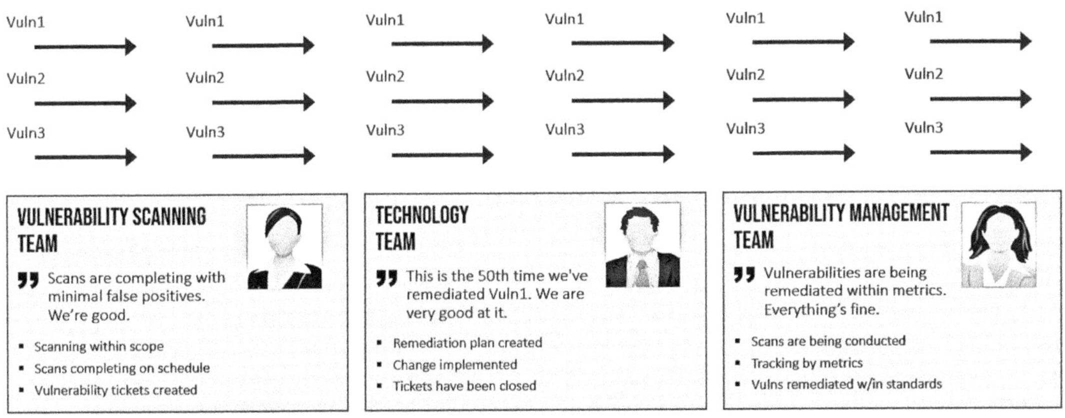

- Vulnerabilities are tracked to closure within standards in this model
- However, reoccurring vulnerabilities are left unchecked
- Siloed teams do not see any issues from within their scope

Figure 7.5 Tactical remediation.

Figure 7.6 Reoccurring issues.

7.15 METRICS AND REPORTING PACKAGE

Generating metrics is the first stage of an end-to-end communications process. Submit a metrics and reporting package to a cybersecurity committee. When metrics or reporting are out of threshold, include that content at the top in a go-to-green section. That makes metrics and reporting easy for board members to review. Provide risk transparency in a manner that is easy to consume. That will pay dividends in meaningful conversations that may influence support and funding.

Populate the reporting package with metrics across domains. Start with vulnerability management, third party risk management, identity and access management and security awareness at a minimum. Include security configuration benchmark reports, patch compliance reports and details from the e-mail security gateway and web content filtering. Provide risk transparency into additional technology and processes such as threat hunting. Include all open risk register entries at the bottom of the report. The core focus is to ensure the board has visibility, risk transparency. Ensure sure that vulnerabilities and risk issues are bubbling up through the management tiers, to executives and the board of directors. Risk transparency is a duty, integrity, doing the right thing. Skeletons in the closet can have significant business impact.

Monthly trend reporting

Provide monthly trend reporting to give context to metrics in yellow or red status. In Figure 7.7 below, remediation of high risk vulnerabilities changed to yellow and red in the past two months. That trend requires explanation. Application penetration tests turned yellow once, four months back. That appears to have been compliance jitter. No action required. Active management of security issue records has trended from yellow to red over the past four months. This is a key performance indicator. There may be an issue with staffing capacity.

The metrics and reporting package is an official document that should stand alone. Include go-to-green commentary with each metric or report that is out of threshold. Board members need that level of detail to evaluate root cause and steps to prevent reoccurrence. Metrics and reporting communicate a problem. Go-to-green narrative presents a solution, which may

#	Metric	Mar 2051	Feb 2051	Jan 2051	Dec 2050	Nov 2050	Oct 2050
1	**Past Due Critical Vulnerabilities - Internet-Exposed Systems** [Internet-exposed systems with one or more past due critical vulnerabilities.]	Green	Green	Green	Green	Green	Green
2	**Past Due High Vulnerabilities - Internet-Exposed Systems** [Internet-exposed systems with one or more past due high vulnerabilities.]	Red	Yellow	Green	Green	Green	Green
3	**Unsupported Operating Systems** Unsupported operating systems no longer have security patches issued by the vendor.	Green	Green	Green	Green	Green	Green
4	**Application Penetration Tests - Systems With Sensitive Data** Penetration tests identify vulnerabilities that can be used to compromise applications.	Green	Green	Green	Yellow	Green	Green
5	**Active Management of Security Issue Records** [Percentage of assessments with 'Last Follow-Up Date' field <= 30 days]	Red	Red	Yellow	Yellow	Green	Green
6	**Self-Identified Issues** Total number of business unit SIIs this year / 2 SIIs required annually by policy X Number of business units	Green	Green	Green	Green	Green	Green

Figure 7.7 Monthly trend reporting.

include a request for support and funding. Providing that complete picture will be welcomed by executives and board directors as they review the package alone, before the committee meeting.

Reporting packages may be reviewed by internal audit and regulators. In the event of a data breach, board-level reporting may be subject to legal hold and discovery. Demonstrate effective risk management by communicating problem and solution.

7.16 BENEFITS OF A METRICS PROGRAM

A metrics program provides monitoring and notification, enabling the team to focus on day-to-day operations, projects, initiatives and strategic planning. Review metrics once a month. If there is something that requires attention, it should be obvious at that time. Add new metrics to adapt to changes in process and technology. Add metrics as a result of risk analysis, incident response and lessons learned.

Metrics can influence the right behaviors and actions. As metrics turn yellow and red, management will ask control owners, why is there an issue with process execution or why is risk exceeding our tolerance in this area? How will you prevent this from happening in the future? Those conversations can influence support and funding.

7.17 CLOSING THOUGHTS

Design your metrics in partnership with process and control owners. Explain the benefits to them and give them options. If their draft metric would be in the yellow or red threshold, mention they start with a grey metric with three months before it enters into production status. There must be a balance. An effective metrics program calls attention to process execution issues and significant operational risk. The thresholds must be set in that context. The grey metric time period must be restricted by policy and should not be used to conceal or suppress material risk.

Generate metrics every month to provide a heads up if a metric is starting to trend the wrong way. That can enable the process or control owner to take appropriate action, mitigating risk and having a better experience before the next governance meeting.

Design	Quality Assurance	Distribution	Discussion	Action
• Metric Name • Description • Measure • Thresholds • Exposure • Scope • Occurrence • Risk Transparency	• Relevance • Calculation • Thresholds • Coverage • Data Source • Separation of Duties • Organization • Automation • Inventory	• Metrics Dashboard • Watch Items Notification • Metric Owner • Process or Control Owner • Manager • Executive • Executive Forums • C-Level Executives • Board of Directors - Reporting package	• Metrics Risk Culture • Draft Metrics • Quality Assurance • Go-to-Green Plan • Metrics Program Meeting • Board-Level Committee Meetings	• Issue Management - Service Desk Tickets - GRC Tickets • Risk Register - Risk Mitigate - Risk Accept

Figure 7.8 Metrics program activities.

If you are establishing a metrics program, provide an introduction by presenting a few slides in existing meeting routines. There are too many cybersecurity program metrics to implement all at once. Start at a moderate pace, with relative few metrics across information security domains. You have time to add metrics in years two and three. Continue to mature the program leveraging peer-reviewed metrics from cybersecurity organizations.

Review Figure 7.8 below for a metrics program overview.

7.18 CALL TO ACTION

Leverage the content in this chapter to establish new metrics. If your organization does not have a metrics program, this is an opportunity for you to design, architect and implement one. It does not matter whether you are an individual contributor or a leader. Raise your hand, start a project and deliver value. If you implement a metrics program, you have demonstrated leadership. That can help prove you ready-now for promotion. If you are already a leader, implementing a metrics program can increase your year-end performance bonus.

Chapter 8

Insider risk monitoring and response

8.1 INTRODUCTION

This chapter provides practical advice to establish insider risk monitoring and response capabilities. Insider threat is discussed in the context of a threat landscape matrix. Provides tips and examples to overcome reluctance to insider risk management due to corporate culture. Provides an order of implementation to influence the next step forward. Data exfiltration controls provide results early-on. Evidence-based inferences give Human Resources a level of comfort. Continuous monitoring detects suspicious activity by an employee or contractor. An incident response process is included. Maturity increases with monitoring triggered by behavioral indicators and when an employee tenders resignation. These practices provide protection for the organization and are likely to produce results. That enables a clear business case for a second phase of program development.

8.2 INSIDER THREAT

Insider threat consists of internal personnel that intentionally cause harm to an organization. Employees and contractors may act for personal gain or because they are disgruntled. They may act due to being compromised by blackmail or threat to a family member. Insiders may seek to commit fraud to steal funds from the organization. There can be corporate espionage where a competitor compromises an existing employee or sends someone to apply for a job. Insiders target assets such as intellectual property, financial accounts, payment cards and strategic plans. Departing personnel will steal customer contacts, especially if they are in sales. They may take an export of mass affluent customers or the entire customer list. Insiders accomplish their goals through authorized accesses approved by management or intimidation of subordinates through their leadership role.

When a threat actor finds it difficult to hack their way into an organization, they may use social engineering techniques to trick an insider into providing access. Disgruntled insiders may seek to cause harm through sabotage or by leaking information (Figure 8.1).

Insiders are our employees, contractors and business partners. These are people that we give access to. They are inside our enterprise. Mitigate the risk by implementing role-based accesses, including the principles of least privilege and separation of duty.

DOI: 10.1201/9781003543619-8

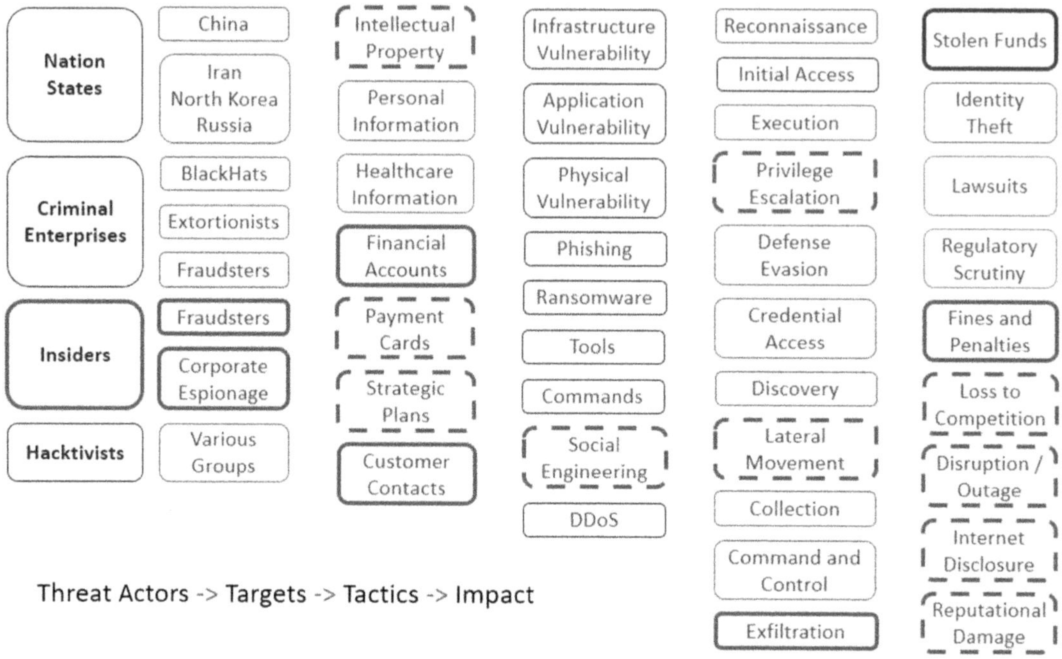

Figure 8.1 Threat landscape matrix - Insider threat.

The Reconnaissance column contains content from the MITRE ATT&CK Framework.

8.3 BE MINDFUL OF THE CULTURE

If you just walk into a meeting with executives and say "I want to establish an insider threat program", it will be very challenging. You have to do a bit of behind the scenes politicking first. The reason is many organizations will communicate 'we care about our employees, we care about your work-life balance'. Executives spend a lot of time developing that culture. It makes sense. That sense of warmth and community is tantalizing. It helps with retention, there are a lot of good business reasons behind that. Sometimes C-level executives are just geared that way, they care about their people and they feel responsible for them. There will be problems if we talk about insider threat versus insider risk and we do it with the wrong audience, cold. Start off by having discussions with your manager and your executive first. Have one-on-one meetings with other executives as necessary, before presenting in a standard meeting routine. It is important to prep your leadership before proposing insider risk monitoring and response.

The potential for insider threat exists within every organization. You know that. Executives often times do not or they may not believe it. We have to prove it to them. One way to do that when you start off, is to talk about facts and data. Reference data breach response reports from reputable firms such as Verizon, Mandiant and IBM. Create a few slides to speak to and to leave behind as reference material. These are real-world events and real-world business impact.

We are about to meet with senior executives that absorb information very quickly. The underlying theme is insider threat poses operational risk to the organization. Insider risk management will be conducted in a discrete way that will not damage the culture.

8.4 PREVENTIVE CONTROLS

Data exfiltration controls

Employees and contractors use common end user techniques to export data from company systems. Therefore, it is necessary to restrict access to prevent sensitive data from being taken:

- Block access to personal e-mail (e.g. Gmail)
- Block access to Internet drive storage (e.g. Dropbox)
- Block access to external drive storage (e.g. USB flash drives)
- Block access to file transfer protocols outbound (e.g. FTP)
- Block external sharing of cloud drive storage (e.g. OneDrive)
- Block external sharing of content management applications (e.g. SharePoint)
- Block download access from office applications to mobile device storage (e.g. Outlook, OneDrive, etc.)
- Block web-based access to office applications (e.g. Outlook Web Access)
- Block file sharing through collaboration tools (e.g. Microsoft Teams)
- Leverage data loss prevention to block or quarantine attempts to exfiltrate sensitive data
- When a laptop is used on an external network, enforce the above data exfiltration restrictions

These are necessary controls from an insider risk management perspective. If a leader is reluctant to implement one or more of them, document that in a risk register entry for transparency to C-level executives and the board of directors.

Access controls: Personally identifiable information (PII)

Employees or contractors may access PII records to commit identity theft. Here are options to mitigate that abuse case:

- Use a customer number versus a Social Security Number (SSN)
- Implement a challenge / response function within the application
  - Customer Service enters an SSN in the field and receives a Yes/No verification response
  - SSNs cannot be viewed by visiting client records
- Display the last four numbers of an SSN
- Store the first six and last four numbers of a payment card number
- If an employee needs to view an SSN, require a click in the application to reveal it
  - Include event logging to capture each time they access an SSN

Monitoring recommendations follow later in this chapter.

8.5 ESTABLISH A RELATIONSHIP WITH HR

If there is a communications gap between Human Resources (HR) and the Information Security team, ask for a touch base meeting. Discuss the intersection between HR and information security practices, such as background checks and insider risk mitigation. Ask for a reoccurring meeting every six months to remain in sync. HR knows about personnel issues, beyond what is visible in security and event logs. Maintain a good relationship so they trust that they can come to you.

8.6 EVIDENCE-BASED INFERENCES

Based on case data shared with the MITRE Center for Threat-Informed Defense, the following inferences were observed:

- Insider threats routinely use unsophisticated TTPs* to access and exfiltrate data. (Tactics, Techniques and Procedures)
- Insider threats routinely leverage existing privileged access to facilitate data theft or other malicious actions.
- Insiders routinely 'stage' data they intend to steal prior to exfiltration.
- External/removable media remains a common exfiltration channel.
- Email remains a common exfiltration channel.
- Cloud storage represents both a collection target for insiders and a common exfiltration channel.[1]

According to MITRE and the data they have analyzed, insider threats typically use unsophisticated tactics to access and exfiltrate data. That makes sense because many employees and contractors do not have a deep technical skill set. In most cases insiders will do relatively simple things to try to get the data out.

Hopefully your organization blocks most common ways to exfiltrate data. Otherwise, that porous security posture does not make sense. Consider how much money is spent on the information security program, technical, administrative and physical controls. If an employee or contractor can just use a USB flash drive to walk out with the data, that poses significant risk of business impact.

There is a theme here. These are conversations you should have one-on-one with an executive, as you are trying to acclimate them to insider threat concepts. It may be best to have a few one-on-one sounding board conversations before proposing insider risk monitoring in a leadership meeting.

8.7 CONTINUOUS MONITORING

Data exfiltration monitoring

Insiders are authorized end users with access to data and the means to transfer it outside of the organization. Insider risk monitoring needs to detect and alert on abuse of those privileges.

Alert when a user attempts 2 of the following within 1 hour:

- Attempts to access personal e-mail
- Attempts to access Internet drive storage
- Attempts to access external drive storage
- Attempts to use a file transfer protocol outbound
- etc. (reference list of controls within Section 8.4)
- Sends a file to a printer

Those data exfiltration techniques are blocked for end users in this scenario. However, information security still needs to know if someone is making a concerted effort to use a few of them. Toxic combinations reduce false positive alerts. We do not want an alert every time someone tries to access their personal e-mail. However, if they try two or more ways to export data from the organization, that is a cause for concern and investigation.

An alert is received by the Security Operations Center. An insider is actively trying to remove data. Upon investigation the insider tried three or four techniques to exfiltrate data, it was blocked, and then they sent the file to a printer to export a hardcopy version of the contents. This scenario depicts why this type of monitoring is worthwhile. When an insider is persistent, sooner or later they will exfiltrate the data. We can monitor for that and alert on those persistent attempts. In this scenario the insider clearly printed to exfiltrate data. That requires further investigation and response.

Scenarios such as this one produce abuse cases, which drive requirements for enhanced monitoring. The insider printed to exfiltrate data. We now care about printer forensics, replicating printer logging to SIEM monitoring, having visibility into the file name printed and visibility into the contents of what was printed.

PII access monitoring

Monitor for excessive viewing of client records. Establish enhanced monitoring for viewing of celebrity records.

- Monitor for process adherence
  - e.g. Call Center Operators speak with up to 15 customers per hour
  - Accessing 20 or more records sends an alert to the supervisor
- Alert on access to two or more celebrity records in an hour
- Monitor event logs for changes in behavior
  - e.g. user account suddenly accesses many more records

Monitoring of this nature may help detect someone writing down PII or taking pictures of it with their phone. Both techniques are used to commit identity theft.

Quality assurance

Insider risk monitoring is dependent on event logging and alert parameter configurations. Test the end-to-end process for each event and monitoring alert:

- Event: User attempts to access personal e-mail
  - <u>Test:</u> Does the event appear in SIEM log and event correlation monitoring software?
- Monitoring: Alert when a user attempts 2 data exfiltration techniques within *1* hour
  - <u>Test:</u> Does a SIEM alert trigger after 2 data exfiltration techniques?
  - <u>Test:</u> Is an alert notification sent to a SOC Analyst for review?
  - <u>Test:</u> Does the SIEM alert open a service desk ticket requiring acknowledgement?

Review monitoring events with severity categories that are below the threshold for alert notification. SOC Analysts may change configurations to suppress alerts of suspicious activity, that management expects to be investigated. Detect and remediate that blind spot before it is noted in the aftermath of incident response.

Assign accountability to SIEM alerts with service desk ticket integration. Require that SOC Analysts document how they investigated the alert and what led them to dismiss it as a false positive or to escalate it for incident response. This approach helps ensure suspicious activity is investigated thoughtfully and deliberately.

8.8 DATA EXFILTRATION BY AN EMPLOYEE OR CONTRACTOR

Establish a process with HR. Schedule a meeting and bring a process diagram to facilitate a conversation about how HR and Information Security will work together.

Frame the conversation with HR referring to the process diagram in Figure 8.2 below. In this scenario, sensitive data has been removed from the network in a manner that appears unethical or malicious. A cybersecurity incident is declared. The employee's accesses are immediately rescinded if that has not occurred already. The incident response team gathers information to determine the extent of data exposure:

- Artifacts such as e-mail message(s), file attachment(s), logs, event notifications and monitoring alerts
- How the data was removed from the network (e.g. e-mail, file transfer, printout, etc.)
- Which data type(s) are in scope (e.g. customer Personal Identifiable Information)
- The volume of records in scope (e.g. 50,000 contact records)
- Last known location of the data (e.g. sent to jsmith@gmail.com)
- Timeline of events

It is often an employee that has submitted a letter of resignation. They may have stolen intellectual property such as research and development information. They may have taken customer contact information to use at a competitor. This activity often goes unnoticed and is first detected as monitoring comes online.

The incident response team calls a meeting with HR to discuss data exfiltration details and next steps. Together we develop a plan to delete data from unauthorized systems and to recover any hard copy printouts.

HR engages the employee. Differing reactions play out:

- The employee gets spooked and agrees to do whatever is necessary to prove that the data has been erased
- The employee decides to engage an attorney and leaves the meeting abruptly
- The employee has already left and will not respond to e-mail or phone calls

In this scenario, the employee meets with HR and members of Information Security (the incident response team). HR discusses techniques to influence the employee to delete the sensitive data:

- Positive Incentive: In return for deleting the data, HR offers a termination package to the employee ('allows the employee to move forward in life with dignity and self-respect intact'*). Insider Threat Mitigation Guide - CISA
- Negative Consequence: If the employee does not cooperate within 24 hours, the incident will be reported to law enforcement.

The influence strategy is the carrot (positive) and the stick (negative). HR and executives may bristle at the thought of a termination package. It can be a relatively small amount of money. We are trying to influence a positive outcome. The stick (negative) is 'We are giving you 24 hours and if you don't do exactly what we are instructing you to do, we will engage law enforcement and let me know how that turns out'. People will tend to take the carrot.

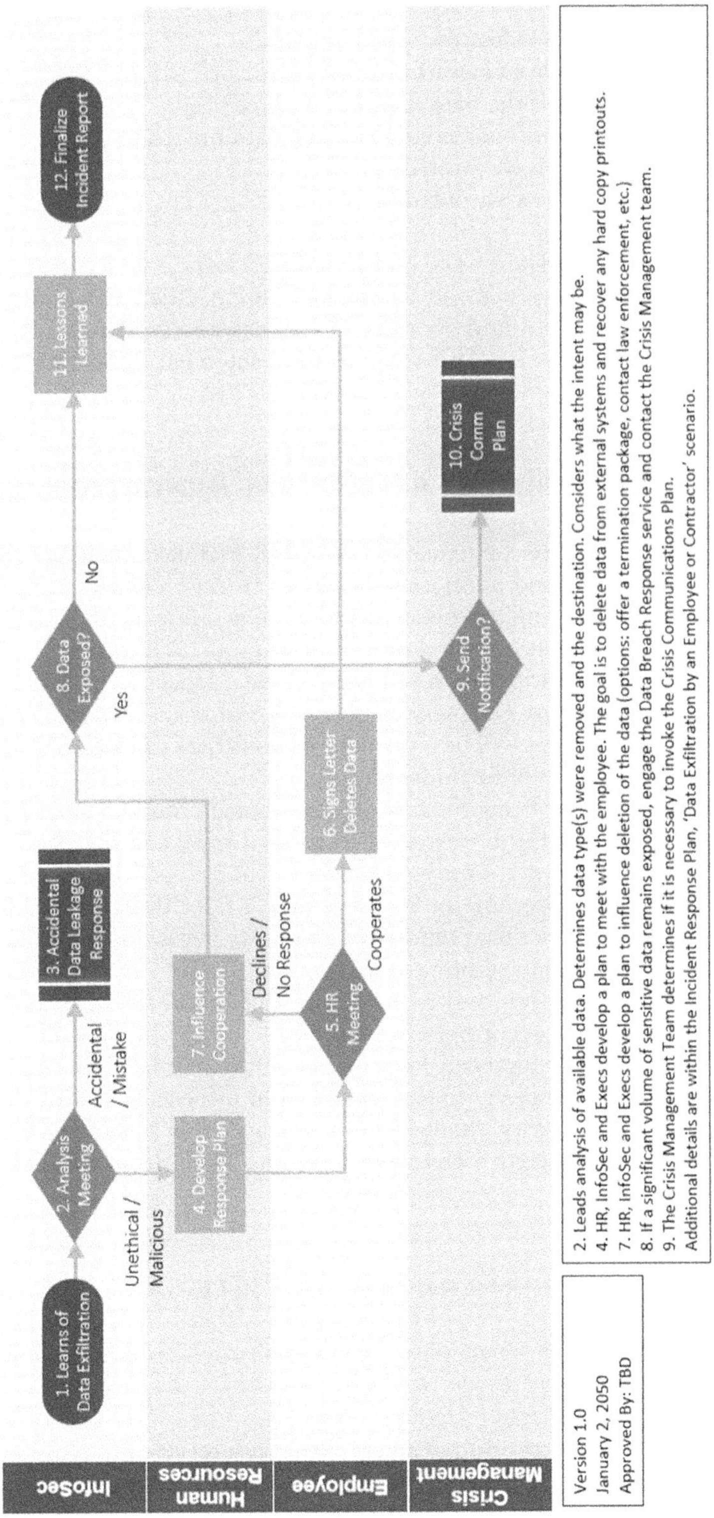

Figure 8.2 Data exfiltration by an insider: Incident response.

HR and the incident response team meet to consider the residual risk:

- **Did the employee agree to delete the sensitive data?**
- **To what extent are we able to confirm the employee deleted the data?**
- Are we able to determine if the data has been viewed?
- Could this incident also be considered a privacy data breach?
  - Is customer notification warranted?
- Is it necessary to contact law enforcement?

The Crisis Management team determines if external notification is necessary depending on the details of the incident (reference the Chapter 11 for details). Once data is no longer exposed, conduct lessons learned and root cause analysis and finalize an Incident Report. The process concludes at that point. This section is not intended to be an incident response playbook.

8.9 MONITORING TRIGGERED BY BEHAVIORAL INDICATORS

At this point we have established a partnership with HR and have included them within an incident response process. Expand upon that success to further identify and mitigate insider risk. Schedule a meeting and bring a process diagram to facilitate a conversation. This is the same approach from earlier in the chapter, standard program architecture.

Start the conversation by mentioning to HR this will be a process where they will be asked to initiate insider risk monitoring. They will be given a list of insider threat behavioral indicators from a reputable source. This will be a menu of options they can select from to determine when enhanced monitoring should be initiated.

Ask HR to accept for the time being that they have adopted criteria from reputable sources, where there is potential for unethical or malicious behavior. We can then discuss the process diagram in Figure 8.3 below.

Mention to HR they will determine in Step # 1 that insider threat behavioral indicators have been met. This is HR-centric. That works well because they are at the helm. HR observes a behavioral indicator and submits a monitoring request. The Information Security Manager reaches out to one Security Analyst and requests enhanced monitoring of that employee or contractor for 30 or 60 days in accordance with policy.

HR does not disclose 'why' enhanced monitoring is requested. There are no scandalous details. There are only three people with this confidential information, HR, the Information Security Manager and the Security Analyst. In most cases this information does not leak because they get used to enhanced monitoring requests. They do not know why they are monitoring.

8.10 ENHANCED MONITORING INITIATION CRITERIA

Provide HR with examples of how they can create their own criteria to request enhanced monitoring.

- **HR requests enhanced monitoring of an employee as a result of the following indicators**
  - When an employee receives significantly negative performance ratings such as 'Unsatisfactory/Needs Improvement'

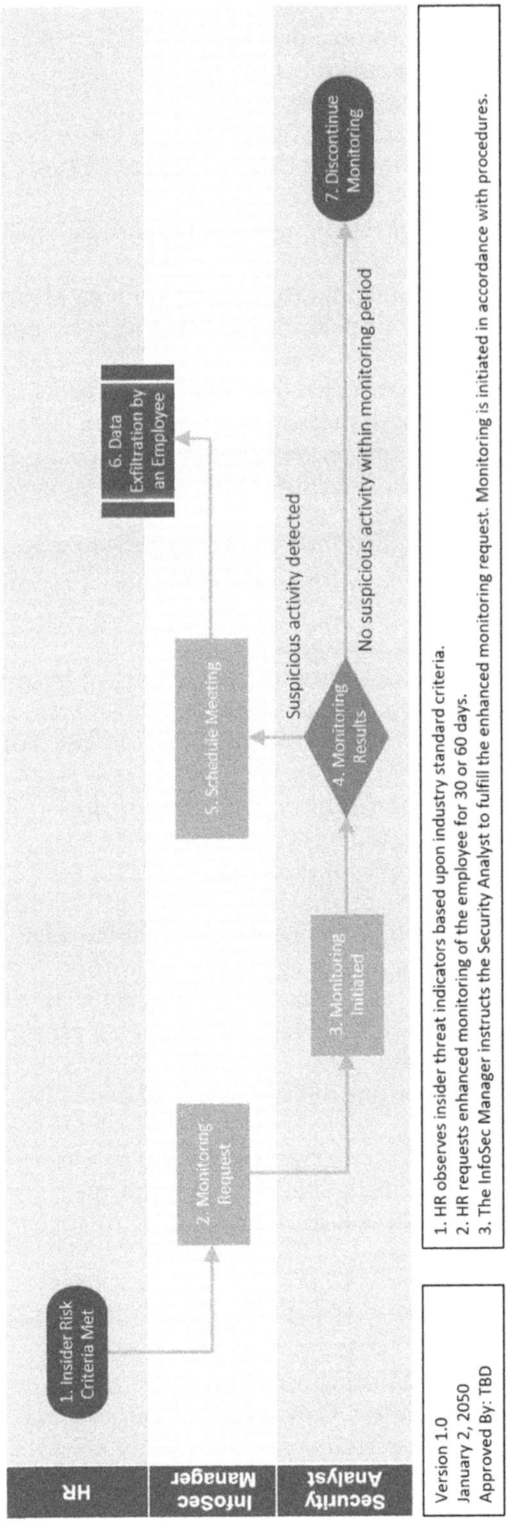

Figure 8.3 Insider risk monitoring - Behavioral indicators.

  - When a significant written warning is issued to the employee from a Supervisor or Human Resources
  - When an employee is placed on a performance improvement plan
  - When an employee may reasonably fear that their employment is in jeopardy
  - When an employee is being terminated
  - When insider threat indicators are observed (two lists follow)
- **Human Resources' Role in Preventing Insider Threats - CISA**
  - Potential Indicators
    - Conflicts with co-workers or supervisors; chronic violation of organizational policies
    - Non-compliance with mandatory security training assignments
    - Disciplinary actions – suspensions, reprimands, removals, or reduction in title or pay
    - Use of social media to threaten the organization or its personnel
    - Observable or vocalized stressors, which may include personal, professional, financial, or unmet expectations that could increase the risk of an 'insider' taking hostile or malicious action
- **Insider Threat Mitigation Guide - CISA**
  - Behavioral Indicator Examples
    - Unwillingness to comply with established rules, procedures, or organizational policies
    - Observable resentment with plans of retribution
    - Making unapproved contacts with competitors or business partners
    - Discussions of new opportunities or of resigning from current position
    - Excessive overtime work, or working odd or late hours without reason or authorization
    - Bringing personal equipment into high security areas
    - Carelessness or impulsiveness
    - Inappropriate statements, jokes, or bragging
    - Poor social interaction or social withdrawal
    - Disgruntlement toward peers due to perceived injustice
    - Increasingly erratic, unsafe, or aggressive behaviors
    - Repeated breaches of rules, procedures, or organizational policies
    - Excessive volunteering that elevates access to sensitive systems, networks, facilities, people, or data
    - Financial difficulties or unexplained financial gains

HR will want to ensure that enhanced employee monitoring is only conducted based on reasonable criteria, based on a need for due diligence and their knowledge of labor laws. Associated processes and procedures will ensure consistent treatment of all employees.

8.11 MONITORING WHEN AN EMPLOYEE TENDERS RESIGNATION

Ask HR to send notification to the Information Security team as soon as an employee tenders resignation, within 24 hours at the latest. Continuous monitoring may not detect subtle activity. Search log and event data for that departing employee for at least 30 days of activity prior to when the letter of resignation was submitted. Search for signs of data exfiltration. Search for unusual activity for someone in their last days of employment:

- Backed up files to ZIP or RAR (potential staging prior to exfiltration)
- Remote login nights or weekend
- Attempts to access office space after hours

We are looking back in logs, back in time, for suspicious or malicious activity. Log and event monitoring should continue until the employee or contractor's access is terminated.

8.12 THE ORDER MATTERS

The order of communication, design and implementation are important when establishing a new program.

- **Step 1. Establish presentation materials:** Create process diagrams to frame a conversation. They visualize how two teams can work together. Prepare a few slides to represent how the new program will identify and mitigate risk. Leverage data breach response reports for real-world events and business impact.
- **Step 2. Request executive support:** Have one-on-one conversations your supervisor and executives to solicit feedback. Request their support for the new program. Review presentation materials with them and leverage them as a sounding board. Finally propose the new program in a leadership meeting.
- **Step 3. Publish an incident response playbook:** Establish response procedures proactively. Review a process diagram with human resources and develop a shared approach to mitigating data exfiltration.
- **Step 4. Implement continuous data exfiltration monitoring:** Start by verifying that common data exfiltration techniques are blocked and associated audit events are visible within SIEM log monitoring and event correlation. Configure monitoring and alerting for two or more data exfiltration events in one hour.
- **Step 5. Implement monitoring for when an employee tenders resignation:** A response playbook and event logging are already in-place. Establish procedures for enhanced monitoring by policy, 30-60 days.
- **Step 6. Implement monitoring when an employee tenders resignation:** Expand on your partnership with human resources. Discuss a new process diagram. Give them behavioral indicators to select from.

8.13 CONTROL ACCESS: DIGITAL RIGHTS MANAGEMENT

Digital Rights Management (DRM) can be used to control access to your organization's information. A file can leave the company and we still control access to the contents within. For example, we can rescind access to a parts list that contains pricing information when a new list has been published.

From an insider risk management perspective, DRM can be configured to disable printing and to only allow access on a company-issued computer:

• Employee salary spreadsheet	– Application source code
• Customer contact list	– Pipeline drug formulas
• Strategic business plans	– Semiconductor chip designs
• Intellectual property	– Aerospace weapons system designs

Those files cannot be opened on an external system. It does not matter if they leave the corporate network. The file content is encrypted.

DRM can be used to restrict access to confidential information. For example, if HR distributes a salary spreadsheet, access can be restricted to groups of employees such as 'HR' and 'Hiring Managers'.

8.14 INSIDER THREAT PERSONAS

Insider risk management comes down to the people who are a threat to the organization. Their means, motive and opportunity can be used to design and implement controls. Reference these five insider threat personas from the Australian Government:

• The Accidental Insider	• The Recruited Insider
• The Negligent Insider	• The Coerced Insider
• The Self-Motivated Insider	

Each persona includes key motivators, red flags and a case study. Access the details in the appendix.

8.15 SUMMARY

The potential for insider threat exists in every organization. Employees and contractors are trusted insiders and have access to systems, data and financial accounts. Motivations that drive insider threat include disgruntled personnel, desire for personal gain and espionage. Insiders target intellectual property, financial accounts, strategic plans and customer contacts. Insider threat must be mitigated as an operational risk, similar to the rationale for cybersecurity and privacy.

8.16 CALL TO ACTION

Establish or enhance an Insider Risk Management Program! When you are thinking about your performance plan for next year, start with the insider risk monitoring piece:

- Continuous monitoring
- Data exfiltration by an employee or contractor
- Monitoring triggered by behavioral indicators

Insider threat activity will be detected once those processes and technologies are up and running. That success will help convince your executives to invest in a second phase of program development. In year two or three, expand scope to an Insider Risk Management Program based on reputable practices.

Some of you wonder how do I get promoted? Raise your hand. Speak one-on-one with your supervisor. Tell them you want to design and implement insider risk management controls in the new year. Bring a few slides with you to tell the story.

This chapter provides a foundation for an insider risk management program. It's up to you as a Program Architect to design and implement the second phase. Apply what you have learned from this book.

NOTE

1 Design Principles and Methodology for the Insider Threat TTP Knowledge Base - MITRE Engenuity.

Chapter 9

Threat landscape and controls analysis

9.1 INTRODUCTION

Threat Landscape and Controls Analysis is organized to start from business management's side of the table. We begin by considering the inherent risk of the organization. Provide an overview of potential adversaries, techniques for compromising data and the cybercrime ecosystem. Describe the potential for impact, while citing reliable sources. Reference the organization's risk tolerance. Describe the organization's assets. Pivot into cybersecurity with protection boundaries, control framework and risk assessments. Provide fair and balanced analysis by documenting risk mitigation and recent accomplishments in that domain. Detail residual risk with recommendations for new processes and controls. Conclude with a summary statement that praises the organization's risk culture, with recognition for conducting risk analysis.

Threat Landscape and Controls Analysis can be used within an assessment report as a preamble for findings and recommendations. It also has utility as stand-alone analysis to present cybersecurity issues to C-level executives and the Board of Directors.

9.2 INHERENT RISK

An organization's inherent risk arises from its industry category and its assets. Consider the details such as digital, financial and physical assets. Include sensitive data types and the number of customers in your analysis.

- Payment card numbers
- Financial accounts
- Personally Identifiable Information (PII)
- Protected Health Information (PHI)
- Customer contacts
- Strategic business plans
- Intellectual property
  - Application source code
  - Pipeline drug formulas
  - Semiconductor chip designs
  - Aerospace weapons systems designs

When asked why he robbed banks, Willie Sutton's response was, "Because that's where the money is." Document the organization's core assets. The intent is to be transparent about what is of value and what is being protected.

9.3 THREAT ACTORS

Transition to the view from the Threat Actor's side of the table. Motivations drive their goals and activities.

DOI: 10.1201/9781003543619-9

Nation states

Nation states are significant adversaries due to government funding and protection from prosecution. When a nation state is subjected to severe sanctions, that may cause an increase in hacking activity. There are at least four nation states actively engaged with the United States (Figure 9.1).

Criminal enterprises

Organized crime is in the business of stealing sensitive data to profit from their efforts. Compromised financial accounts provide an immediate return. PII and healthcare records can be sold on the dark web. Social engineering tactics such as business e-mail compromise and deepfake videos may be used trick an employee into wiring funds to an offshore account.

Criminal enterprises are formidable because they team up to overcome obstacles as detailed in the Cybercrime Ecosystem section below.

Insiders

The potential for insider threat exists in every organization. Employees and contractors are trusted insiders and have authorized access to systems, data and financial accounts. Motivations that drive insider threat include disgruntled personnel, desire for personal gain and espionage.

Hacktivists

Hacktivists are idealistic and use hacking and denial of service attacks to influence change. Most organizations are not targeted by Hacktivists. However, that can change quickly if a senior executive or the organization itself is discovered to have acted in a manner that is corrupt or morally wrong. Hacktivists are also known to conduct 'doxing' operations, releasing

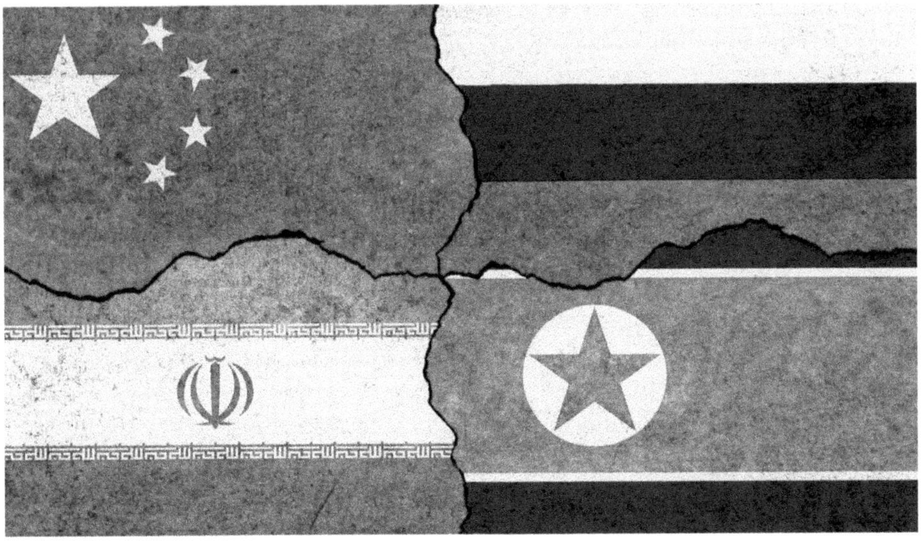

Figure 9.1 Flags of Iran, China, Russia and North Korea. Image licensed from Shutterstock (Asset id: 2200210289).

sensitive business communications to the Internet to cause embarrassment. Doxing may also be used to release executives' home addresses, e-mail and mobile phone numbers.

9.4 TACTICS, TECHNIQUES AND PROCEDURES

Techniques for compromising data

Malicious hackers leverage attack frameworks when targeting an organization. The process begins with reconnaissance, conducting research on the Internet and within social media. Scans of the organization's Internet-facing technology are also conducted. A plan is developed including which tools and configurations will be used. Hackers use penetration testing suites that contain many software applications, similar to a Swiss army knife. Phishing attacks may be used to deploy and install malware, which can provide a hacker with initial access and a foothold in the IT environment. The hacker pivots and moves laterally across the network from system-to-system, searching for sensitive data. The path to exfiltrate data from the organization will depend on network traffic flow restrictions. Hackers may persist in an IT environment for many months without being detected.

Cybercrime ecosystem

Cybercrime is committed through an ecosystem of criminal enterprises. Tool makers create software for detecting and exploiting vulnerabilities. They also sell zero day exploits, which take advantage of undisclosed vulnerabilities. Malicious hackers compromise systems and exfiltrate valuable information such as PII or intellectual property. Hackers sell information to Data Brokers, who in turn use Money Mules to monetize it. A Money Mule may use stolen payment card numbers to make purchases and resell the items to launder money. A portion of the funds are returned to the Data Broker to complete the process.

Criminal enterprises specialize in double extortion. They first exfiltrate sensitive data and then execute ransomware to encrypt systems. The organization is required to pay a ransom to prevent data from being publicly disclosed and to regain access to systems taken offline. Ransomware countermeasures may be disabled by hackers, such as gaining administrative access and deleting offline backups.

9.5 THREAT LANDSCAPE ANALYSIS

Document an analysis of the threat landscape, threat actors and their motivations. Include services and assets that are likely targets. Here is an example:

Acme has assets that are of value to threat actors. Nation states target *industry* when subjected to significant sanctions. Criminal enterprises seek to generate revenue through ransomware and illicit wire transfers. Insiders target company funds, PII and customer contacts. There is potential for fraud by those authorized to approve fund transfers. Hacktivists rarely take action but should not be discounted in the event of a public relations incident.

Service1 and *Service2* are prime targets for adversaries. Those services are hosted by *Vendor*. It is also important to focus on digital assets within *Acme*'s span of control as detailed within the Protection Boundaries section below.

9.6 POTENTIAL IMPACT

Executives strive to make decisions based on data and facts. Leverage real-world statistics from reputable sources to determine potential impact to the organization. Here is an example:

> Disclosure of names, birthdates and social security numbers can harm *Acme's* clients through fraud and the pain of recovering from identity theft. E-mail addresses can be used to conduct phishing campaigns under *Acme's* brand, resulting in further compromises and damage to customers. A data breach incurs costs of legal fees, unfunded remediation efforts, credit monitoring and identity theft protection. A breach may result in a class-action lawsuit. In aggregate, impact to the organization would be significant.
>
> The average cost of a data breach 20##-20## was $#M. The average cost per lost PII record was $###. The average time to identify a breach was ### days.
>
> In 20##, there were #,### cases of occupational fraud, totaling $#.# billion in losses. The average loss per case was $#M. Typical fraud cases last ## months before detection.

Reference section '5.2 Sources - Input' for a listing of threat landscape reports. ACFE's Occupational Fraud Report is also a good resource.

9.7 RISK TOLERANCE

Risk tolerance is management's tone from the top, under what circumstances they are willing to accept risk. That establishes risk context as the analysis moves forward.

If a Risk Tolerance Statement has been published in your organization, copy-and-paste it into this section of the report. Otherwise, leverage Figure 3.2 as a template and update as necessary with your executives.

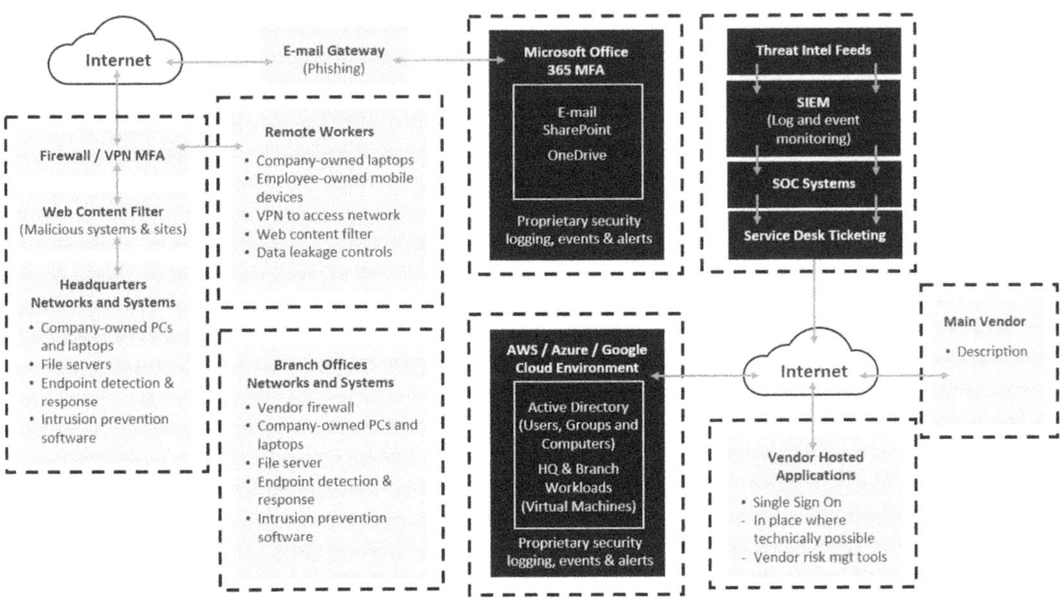

Figure 9.2 Protection boundaries.

9.8 PROTECTION BOUNDARIES

Detail where sensitive data is stored, processed and transmitted within this section. Protection boundaries are a visualization of the information security program's scope (Figure 9.2).

Include an overview of the diagram so that it stands alone. An executive or Board Director should be able to review and comprehend the diagram on their own. Here is an example:

> The majority of *Acme's* data is hosted with third party service providers such as *ServiceProvider1*, *ServiceProvider2*, *ServiceProvider3* and *ServiceProvider4*. *Acme's* operational span of control consists of the headquarters building, branch offices, employee laptops, Microsoft Office 365 and *AWS/Azure/Google* cloud computing. Sensitive data is hosted within each of those IT environments. Therefore, it is necessary to focus preventive and detective controls where that data is stored, processed or transmitted.

9.9 CONTROL FRAMEWORK

Describe the internal control framework within the organization. Here is an example:

> *Acme's* information security program leverages the *NIST Cybersecurity Framework* as a foundation for technical, administrative and physical security controls. *Acme* also adheres to *regulations, laws and contractual obligations*. Acme *has / has not* published an internal control framework.

Insert a visualization of control functions here, such as those depicted in 'Figure 10.1 - NIST Cybersecurity Framework'.

9.10 THREAT LANDSCAPE MATRIX

Provide a visualization that depicts threat landscape analysis for the organization (Figure 9.3).

Here is sample narrative based on the matrix above:

> Threat Actors: Criminals enterprises target organizations in *Acme's* industry. Nation states and insiders are likely threat actors.
>
> Targets: Threat actors target data that can be monetized, including client PII and Acme's financial accounts. Customer contacts may be a target by departing personnel. Strategic plans are of value to competitors.
>
> Tactics: Infrastructure and application vulnerabilities may be exploited with penetration testing tools and operating system commands. Phishing and social engineering may provide access to the network. Ransomware is used to extort funds.
>
> Outcomes: Criminal enterprises and insiders strive to commit fraud. The ultimate goal is to wire funds overseas, where they are difficult to claw back. Competitors may take advantage of strategic plans and customer contacts. The business impact may never be known.

For corroborating details, reference section '9.5 Threat Landscape Analysis' above.

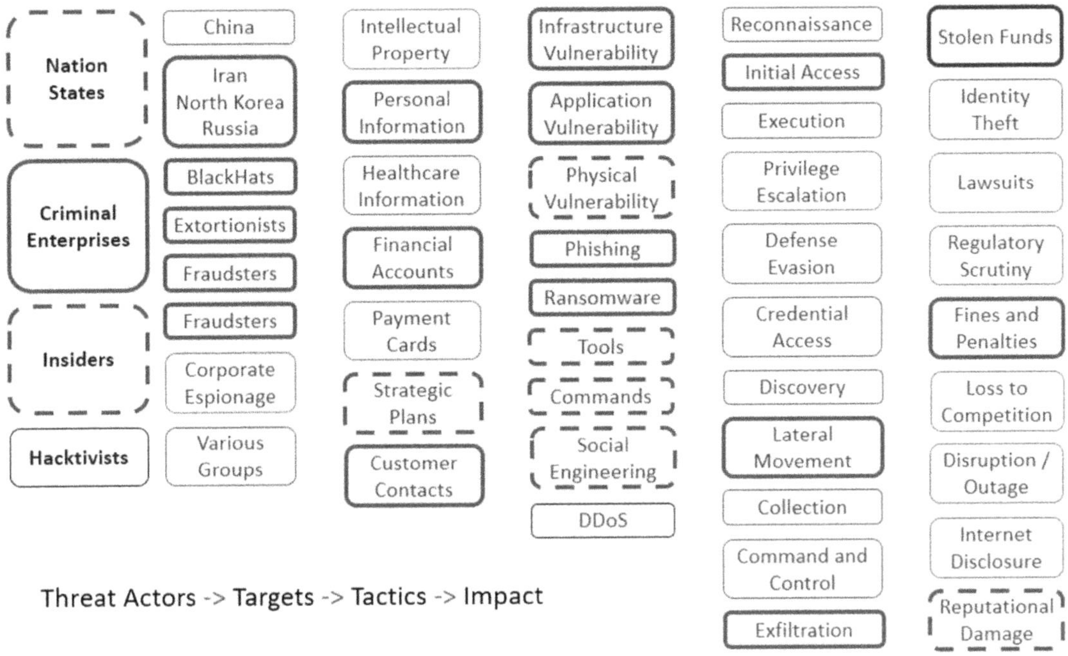

Figure 9.3 Threat landscape matrix.

The Reconnaissance column contains content from the MITRE ATT&CK Framework.

9.11 NATURAL DISASTERS

Severe weather causes service disruptions and business impact. Locate production and disaster recovery data centers at least 300 miles apart. That distance reduces the risk of a natural disaster impacting both facilities. Host data centers east-to-west in the United States to avoid coastal hazards such as hurricanes, tsunamis and earthquakes (Figure 9.4).

Reference the FMEA National Risk Index. Compare Hazard Types and Expected Annual Loss Ratings between the two data centers.

9.12 RISK ASSESSMENTS

The term 'Risk Assessments' is used loosely within this section. Provide an executive overview of technical, administrative and physical security processes used to identify risk to the organization. Here are examples to consider:

- Cybersecurity program assessments conducted by a third party
- Penetration tests conducted by a third party
- Vendor cybersecurity assessment reports
- Risk self-assessments such as
  - Ransomware preparedness
  - Zero trust controls analysis
  - Risk control self-assessments
  - Threat landscape and controls analysis
- Vulnerability scans
- Incident response tabletop exercises
- Business continuity exercises
- Disaster recovery exercises
- Internal IT audit assessments

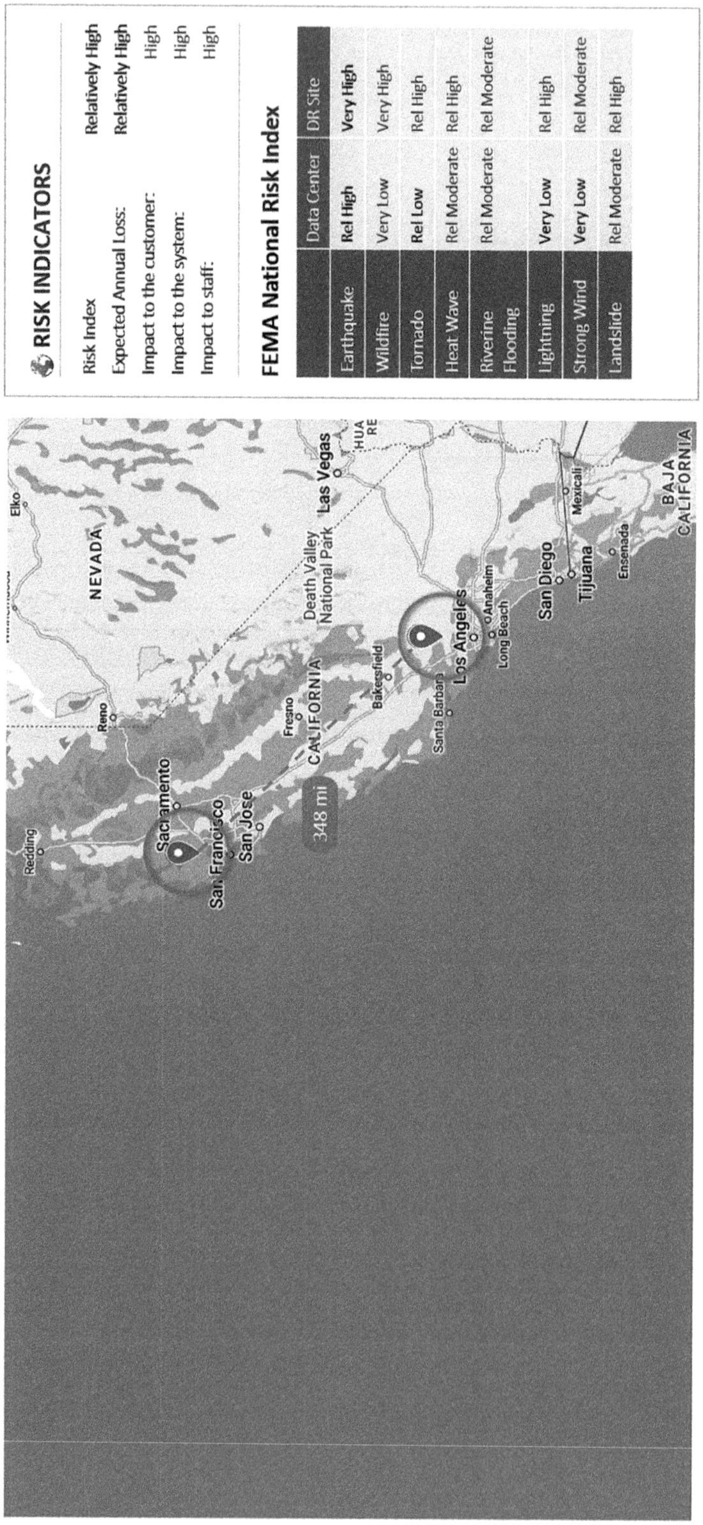

Figure 9.4 Natural disasters - Acme – 2050.

Describe in a paragraph each of the entries that are in-place. Include how often they are performed. If a control is missing, note that in the Residual Risk section below.

9.13 RISK MITIGATION (STRENGTHS)

It is important to be fair and balanced in this analysis. Document in-place controls that mitigate risk. Here are common controls to consider:

- Business continuity/Disaster recovery
- Conditional access
- Cybersecurity insurance
- Data breach response services
- Data loss prevention
- Identity and access management
- Incident management process
- InfoSec management routines
- Multi-factor authentication
- Physical security
- Privileged access management
- Ransomware preparedness
- Security awareness training
- Security monitoring
- Third party risk management
- Vulnerability management
- Web content filter

Include a section header for each control, with a brief description of the value-add in laymen's terms. If there is partial coverage of a control, provide details of where it is in-place in this section and a recommendation for improvement in the Residual Risk section below.

9.14 RESIDUAL RISK (OPPORTUNITIES FOR IMPROVEMENT)

Analysis concludes with opportunities for improvement in an operational risk context. Here are opportunities to identify and mitigate risk in a way that makes sense:

> Given the threat landscape and Acme's control environment, below are practices to reduce residual risk to align with management's risk tolerance.

Assessment report

If you are using Threat Landscape and Controls Analysis within an assessment report, provide a table of findings and recommendations in this section. Stack rank entries in order of risk severity such as high, moderate and low.

Analysis report

If you are conducting Threat Landscape and Controls Analysis to present existing cybersecurity issues, provide control recommendations that mitigate significant risk. Here is a sample listing of controls to consider:

- Allowlisting
- Cloud access security broker
- Crisis management program
- Cyber threat intelligence program
- Data exfiltration controls
- Deception technology
- Digital rights management
- Insider risk management program
- Metrics program
- Micro-segmentation
- Role based access control
- Privacy management program
- Risk register process
- Security architecture reviews
- Tabletop exercises
- Threat hunting program
- Tokenization
- Zero trust architecture

Provide a paragraph for each recommendation. Answer the 'so what' question, describing how the proposed control will identify or mitigate significant risk. Executives and Board Directors may not have technical backgrounds. Document recommendations in laymen's terms as a matter of courtesy and to influence support and funding.

9.15 CONCLUSION

Provide an executive summary that represents risk mitigation (strengths) and residual risk (opportunities for improvement). Here is an example:

> **Acme actively manages its Information Security Program as evidenced by the significant risk mitigation and analysis noted above.** Our program must be kept current to adapt to emerging threats and changes in technology. The residual risk section provides recommendations aligned to management's risk tolerance statement.
>
> There is opportunity to enhance operations within *Recommendation1*, *Recommendation2*, *Recommendation3*, *Recommendation4*, *Recommendation5 and Recommendation6*.
>
> The threat landscape and adversary attack techniques will continue to evolve. **While there are areas of risk that require consideration, continued analysis and remediation are a sign of active risk management.**

9.16 CALL TO ACTION

Conduct your own analysis on a backlog of cybersecurity issue records. Present to senior leadership in an executive forum or a board-level committee. Threat Landscape and Controls Analysis is an effective way to influence support and funding because it starts from the executive's side of the table. Take the time to develop business acumen. It will pay off for you.

Want to demonstrate leadership? Opportunity knocks!

Chapter 10

Conduct an assessment

10.1 INTRODUCTION

This chapter provides practical advice to conduct cybersecurity assessments. It details the end-to-end process including: scoping, 15 steps to develop work papers, scheduling, on-site assessment, report preparation and presentation. The first assessment example leverages the NIST Cybersecurity Framework for coverage across security domains. This chapter also addresses follow-on assessments. Readers are encouraged to evaluate lines of business and to take deep dives into critical functions. Tips and examples are provided to create testing procedures. The chapter also provides an assessment report framework. The assessment presentation phase includes a slide deck framework covering the threat landscape, assessment methodology, findings and recommendations, Strengths, Weaknesses, Opportunities and Threats (SWOT) and next steps.

10.2 ASSESSMENT FRAMEWORK

Leverage the NIST Cybersecurity Framework (CSF) when preparing to conduct an information security program assessment. NIST CSF has 100+ controls. When you are evaluating cybersecurity, that is a reasonable number to start with, something manageable. NIST CSF establishes a foundation of common controls for your assessment.

NIST CSF provides a good presentation layer for executives. Consider Figure 10.1 below. 'We identify threats and vulnerabilities. We implement preventive controls. We detect suspicious activity. We respond, leveraging our incident response plan. We recover, go through lessons learned and return to a normal state business as usual.' That could be a conversation in an elevator. NIST CSF addresses cybersecurity in non-technical terms. That is an inclusive form of communication for executives with business and financial backgrounds.

10.3 SCOPING

Next, we need to learn more about the organization. Scoping is process to determine what will be evaluated within an assessment, such as an organization, an operational function or a line of business (in-scope). Scoping also identifies areas that will not be included within the assessment (out-of-scope). That helps prevent scope creep, a condition where assessment activity strays beyond what is intended.

In this chapter we are preparing for an information security program assessment. Scoping activity will be focused on understanding the organization, their assets and their critical services. Start by conducting research on the Internet as an adversary might do. Review the

DOI: 10.1201/9781003543619-10

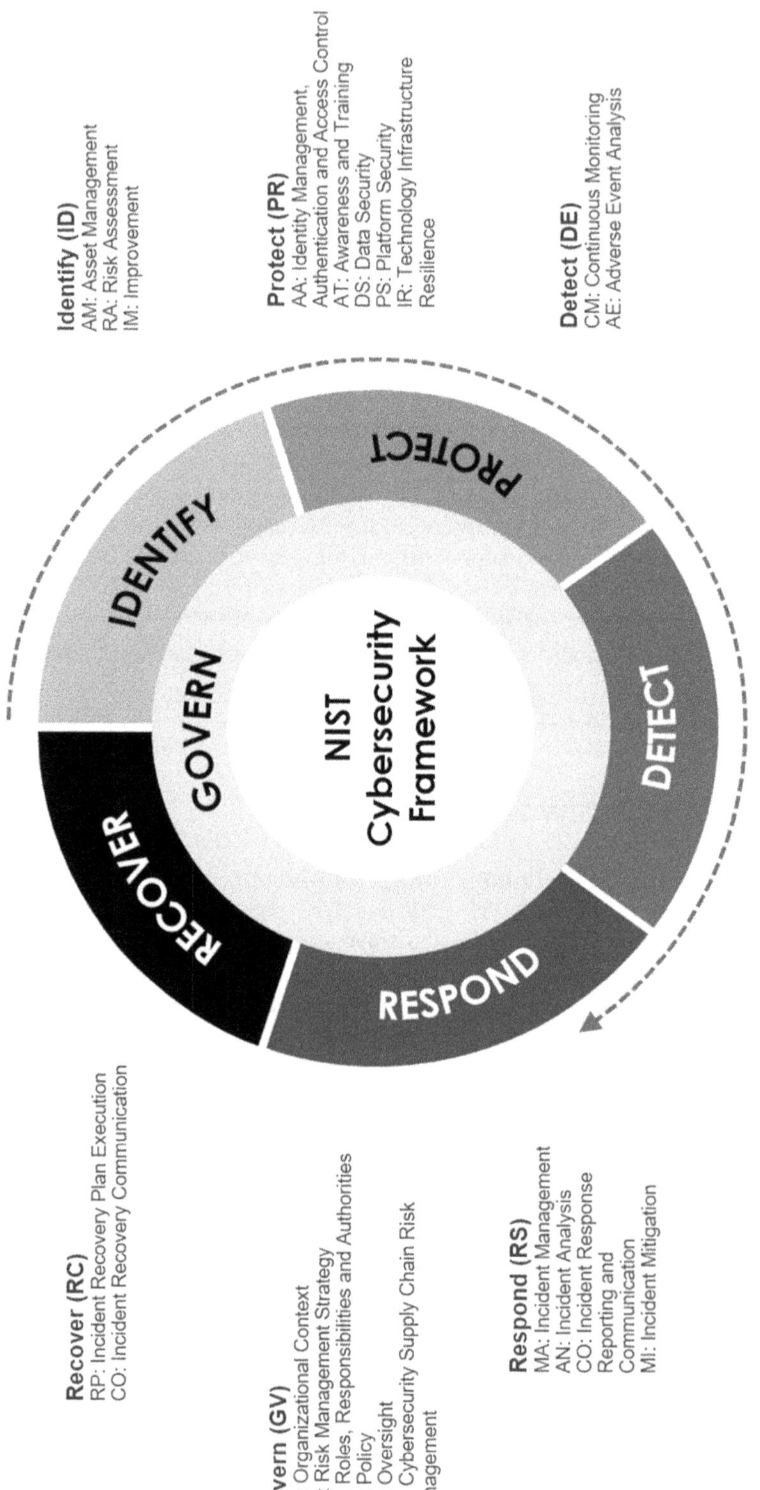

Figure 10.1 NIST cybersecurity framework.

organization's website, the products and services they offer. Review news, events and press releases. Determine if there are new services, technology implementations or mergers and acquisitions activity. Review LinkedIn profiles and employee commentary on Glassdoor.com.

Next, ask for 60 minutes with technology and business leaders of the organization. Prepare scoping questions to frame the conversation. Start with the partial list in Figure 10.2 below.

Go deeper than what you can find on the Internet. Ask about the organization's sensitive data and assets. It may be necessary to lead meeting participants through what categories of sensitive data might be present, such as Personally Identifiable Information (PII), Protected Health Information (PHI) or intellectual property. Ask where that data is stored, in on-premises data centers or within cloud hosting such as Microsoft Azure or AWS. Determine if third parties are heavily utilized. Gauge where sensitive data is stored, processed or transmitted. Leave time at the end of the meeting to ask 'what are a few nightmare scenarios for your organization'. Be mindful that these technology and business leaders have worked in the organization for years. They know of skeletons in the closet. It makes sense to ask what keeps them up at night. Determine where they feel exposed. Ask if there have been any security incidents with significant business impact within the past three years. The information gained in this scoping meeting will help craft assessment work papers, which we will get into soon.

10.4 THREAT ACTORS

Threat actors operate based on means, motive and opportunity. Determine which threat actors are likely targeting the organization's data and assets. Reference Figure 10.3 below for an overview of threat actors, their motivations and targeted data.

Hostile nation states strive to grow their countries economically, compromising intellectual property such as pipeline drug formulas. When that occurs, companies can bring that product to market without incurring the costs of research and development. Sanctions motivate countries to compromise data to shore up their economies. Foreign actors are also known to go after human resources and clearance records within government organizations. They may also target critical infrastructure such as election systems. We may have to contend with cyber warfare at some point.

Many organizations need to protect themselves from criminal enterprises. Their motivations are profit. Criminal enterprises target financial processes with social engineering and to convince someone to send a wire transfer overseas. There is a cybercrime ecosystem, with tool makers, black-hat hackers and data brokers. They target payment cards so if your

What is Acme's Mission/Vision?	**Which locations are involved in providing services?** Corporate office locations, data centers, etc.
Which services are provided by Acme?	Are services provided out of distributed locations such as branch offices?
Which categories of sensitive data or assets are present?	May I have a list of Internet facing websites, web applications and Software as a Service implementations?
Where does the data and/or assets reside?	Which web applications process sensitive information?
Which services must be highly available?	**How does Acme leverage cloud services such as AWS or Azure?**
Who provides IT support for Acme internally?	Are there services which include distribution of funds?
Which IT services are procured from vendors?	Who conducts software development for Acme?

What are a few nightmare scenarios for your organization?

Figure 10.2 Scoping questions.

Role	Motivation	Targeted Data
Nation States	• **Economic growth of their country** – Innovation without R&D • Response to sanctions • Cyber warfare	• **Intellectual property** • Military secrets / designs • **HR and clearance records** • Critical infrastructure • Election systems
Criminal Enterprises	• **Profit**	• **Financial accounts** • **Payment card data** • **Personally Identifiable Information (PII)** • Healthcare records
Insiders	• **Disgruntled** • **Personal gain** • Awe of rank • Espionage	• Intellectual property • Strategic plans • **Customer contacts** • **Company funds**
Hacktivists	• **Idealism** • Influence change • Service disruption	• **Sensitive business communications** • Executive documents that could cause embarrassment

Figure 10.3 Threat actors.

organization processes credit or debit card numbers take note. They also target PII, looking to monetize it by committing identity theft and fraud.

Every organization needs to worry about insider threat. There are a variety of motivations. An employee or contractor may be disgruntled or upset with the organization. An employee may commit fraud to benefit themselves financially. Corporate espionage targets intellectual property. Customer contacts may be taken as an employee resigns and leaves for a competitor.

Hacktivists strive to influence changes in behavior through punitive damages. When the news media reports unethical activities, Hacktivists may become upset and use computer hacking to cause harm to the organization. They may conduct denial of service attacks or disclose sensitive documents. Crisis communications are a mitigating control.

10.5 WORK PAPERS

Work papers are used to prepare for an assessment. Reference Figure 10.4 below as an example of how work papers are organized.

Create your own work papers starting with a blank spreadsheet. Enter column headers as fields, referencing Figure 10.4 above. Next, populate your work papers with NIST CSF entries as foundational controls for your cybersecurity program assessment.

Enter the appropriate testing procedure for each control in the 'Question/Test' field. The goal is to determine if necessary controls are in-place. Assessors verify controls by asking questions, by observing controls and by reviewing artifacts, such as documents or screenshots. The most effective test is to observe a control to determine whether it is in-place or not. Reviewing artifacts can also contribute to a fact-based assessment. Conducting interviews and asking questions has value, though the results can be less reliable.

Create a 'Response/Results' field to capture notes. There will be many hours of assessment activity. Work papers document whether each control was in-place or not as the Assessor was verifying controls. Those contemporaneous notes enable the Assessor to reconstruct the

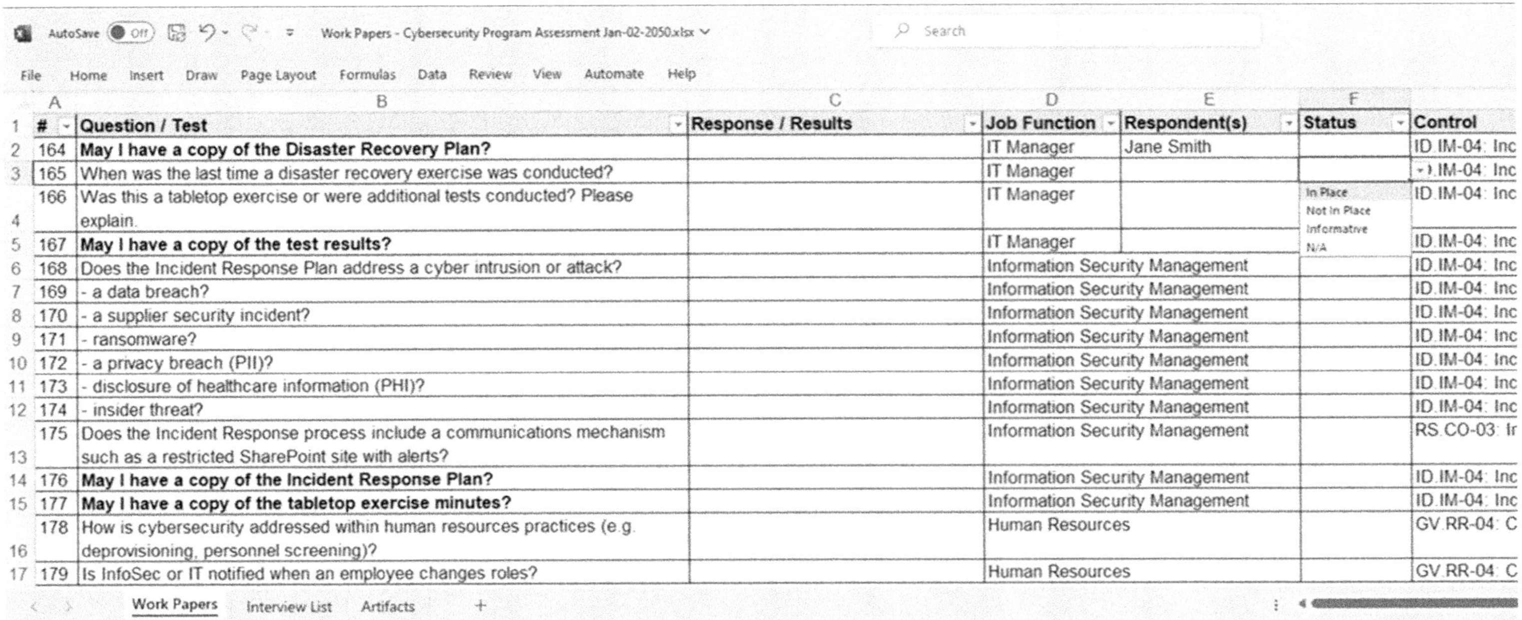

#	Question / Test	Response / Results	Job Function	Respondent(s)	Status	Control
164	**May I have a copy of the Disaster Recovery Plan?**		IT Manager	Jane Smith		ID.IM-04: Inc
165	When was the last time a disaster recovery exercise was conducted?		IT Manager			ID.IM-04: Inc
166	Was this a tabletop exercise or were additional tests conducted? Please explain.		IT Manager		In Place Not In Place Informative N/A	ID.IM-04: Inc
167	**May I have a copy of the test results?**		IT Manager			ID.IM-04: Inc
168	Does the Incident Response Plan address a cyber intrusion or attack?		Information Security Management			ID.IM-04: Inc
169	- a data breach?		Information Security Management			ID.IM-04: Inc
170	- a supplier security incident?		Information Security Management			ID.IM-04: Inc
171	- ransomware?		Information Security Management			ID.IM-04: Inc
172	- a privacy breach (PII)?		Information Security Management			ID.IM-04: Inc
173	- disclosure of healthcare information (PHI)?		Information Security Management			ID.IM-04: Inc
174	- insider threat?		Information Security Management			ID.IM-04: Inc
175	Does the Incident Response process include a communications mechanism such as a restricted SharePoint site with alerts?		Information Security Management			RS.CO-03: Ir
176	**May I have a copy of the Incident Response Plan?**		Information Security Management			ID.IM-04: Inc
177	**May I have a copy of the tabletop exercise minutes?**		Information Security Management			ID.IM-04: Inc
178	How is cybersecurity addressed within human resources practices (e.g. deprovisioning, personnel screening)?		Human Resources			GV.RR-04: C
179	Is InfoSec or IT notified when an employee changes roles?		Human Resources			GV.RR-04: C

Figure 10.4 Work papers.

assessment long after it is completed. Work papers can be used to answer why a finding was written up or why a control was determined to be in-place at the time of the assessment. Contemporaneous notes are especially important when someone answers a question during assessment interviews.

Create a 'Job Function' field to identify which role to verify the control with. This would be the person that does the work, the person that maintains or uses the control. Populate the 'Respondent(s)' field with the name(s) of the people interviewed during assessment activity.

The assessment will have many testing procedures, often in the hundreds. Therefore, it makes sense to create a 'Status' field to label each control as in-place or not-in-place. That makes it easier to create the assessment report.

Create a 'Control' field to map assessment findings to NIST CSF, laws, regulations and contractual obligations. That context can help influence risk mitigation, including support and funding from executives.

Abraham Lincoln is quoted as having said, "Give me six hours to chop down a tree and I will spend the first four sharpening the axe". This chapter includes 15 steps to flesh out work papers. That enables you to focus on whether controls are in-place, minimizing stress in the process.

10.6 FLESH OUT CONTROLS

Continue to flesh out your work papers. The first main bullet below is a NIST CSF control.

- GV.SC-05: Requirements to address cybersecurity risks in supply chains are established, prioritized and integrated into contracts and other types of agreements with suppliers and other relevant third parties.
  - Is default contract language in place to mandate compliance with security requirements?
  - May I have a copy of the default language?
  - What is the process if a vendor wants to redline contract security language?
  - Does process require the security team to review contracts pertaining to IT services?

The four testing procedures above are necessary to verify the extent of the control. We ask for a copy of the default contract language. Review artifacts to determine the coverage and the effectiveness of the control. It may take 2-3 hours to review default contract language. There may be significant security requirements missing. Depending on the severity, the details may be written up in an assessment finding or a recommendation. Have that attention to detail. It is necessary to review many artifacts during an information security program assessment.

The testing procedures address the process if a vendor wants to redline contract security language. The legal team or the third party risk management team should have an information security professional involved in review. In some cases, a vendor may want to redline services they are not providing. In others, a vendor may want to strike a data security control that should be in place. That will cause concern if someone with an information security skill set is at the table.

The testing procedures question whether the security team reviews contracts pertaining to IT services. This is in cases where the contract is written by the vendor. Default contract security language needs to be added. If the vendor resists inserting an addendum due to duplicate or similar requirements in the contract, a security professional should conduct analysis and insert necessary security requirements in-line throughout the contract.

These are examples of how one control framework entry should be evaluated to verify to what extent the control is in-place. That level of detail is necessary to identify material risk throughout the assessment.

10.7 SECURITY MONITORING

Continue to flesh out your work papers. This is an example of how the Assessor can leverage their knowledge and experience to verify controls in an area of focus (Figure 10.5).

These are examples of security monitoring, increasing in maturity from A through F. Testing procedures should verify that security logging and events are centralized, including operating systems, commercial software and custom applications. Confirm that SIEM log monitoring and event correlation parses through logging and events, with suspicious activity alerts configured. Determine if there is a Security Operations Center (SOC) with cybersecurity personnel monitoring and responding to suspicious events 24/7/365. Testing procedures should focus on the end-to-end process, starting with a security event being logged, to a SOC Analyst acknowledging an alert ticket as a false positive or escalating for further investigation.

The testing procedures transition into a higher level of maturity. These controls may be documented in the assessment report as recommendations based on operational risk and reputable practices. Determine if threat hunting is conducted, where cybersecurity professionals actively search for threat actors within the IT environment. Threat hunting is a search for Tactics, Techniques and Procedures (TTPs) and Indicators of Compromise (IoCs). The goal is to identify suspicious activity that was not detected by security monitoring.

Determine whether behavior analytics software is used to detect unusual activity from a login account or system. An employee that has given notice may login late at night. A login account may move laterally across the network, connecting to multiple servers when that is not the norm. It is difficult for a threat actor to change their tactics, how they conduct hacking activity. Behavior monitoring can pick up on that.

The assessment report makes optional recommendations if these last few controls are not in-place. Recommendations entries call attention to common controls or reputable practices. They have utility for strategic planning as well.

#	Control	Description
A	Security Logging & Events Centralized	• Operating systems, commercial software and custom applications
B	SIEM Configurations	• Configure the SIEM leveraging the MITRE ATT&CK framework • Ticket integration / Automated response actions
C	Security Operations Center (SOC)	• InfoSec personnel monitor and respond to suspicious activity 24x7 • Threat Actors are on different time zones, active after hours
D	Threat Hunting	• InfoSec actively searches the SIEM for Tactics, Techniques and Procedures (TTPs) and Indicators of Compromise (IoCs)
E	User Behavior Analytics	• Monitors patterns of user activity for anomalies that can indicate potential threats
F	Cyber Fusion Center	• Shares threat intelligence information between SecOps, ITOps, DevOps, etc.

- A sampling of security monitoring controls, order and priority are subjective
- Some controls may be documented as recommendations

Figure 10.5 Flesh out controls - Security monitoring.

10.8 ALERTS BASED ON ADVERSARY TOOLS

It is difficult for threat actors to swap out their tools. They have a trend of using commercial, freeware and open-source tools to avoid detection by security software. Review monitoring alert configurations for administrative software that is not in use within the IT environment. If an organization does not use a certain brand of remote management or file compression software, monitoring should be in place to alert when it is detected. Flesh out testing procedures with threat actor tools based on 'living off the land' cyber threat intelligence. Verify an alert is sent if one of these tools is detected.

10.9 MONITORING FOR SUSPICIOUS COMMANDS

Create testing procedures to (1) verify operating system command logging to SIEM monitoring software and (2) configurations to alert on use of suspicious commands. Monitor for rarely used commands such as those that determine which account is logged in or the host name of the system. Flesh out testing procedures with suspicious commands based on cyber threat intelligence. Ask for a copy of the configurations, compare them to your list of suspicious commands and call out the gaps as recommendations for improvement.

10.10 INSIDER THREAT

Insiders are one of the four types of threat actors. An assessment needs to account for them. Tread lightly in this space, especially in organizations that foster a sense of warmth and community within work-life culture. Use the term 'Insider Risk Management' within the assessment report and related materials.

Flesh out your work papers with testing procedures for core insider risk management controls such as:

- Continuous monitoring
- Data exfiltration by an employee or contractor
- Monitoring triggered by behavioral indicators

Reference the 'Insider Risk Monitoring and Response' chapter for additional details. Resist the urge to include many insider threat controls in your work papers. The scope of this assessment is the information security program. There is opportunity to focus on insider threat vulnerabilities in a future assessment.

10.11 ATTACK-CENTRIC CONTROLS

Include testing procedures with an attack-centric focus. Move beyond framework and common controls. Include controls that identify or mitigate risk in a modern context. Reference Figure 10.6 below for inspiration.

Think in terms of how a threat actor operates, how they conduct their work. When an adversary tries to gain access to an organization, they start by sending a phishing message. The adversary wants to trick an employee or contractor into clicking on a malicious link or a file attachment with malware embedded. Assessment work papers should verify the organization has a phishing test messages program to mitigate that risk. Test messages help

Tactics and Response	Control Options	
Malware delivery	• **Phishing test messages** • Web content filtering • Advertisement blocking	• External message warning • E-mail authentication (DMARC, SPF and DKIM)
Gain system access	• Restrict workstation admin access from end users • **Known Exploited Vulnerabilities Catalog - CISA** • **Lock down PowerShell**	• Require Admins to leverage their end user account • Unique passwords for each server • **Allowlisting software** • **Multi-factor auth for servers**
Pivot and move laterally	• **Network segmentation** • **Jump box - Bastion host**	• Micro-segmentation
Data exfiltration	• **Granular source/destination firewall rules (network)** • Web application firewall • Resolve from internal DNS servers	• Monitor length of DNS queries and responses • **Research other forms of exfiltration and implement controls**
Detect	• **Suspicious command monitoring** • Threat hunting	• **Honeypots and honeytokens** • 24x7 SOC monitoring
Respond	• **Incident response plan** • Automated security response	• **Incident response exercises** • Crisis management team

- **A sampling...**
- **80/20 rule**
- **Establish a matrix for your organization**
  - Critical few controls
  - In addition to frameworks and standards
  - Be mindful of productivity impact
- **Tell the story**
- **Mature risk management**

Figure 10.6 Work papers - Attack-centric controls.

end users learn what a true phishing message looks like, not to click and how to report the suspicious message to the information security team. Testing procedures also need to verify if web content filtering and advertisement blocking are in place to protect from malicious links.

Threat actors strive to gain system access to compromise sensitive or valuable data. The information security program should have controls in place to make that difficult. Testing procedures should verify that end users do not have administrative access to their company-issued desktop PCs and laptops. That access privilege restriction makes it harder for malware or ransomware to execute.

Threat actors are reluctant to bring hacking tools into their target environment. They seek to avoid detection by using software that is already available, referred to as 'Living off the land'. PowerShell software is included within Microsoft operating systems. System administrators use it to conduct their work. Testing procedures should verify if Microsoft's PowerShell security configurations have been implemented.

Verify if server access has been hardened against attack. Allowlisting software is a preventive control against ransomware and other malware. It permits authorized programs to run and blocks all others. It is relatively easy for threat actors to bypass login ID and password authentication through credential stuffing. Multi-factor authentication (MFA) provides an additional layer of protection, such as a random number generator within a mobile phone application. Determine if MFA has been enabled for servers. That makes it difficult for an adversary to hop from system to system while looking for sensitive data.

When an adversary gains access to their first system, it is not likely to contain the data they are looking for. Therefore, it is necessary for them to pivot and move laterally, east to west across the network. The information security program should have controls to make that difficult. Verify that network segmentation is in place to protect sensitive information such as research and development data and payment card numbers. Network segmentation must include access restrictions such as a jump box or bastion host. A user must authenticate to the jump box to gain access to sensitive information. It is a good practice to require MFA to the jump box to further restrict access from the common use network.

An adversary may gain access to a system with sensitive data. The information security program should make it difficult to transfer sensitive data from the IT environment to a system out on the Internet. Verify that network firewall rules include granular source and destination restrictions. Verify the use of internal Domain Name System (DNS) servers to limit the need for system access straight out to the Internet, which an adversary could use to steal data.

A critical metric within cybersecurity is 'dwell time'; the time between when a threat actor gains access to an IT environment and the time they are detected. Behavior monitoring alerts of suspicious activity by end users or systems. Deception technology mimics servers and files. If a threat actor connects or opens them, an alert is sent to the Security Operations Center. Create testing procedures to determine whether these technologies are in place.

Early detection and incident response can mean the difference between an incident and a data breach. Submit artifact requests to evaluate the Incident Response Plan and tabletop exercise meeting materials. Incident response should occur at machine speed where technically feasible. Verify to what extent automated security response is in place, such as conditional access and automated isolation of systems and accounts.

This section is not intended to provide comprehensive coverage of how threat actors compromise data and which controls should be in place. It is an example of a way of thinking, a mindset when preparing for an assessment. Design tests, questions and artifact requests to verify controls in an attack-centric context.

10.12 THREAT LANDSCAPE

An information security program assessment should be informed by cyber threat intelligence. Assessors must keep current with how threat actors are gaining access to IT environments and how they exfiltrate data. Attend webinars that discuss the aftermath of data breaches. Review reports and articles from data breach response firms. Participate in local information security chapter meetings, ISACA, ISC2, ISSA and FBI InfraGard. Participate in industry groups such as Information Sharing and Analysis Centers (ISACs). Reference the Cyber Threat Intelligence chapter for additional details.

When attending a briefing on a recent data breach consider the tactics, techniques and procedures used by the threat actor. Which vulnerabilities or control gaps were exploited? Which software tools were used by the adversary? What mitigations should be in place, preventive, detective and corrective controls? Create corresponding testing procedures within your work papers.

10.13 EMERGING TECHNOLOGIES

Keep current with emerging technologies. Generative and Agentic AI increase the capabilities of threat actors. Include relevant governance controls within testing procedures:

- **Artificial intelligence policy and awareness training**
- **Security architecture reviews**
- **Project management**
- **Change management and**
- **Incident response playbook**
- **Third party risk management program**
  - Vendor contract addendum
  - Vendor assessment report analysis
  - TPRM questionnaire
  - Shared responsibilities matrix
- **Risk scenarios**
  - AI hallucinations
  - Intellectual property violations
  - Data leakage
  - Software integration
  - Downloading fake AI software
  - AI chatbot

Quantum computing will have the ability to break current encryption methods. Artificial general intelligence will have cognitive abilities, a powerful tool threat actors will use to compromise data.

Establish testing procedures to make control recommendations based on current and future state. Reference the zero trust security model for inspiration.

10.14 ID ACCESS CARD SYSTEM

Continue to flesh out your work papers by establishing testing procedures for physical security. Verify a process is in place to compare a list of employees and contractors with active ID access badges. That simple quality assurance process will detect if someone resigns or is terminated and somehow their access badge privileges were not rescinded. Review cards with extensive access such as 'computer room', 'network equipment closets' and 'all access' badges. Groups and role-based access should be used as a reputable practice. Determine who has access to issue badges.

10.15 RESISTANCE TO BREACHING TOOLS

Determine if controls are in place to protect against physical breaching tools.

In Figure 10.7, the two tools at the top are the Seattle Rapid Access Tool (SEARAT) and the FirePik. They can be used to open doors without a key. A door can be opened quickly

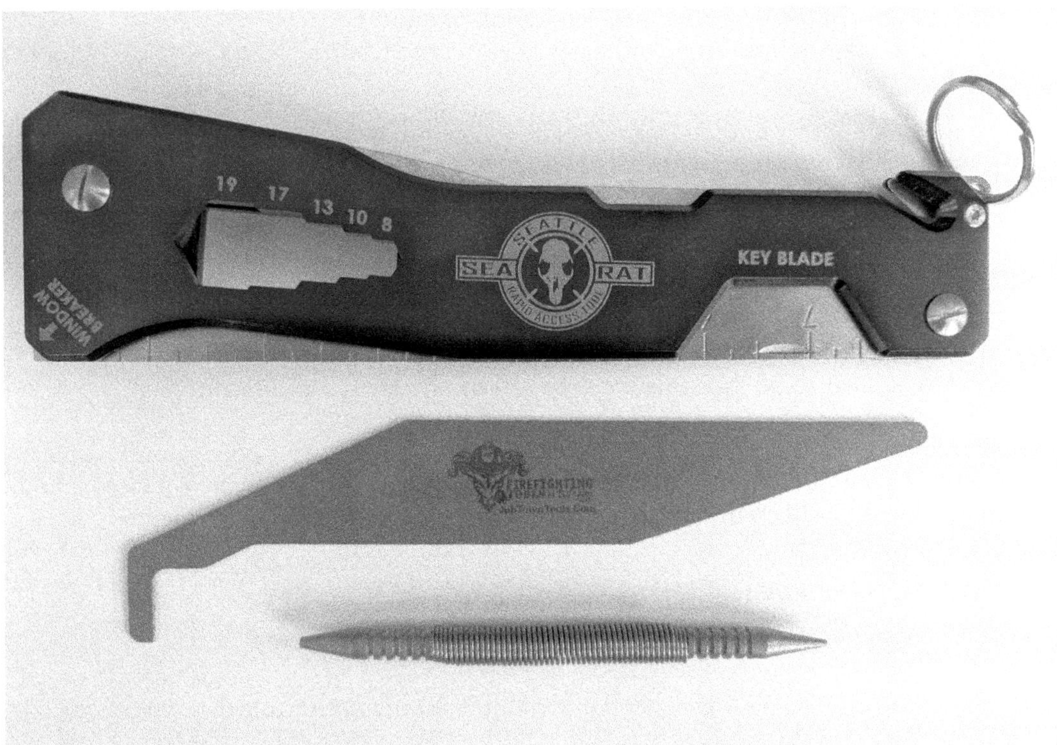

Figure 10.7 Resistance to breaching tools.

and easily by sliding the tool between the door and the frame to retract the latch. Verify that a door latch protection plate is in place to cover the latch so it cannot be retracted by a breaching tool.

Doors that have hinges facing outward are vulnerable to a hinge pin removal tool. Hinge pins are easy to remove. Just pop the hinge pins out with the tool and pull the door out of the frame. Protect against this vulnerability by installing door hinges facing inward from within the room being secured. Another option is security door hinges, which use a metal tab to interlock hinges when closed. That prevents a threat actor from removing the door.

A threat actor may use these tools to open perimeter doors, stairwell doors, office doors, network closet doors and computer room doors. Become familiar with door breaching tools and countermeasures. Do not use these tools during an assessment to prevent damage to the door.

10.16 RESULTS OF SCOPING

At the beginning of the chapter there was a 60 minute scoping call with IT and business leaders. The Assessor learned of nightmare scenarios and other information that can be used to focus the assessment. Continue to flesh out your work papers with those details. Create custom testing procedures based on service offerings and assets.

- **Sensitive data present - Evaluate data protection controls in that environment**
  - How are access requests for the Research and Development (R&D) systems approved and documented?
  - Is multi-factor authentication required to access R&D systems?
  - How are access permissions managed within the R&D systems, incorporating the principles of least privilege and separation of duties?
  - Is there an Administrative or 'Super User' account for the R&D systems? Who has that access?
  - Do R&D systems reside on their own network segment?
- **Large sums of money present - Evaluate fraud prevention controls**
  - What types of fraud prevention measures are in place?
  - What types of fraud detection measures are in place?
  - Is fraud examination conducted to monitor for common fraud schemes?
  - Do any employees have the ability to create an account and make a payment?
  - Does Acme have formal and regularly scheduled procedures to perform fraud risk assessments?
  - Is an annual fraud assessment conducted by an external audit firm?

Request artifacts to validate answers to the questions above. Fraud prevention is typically out-of-scope for an information security assessment. Acme's management requested a high-level evaluation of fraud analysis and prevention controls in the example above.

10.17 INTERVIEW TECHNIQUES

Bad practices

At this point the assessment is grounded in reputable practices, controls that we expect to be in-place. Create testing procedures that search for bad practices, to prevent security incidents, outages and associated business impact. Here are examples for inspiration:

- Do end users have administrative access to their workstations?
- Are any shared accounts in use?
- Is a second person required to sign-off on all fund disbursements before a payment can be made?
- Do protections against data leaks remain in place when a laptop is not connected via VPN?
- Are development and testing environment(s) separate from the production environment?
- Do Developers have access to the Production Environment?
- How do you know if each system is replicating logs to the SIEM?
- Are there 'Any/Any' firewall rules in place?
- Is there a Deny All rule at the bottom of the firewall rule base?

Request artifacts or screen sharing sessions to verify current state.

Survey questions

While preparing for the assessment ask the information security leader if there are any vulnerabilities or control gaps they are having trouble addressing. These are scenarios where material risk exists and senior executives will not support mitigation. For example, some organizations still allow employees and contractors to access personal e-mail from their company-issued computer. That provides an easy way to exfiltrate or steal information.

Use survey questions to influence change. Create testing procedures that ask questions of each person interviewed throughout the assessment. Here are examples for inspiration:

- Does your job require access to external drive storage (e.g. USB flash drives, external hard drives or smart phone storage)?
- Does your job require access to personal e-mail (e.g. Gmail)?
- Does your job require access to Internet drive storage (e.g. DropBox)?
- Are there any security or risk concerns that should be raised?
- Are there process and procedure documents for the areas we have discussed? May I have a copy?
- Are you the Primary for this function? Who is the Alternate?

The assessment report will document the known vulnerability or control gap. That same finding should include context gained from the survey questions such as, 'Of the 20 people interviewed during the assessment, all of them said they did not need personal e-mail access in performance of their duties'. That level of detail documented in a formal report may be sufficient to influence remediation.

Consider asking 'Are there any security or risk concerns that should be raised'. It is a similar approach to the nightmare scenario question in scoping. An open-ended question gives voice to known or suppressed risk issues.

10.18 CONTROLS ACROSS ROLES AND FUNCTIONS

Some controls must be verified in more than one place to determine if there is adequate coverage. Here are examples for inspiration:

- **System hardening within operating systems and commercial applications**

  - System Administrator, Cloud Administrator, Network Administrator and Database Administrator
- **Access control across critical systems, applications and functions**
  - Identity & Access Management and Application Governance
- **Documentation of where sensitive data resides**
  - Data Governance, IT Operations, Information Security and Privacy

The assessment is designed to comprehensively verify these controls, not just in one place.

10.19 FINISHING TOUCHES - WORK PAPERS

Good news, your work papers are almost complete. One last step to conduct quality assurance:

- **Filter work papers by Job Function**
  - Question/Test flow, reorder if necessary
  - Reword questions for conversational tone
  - Add questions to fill in gaps, better address risk
  - Copy question to another Job Function
- **Confirm artifacts are requested where appropriate**
- **Ask to observe - Confirm a control is in place**
- **Assessment Techniques**
  - Observe whether a control is in place
  - Review documents
  - Interview staff
- **Trust, but verify**

Start by filtering your work papers by job function. Some roles such as the Backup Administrator will only have a few testing procedures at this point. Each interview session is at least 30 minutes. Make use of that time and add testing procedures to verify controls. You may make edits for a more natural conversation such as reordering testing procedures and rewording questions.

You will also notice testing procedures that should be copied to another job function for comprehensive coverage of the control.

Consider how the three assessment techniques are used throughout the testing procedures. Observe whether a control is in-place. Review artifacts, such as documents or screenshots. Interview staff and ask questions. The goal is a fact-based assessment. Observe controls and review evidence as much as possible.

10.20 INTERVIEW LIST

Prepare an Interview List based on the functional roles required to conduct the assessment. Determine the duration of each interview by filtering your work papers by job function. The number of testing procedures that appear help determine how much time is needed for each interview, 30 or 60 minutes. Reserve two hours for physical security building tours (Figure 10.8).

Schedule an Assessment Status Call at the end of each week. That leaves time to adapt to challenges in the assessment. If someone called out sick, reschedule the interview. The status call can also be used to escalate submission of assessment artifacts that are past due.

In some cases, a manager will say they can be the respondent for multiple interviews. The Assessor needs to meet with the people that do the work, people that know whether a control is in place or not. Managers are welcome to join and listen in.

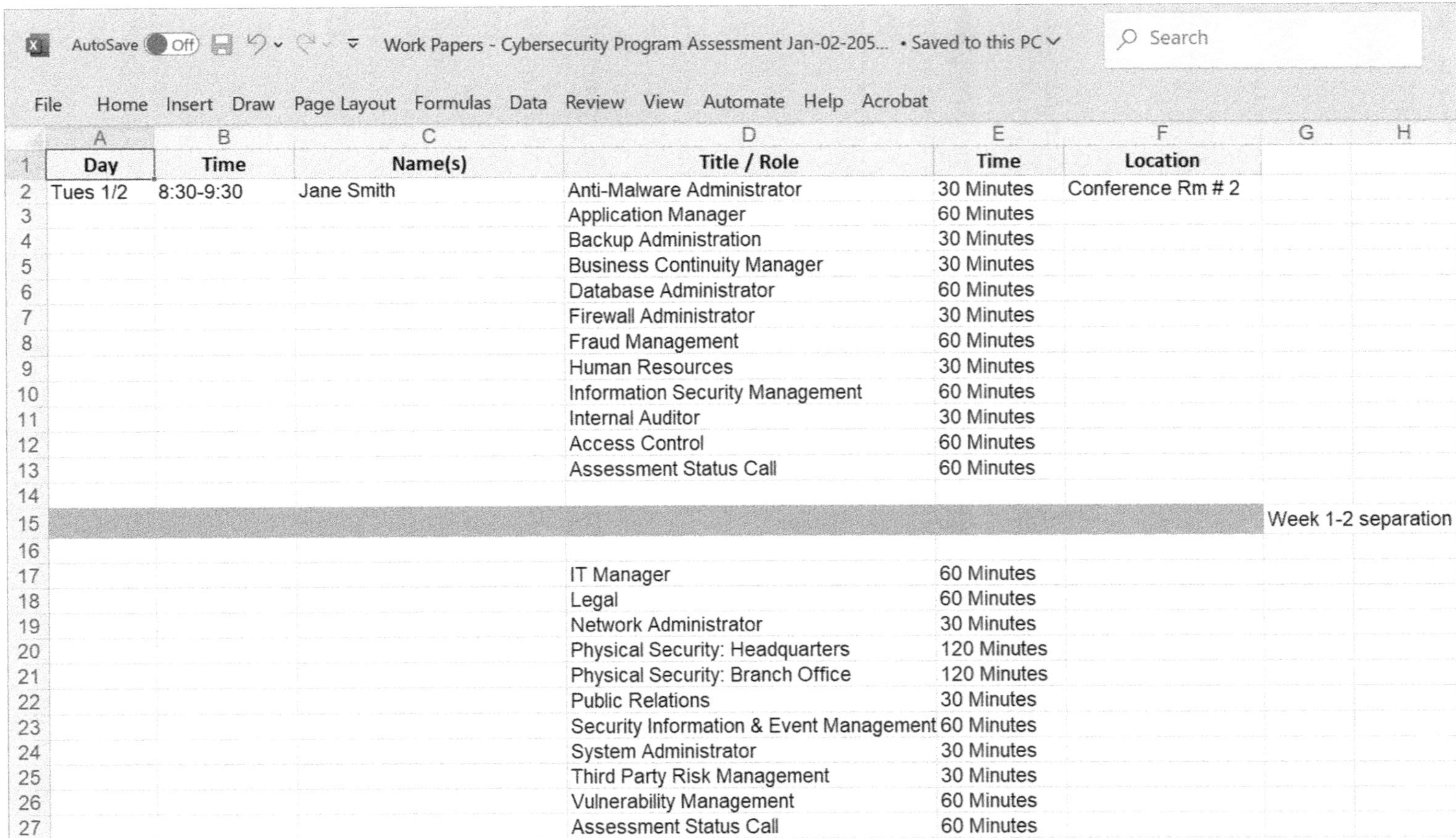

	A	B	C	D	E	F	G	H
1	Day	Time	Name(s)	Title / Role	Time	Location		
2	Tues 1/2	8:30-9:30	Jane Smith	Anti-Malware Administrator	30 Minutes	Conference Rm # 2		
3				Application Manager	60 Minutes			
4				Backup Administration	30 Minutes			
5				Business Continuity Manager	30 Minutes			
6				Database Administrator	60 Minutes			
7				Firewall Administrator	30 Minutes			
8				Fraud Management	60 Minutes			
9				Human Resources	30 Minutes			
10				Information Security Management	60 Minutes			
11				Internal Auditor	30 Minutes			
12				Access Control	60 Minutes			
13				Assessment Status Call	60 Minutes			
14								
15							Week 1-2 separation	
16								
17				IT Manager	60 Minutes			
18				Legal	60 Minutes			
19				Network Administrator	30 Minutes			
20				Physical Security: Headquarters	120 Minutes			
21				Physical Security: Branch Office	120 Minutes			
22				Public Relations	30 Minutes			
23				Security Information & Event Management	60 Minutes			
24				System Administrator	30 Minutes			
25				Third Party Risk Management	30 Minutes			
26				Vulnerability Management	60 Minutes			
27				Assessment Status Call	60 Minutes			

Figure 10.8 Interview list.

- AWS trusted advisor report
- Microsoft secure score reports
  - Microsoft secure score (Office 365)
  - Microsoft secure score for Identity
  - Microsoft defender for cloud
- Patch management report
- Incident response plan
- Crisis communications plan
- Tabletop exercise minutes
- Business continuity plan
- Disaster recovery plan
- BC/DR exercise minutes
- Listing of InfoSec policies and standards
- InfoSec program metrics, KPIs and KRIs
- Risk tolerance statement
- Vendor security contract addendum
- Help desk authentication procedures
- Wire transfer authentication procedures

Figure 10.9 Assessment artifacts.

10.21 ARTIFACTS

Artifacts contribute to a fact-based assessment. Artifacts include documents, screenshots and any type of evidence that proves whether a control is in-place or not. A partial listing of artifacts is included in Figure 10.9 for illustration purposes.

An Assessor may request 50+ artifacts aligned to the controls of an information security program assessment. Request artifacts before the assessment and within work papers. Feel comfortable asking for artifacts by discovery, things that occur to you in the conversations as you go along in the assessment.

You should spend as much time preparing for the assessment as time spent conducting the assessment, documenting the report and presenting the results.

10.22 ASSESSMENT REPORT

The assessment report begins with an executive summary, typically one page. It provides high level trends observed during the assessment and areas where security controls could be improved. The report includes assessment methodology and scope, with names of staff members that were interviewed. The report concludes with findings and recommendations. Findings document a violation of the NIST Cybersecurity Framework, or a policy or standard of the organization. Recommendations are made based on reputable practices or in some cases just good common sense.

Submit the assessment report to one person within the organization. Start with a draft report and request feedback. Ask if there are any significant issues, such as a finding that is not valid, perhaps miscommunicated by someone that did not have visibility into the control. Once feedback and edits are complete, give that person the final report. They control distribution internally, not the assessment team. If someone requests a copy of the report, gently refer them to that internal point of contact.

10.23 ASSESSMENT PRESENTATION

You may be asked to present an assessment briefing to executives. Leverage content from this book to discuss threat actors, assessment methodology and the NIST CSF. Conduct a findings overview, that is what the executives are interested in. Cover high risk assessment findings and the highest risk moderate findings. SWOT analysis is great to conclude with, strengths, weaknesses, opportunities and threats. Remember that you are speaking with C-suite or senior executives. They are focused on risk management. Speak in terms of risk versus security. The executives will want to discuss remediation plans. Ask the information security team to provide the requested details, including target dates.

10.24 FOLLOW-ON ASSESSMENTS

Frederick II is quoted as having said, "He who tries to defend everything, defends nothing". Accept risk as you conduct future assessments beyond the information security program assessment in this chapter.

Line of business assessment

• Access Control
• Process Design
  – Insider Threat
  – Fraud Prevention
• Call Center
	• Application Governance
	• Data Management
	• Third Party Risk Management
	• LOB Service Offerings

Some lines of business are as large and complex as a mid-sized company. Verify how they manage access control. Request process diagrams for critical processes where sensitive data or assets are present. Determine if controls are in-place for insider risk management and fraud prevention. Verify how callers are authenticated by customer service. Determine how the line of business is addressing each vendors' shared security model. Reference the 'Third Party Risk Management' chapter for inspiration.

Future assessments

Follow the data, follow the risk. There are many options for future assessments beyond a line of business (Figure 10.10).

Leverage the list of topics above to create a multi-year assessment plan. There can be good return evaluating business processes, conducting risk assessments and with Failure Modes and Effects Analysis (FMEA).

An information security assessment reveals threats and countermeasures that have not been considered. Controls thought to be in place may not be. Commissioning an assessment is a proactive approach, a sign of ownership. An assessment shines a bright light into dark places.

• Application Security	• Ransomware
• Business Process Risk	• Line of Business Risk
• Security Operations Center	• Insider Threat
• Mergers and Acquisitions	• Zero Trust Security Model
• Security Awareness	• Third Party Risk Management
• Incident Response	• FMEA Process Risk
• Fraud Prevention	• Threat Landscape & Controls
• Data Security	• Generative AI

Figure 10.10 Future assessments.

Chapter 11

Crisis communications

11.1 INTRODUCTION

This chapter provides practical advice to support crisis communications in a cybersecurity context. Provides rationale for establishing a Crisis Management Program from an operational risk perspective. The compliance validation section references requirements from NIST cybersecurity and privacy frameworks. Details how incident response and crisis management teams work together. Includes recommendations for a crisis communications plan, holding statement templates, a data breach notification matrix and a distribution plan. Provides lessons learned and ten reputable practices to communicate effectively. The chapter begins to conclude with legal considerations for an Incident Response Plan. The call to action section outlines a three year plan.

11.2 RATIONALE

Many organizations do not have a Crisis Management Program. When a significant event kicks off, management observes 'It's a bit chaotic'. A message template has not been prepared, everyone chimes in with an opinion. It is not clear how external notification must be conducted in accordance with laws and regulations. The local news media asks for an update from executives...

Every organization needs a Crisis Communications Plan and Holding Statement Templates, within the direction of a Crisis Management Team. In the absence of that, significant support from the Information Security Team will be demanded during a time of incident response. It is difficult to focus on those two activities at once. Communications and incident response will suffer as a result.

The Crisis Management Team must practice to be effective. Invite them to cybersecurity tabletop exercises. That enables them to use their Crisis Communications Plan and Holding Statement Templates during a simulated cybersecurity incident. The Information Security team will provide support, with periodic updates on incident response developments. Crisis Management and Information Security learn how to work together effectively during those exercises.

11.3 COMPLIANCE VALIDATION - INFLUENCING CHANGE

There are differing ways to influence. If your organization is compliance focused, you can discuss reputable practices, laws, regulations and contractual obligations (Figure 11.1).

DOI: 10.1201/9781003543619-11

NIST Cybersecurity Framework	
RS.CO-02	Internal and external stakeholders are notified of incidents Ex1: Follow the organization's breach notification procedures after discovering a data breach incident, including **notifying affected customers** Ex2: **Notify business partners** and customers of incidents in accordance with contractual requirements Ex3: **Notify law enforcement agencies and regulatory bodies** of incidents based on criteria in the incident response plan and management approval
GV.SC-08	Relevant suppliers and other third parties are included in incident planning, response, and recovery activities Ex4: Define and coordinate crisis communication methods and protocols between the organization and its critical suppliers
RC.CO-04	**Public updates on incident recovery are shared using approved methods and messaging** Ex1: Follow the organization's breach notification procedures for recovering from a data breach incident Ex2: Explain the steps being taken to recover from the incident and to prevent a recurrence
NIST Privacy Framework	
CM.AW-P7	**Impacted individuals and organizations are notified about a privacy breach or event**
CM.AW-P8	Individuals are provided with mitigation mechanisms (e.g., credit monitoring, consent withdrawal, data alteration or deletion) to address impacts of problematic data actions

Figure 11.1 Compliance validation - Influencing change.

If there is a data breach, we need to notify affected customers, business partners, law enforcement agencies and regulatory bodies. We would have to keep the public updated on incident recovery. We would have to use multiple communications mechanisms. If there is a privacy breach, impacted individuals and organizations must be notified. It makes sense to incorporate these practices into a plan.

Each organization must consider compliance obligations from organizations such as the Securities and Exchange Commission and the Cybersecurity and Infrastructure Security Agency (CISA). Data breach reporting for initial notification to regulators are aggressive, typically three to four days. There are materiality and message content requirements to account for.

11.4 ROLES AND RESPONSIBILITIES

Public relations typically has responsibility for the Crisis Management Program. Its scope expands beyond data breaches to other crisis events, such as pandemics and natural disasters. The company needs this communications capability for a number of common issues that occur over time (Figure 11.2).

Crisis management teams include representatives from public relations, marketing, c-level executives, business leaders, legal, information security, privacy and specialized functions based on the crisis event.

11.5 CRISIS COMMUNICATIONS PLAN

From a cybersecurity perspective, the Crisis Communications Plan has a data breach notification matrix and holding statement templates. There are procedures for how the crisis management team should respond, including assess, prepare, distribute and lessons learned. The plan should also contain contact information maintained for the Crisis Management Team, including mobile phone numbers and e-mail addresses (Figure 11.3).

11.6 HOLDING STATEMENT TEMPLATES

A Holding Statement Template contains pre-approved content to respond to a crisis scenario such as a natural disaster. Fill in the blanks to issue a statement as quickly as possible. 'On X

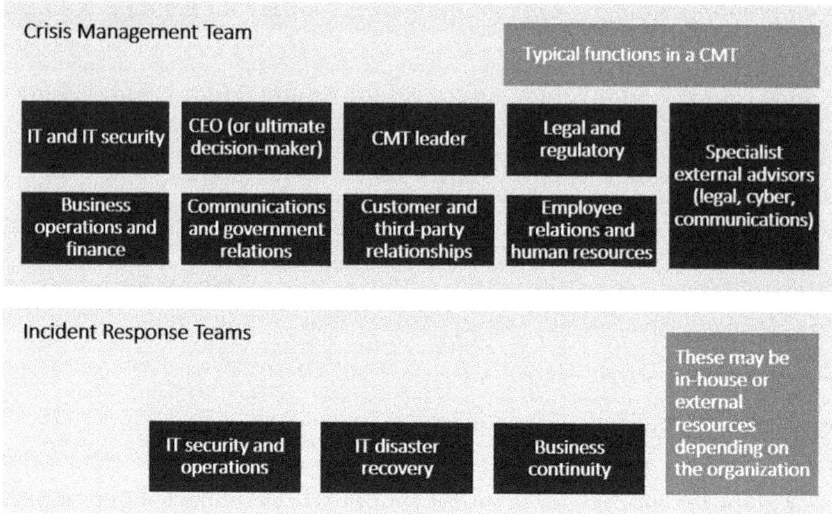

Figure 11.2 Roles and responsibilities Governing Through a Cyber Crisis - Australian Institute of Company Directors.

date, we discovered *Y* data category was compromised within *Z* service', for example. The templated content has been vetted and approved by senior executives and legal in advance. When and if that crisis scenario occurs, it is straightforward to fill in the blanks, conduct final approval and send a communication. That interim message buys the Crisis Management Team time to better understand the situation, collect the facts and ultimately issue something more detailed.

The Information Security Team should author 'data breach' and 'threat party data breach' holding statement templates at a minimum. The Crisis Management Team is responsible for holding statements with a broader context, such as a service outage.

The goal of holding statement templates is to quickly distribute a message in response to a crisis event. Many of us have seen breaking news when it is first announced. There has been a data breach at a company. The News Anchor is just finding out about it. They may barely know how to pronounce the company's name. They are either handed a piece of paper or they are looking at a teleprompter. The Anchor will start with '*Acme* has experienced a data breach'. The Anchor does not have details because it is breaking news and this a 24/7 newscast. The Anchor will start to riff or try to come up with ideas about what 'may' have happened. You will hear that word used often. 'This may have been as a result of some failed processes or failed technology within this company. That company may have been negligent.' There is reputational damage being done to that company because the Anchor does not know what is going on. They are just guessing. When an Anchor reads a press release, they are providing an update with appropriate details and facts, based upon what is known now. Distributing a press release quickly controls the narrative and minimizes reputational damage that news outlets can give rise to.

11.7 DATA BREACH NOTIFICATIONS MATRIX

Data breach notification requirements are complex when viewed in aggregate. The matrix example in Figure 11.4 below provides an overview, such as the deadline to send notifications to each governing body.

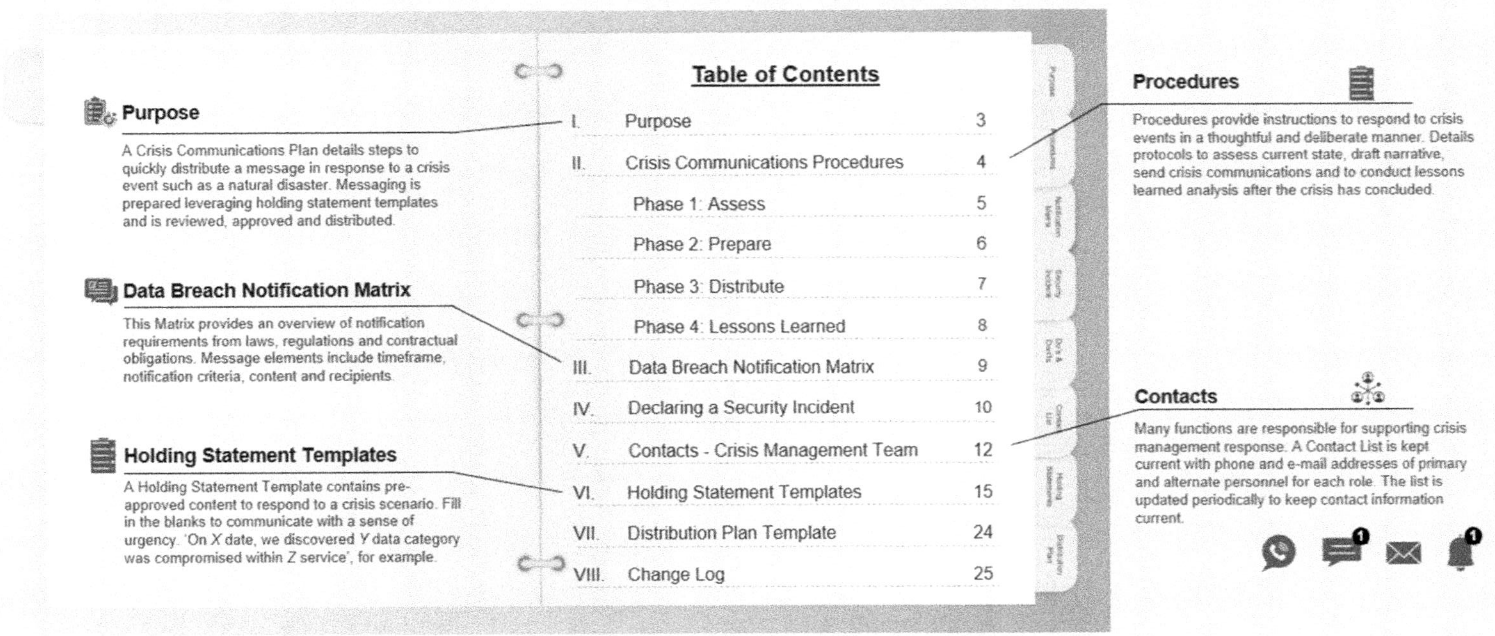

Figure 11.3 Crisis communications plan.

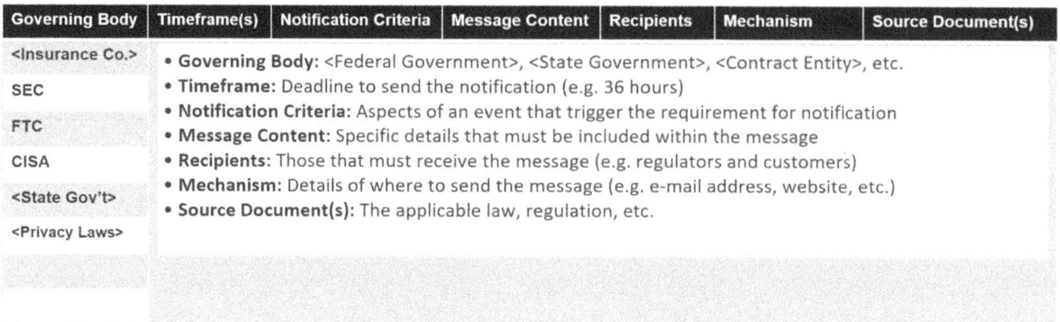

Figure 11.4 Data breach notifications matrix.

It takes significant time to gather data breach notification requirements. The matrix starts with the governing body, such as an insurance company, regulators and federal and state government. If personally identifiable information has been compromised, there will be privacy laws to contend with. There is a timeframe for when notification must be sent to each entity. There are specific details for what must be included in the message.

A notification matrix is a cheat sheet, a quick reference guide. It provides an overview of who needs to be contacted and when. Source documents are referenced for detailed requirements.

Be proactive. Gather notification requirements in advance. Discuss with legal counsel to ensure laws, regulations and contractual obligations are accounted for.

11.8 DATA BREACH NOTIFICATION WORKFLOW

Data breach notification begins by following the Crisis Communications Plan. Refer to the workflow in Figure 11.5 below.

Reference the Data Breach Notification Matrix to determine who needs to be contacted and when the first wave of communications is due. Leverage a holding statement template to

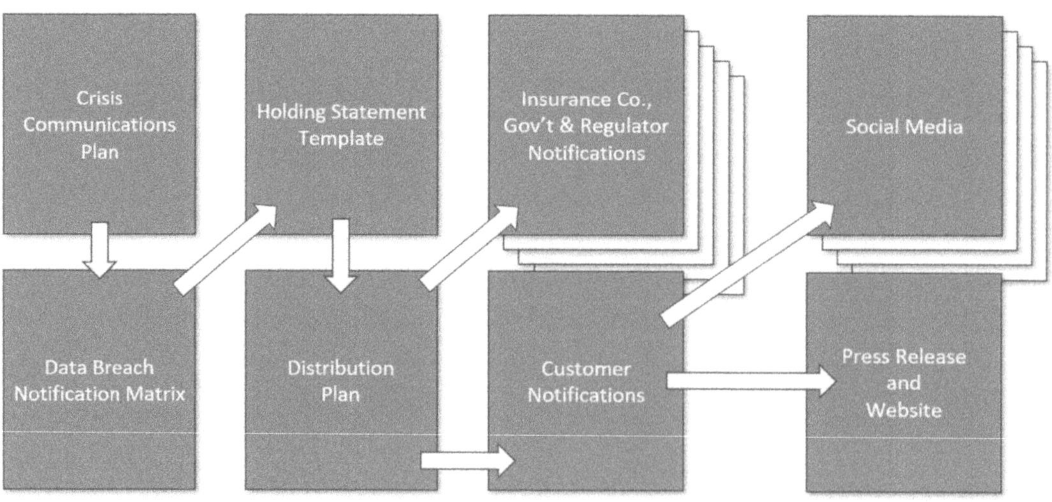

Figure 11.5 Data breach notification workflow.

create a message quickly. Reference the Communications Distribution Plan to track the status of each message and when it will be sent. Prepare messaging for customer service as well.

Send notification to the insurance company within the first day or two. Modern cybersecurity insurance extends beyond coverage amount to include services such as data breach response, forensics, legal and crisis communications support. Notify the insurance company first, followed by governing bodies as required by laws, regulations and contractual obligations.

11.9 DISTRIBUTION PLAN - CUSTOMERS AND THE PUBLIC

The second wave of communications follows with customer notifications and a press release. Reference the Distribution Plan in Figure 11.6 below as an example of how to coordinate those communications.

If a data breach has been kept confidential up until this point, customers and employees may be notified at the same time. Reference the Status field options above as an example of how messaging is created, reviewed, approved, queued and distributed.

11.10 LESSONS LEARNED (FROM PAST LIVES)

At some point you may want to discuss the need for a Crisis Management Program with senior executives. Reference Figure 11.7 below as a summary slide.

Assemble the Crisis Management Team when a crisis event occurs. Reference the Crisis Communications Plan. Select a holding statement template and begin to draft a message. If there is a data breach, the Crisis Management Team still has point. Executives, legal and public relations are actively engaged. The Information Security Team provides periodic updates of what is known now. Incident response remains the primary focus. The Crisis Management Team moves forward with communications procedures.

The Crisis Management Team leverages the Distribution Plan to ensure messages are sent at appropriate times and through the proper communications channels. The Crisis Management Team prepares to respond to questions. When the first wave of communications goes out, the

Recipient	Message Type	Responsible	Target Date	Status	Notes
Customers	Initial Notification	Jane Smith	Jan-02-2050	Not Started	
Employees	Initial Notification			In Draft	
Press Release - Website	Initial Notification			Content Approved	
LinkedIn	Initial Notification			Distribution Approved	
X / Twitter	Initial Notification			Published	
Facebook	Initial Notification				
Instagram	Initial Notification				

Figure 11.6 Distribution plan - Customers and the public.

Lessons Learned

- **Assemble the Crisis Management Team**
- **Reference the Crisis Communications Plan**
  - Data Breach Notification Matrix provides requirements
    - What constitutes an incident
    - Earliest deadline for data breach notification
    - Message content elements
  - Select the appropriate holding statement template
- **Begin to draft the message body of the communication(s)**
  - Crisis Management Team has point (execs included)
  - **Incident response supports, provides details**
  - Legal support is necessary
- **Leverage a distribution plan**
  - Entries for which communications will be sent and when
- **Prepare to respond to questions**
  - From the insurance company and regulators
  - From customers, the media and employees

Figure 11.7 Lessons learned. Image licensed from Shutterstock (Asset id: 322892825).

insurance company and regulators are going to want meetings almost immediately, certainly within the first 24 hours. If there is an insurance company and two regulators in scope, there will need to be three 60-minute meetings with senior executives and legal at a minimum. In the second wave, customers and the media will have questions.

11.11 EFFECTIVE CRISIS COMMUNICATIONS

Customers, the media and regulators will judge the effectiveness of communications. There are high expectations. Mistakes and mixed messages will be noted, incurring frustration and reputational damage. The atmosphere is unforgiving.

A proactive approach to crisis communications will reduce the stress level of the team and external stakeholders. Here are tips for effective crisis communications and the best possible outcome.

Provide a quick statement - Service outage

If there is something that is known to the public, provide a high-level statement as quickly as possible. For example:

> Some of our customers are experiencing a service outage within <service>. Our technical team responded immediately. We are working as quickly as possible to restore service.
>
> These are preliminary details, what is known now. Additional information will be provided as it becomes available.

Provide updates - Service outage

That first message was sent quickly, which is good. Continue with updates as more information becomes available:

• An estimate of service restoration • Service has been partially restored • Service has been restored	• The cause of the outage • Actions to prevent reoccurrence

Err on the side of providing too many updates. That demonstrates transparency, ownership and integrity, doing the right thing when no one is looking. Periodic updates also minimize reputational damage because customers do not feel like they are being ignored.

Own the narrative

Reputational damage begins to occur when a crisis event is known to customers and the public. Leverage a holding statement template and issue a press release with a sense of urgency. Provide a message that describes the crisis event and what is being done in response.

Distribute the press release to the media so they have something to read from. Otherwise, customers and the media are left to imagine what *may* have happened and what is *possible*. That condition results in reputational damage.

Tell customers if they have been impacted

Consider the view from the customer's side of the table. When there is a cybersecurity incident, they want to know what their exposure is. Let customers know early-on if there is evidence that their information has been accessed. If it is too early to know for sure, provide a caveat that there is an ongoing investigation or something to that effect.

Answer frequently asked questions

As soon as a press release is distributed there will be frequently asked questions from customers and the media. It makes sense to make that information available on a website.

• What happened? • What type of data was accessed? • What prevents reoccurrence?	• What should I do to protect myself? • For more information

A Frequently Asked Questions page can reduce the number of calls and e-mail from customers if they are receiving the information they need.

Say you're sorry

Take ownership of customer impact and apologize throughout crisis communications. Apologize in the first message and in the communications and press releases that follow. That theme is critically important. Whether there is severe weather or a cybersecurity incident, people depend on services and expect them to be up, available and resilient. If there is a service disruption as an example, it makes sense to say you're sorry. That can go a long way with customers if it is heart-felt, it does not happen often and the organization is quick to respond.

Hostile nation states

A hostile nation state is an 'Advanced Persistent Threat' that is government funded. Disclose publicly if your organization experiences a nation state inflicted data breach. Nation states are known to be formidable threat actors. Mentioning the term 'nation state threat actor' may reduce reputational damage and it is appropriate to include that in a press release.

Use multiple forms of communication

Use a multi-channel approach to send crisis communications. Preferences vary by age group and generation. Communicate through text messages, social media, e-mail and your organization's website. Monitor each communication channel for questions and negative commentary.

Address your employees

The Crisis Management Team must be thoughtful and deliberate when sending messages to employees. Anticipate that internal crisis communications may be leaked to news outlets or within social media. Leverage a Distribution Plan to determine in which order crisis communications will be sent and at what time. In the event of a cybersecurity incident or a data breach, consider sending crisis communications to customers, the media and employees all at once. Customer service will need to be briefed in advance.

Archive crisis communications

Save real-world examples of crisis communications as breaking news occurs. Learn from crisis events at other organizations. Reference Figure 11.8 below for areas of focus.

Sample content reveals commonly-used crisis communications frameworks and messaging. Real-world events may also inspire development of new holding statement templates.

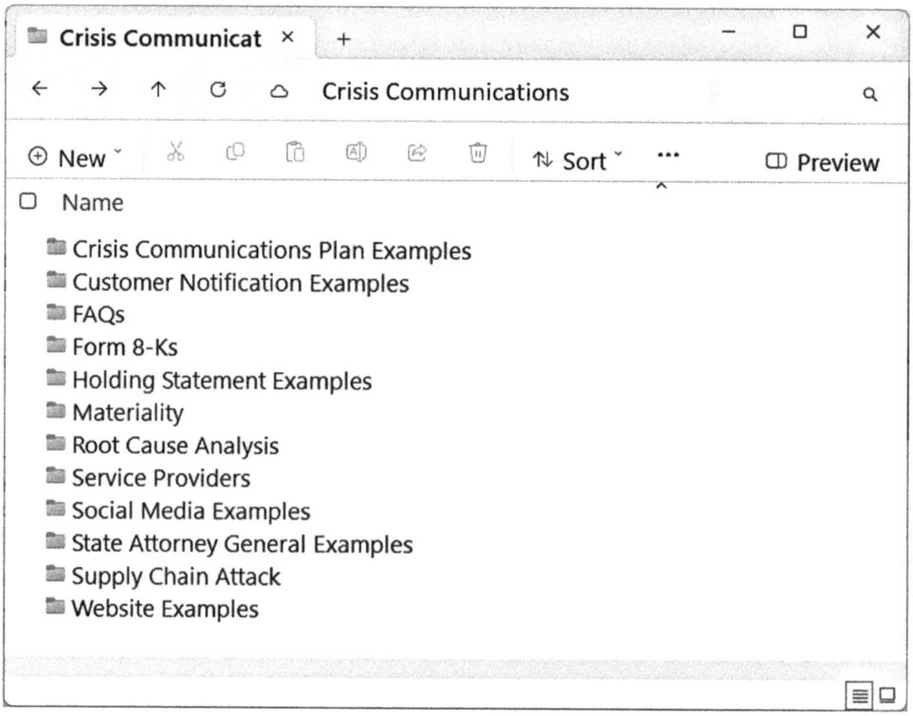

Figure 11.8 Archive industry crisis communications.

11.12 INCIDENT RESPONSE PLAN - LEGAL CONSIDERATIONS

Lawsuits may occur in the aftermath of a significant cybersecurity incident or data breach. In that scenario, the Incident Response Plan is subject to legal discovery and may be referenced as evidence in a court of law.

An Incident Response Plan should distinguish between 'technical incident response' and security incident declaration criteria:

> Declaring a security incident
>
> The incident response process and procedures within this plan are initiated when suspicious activity occurs. Formal declaration of a security incident is a separate and distinct process. **The criteria of what constitutes a security incident and requirements for notification varies depending on laws, regulations and contractual obligations.** There is legal criteria to consider such as materiality and business impact. That analysis falls outside of technical incident response and must be conducted by the Crisis Management Team, which includes legal representation and C-level executives. **A security incident and/or a data breach may only be declared in writing by the Crisis Management Team.**

The narrative above is a proof-of-concept. Consult your attorney to develop legal language suitable for your organization.

11.13 CALL TO ACTION

Have a conversation with your supervisor if your organization does not have a Crisis Management Program in place. Discuss the benefits of crisis communications from a business perspective. The rationale is included in this chapter, along with reputable practices from NIST's cybersecurity and privacy frameworks. You can also cite laws, regulations and contractual obligations that are specific to your organization.

The Crisis Management Team has responsibility for external communications. Public relations, executives and legal work together for a positive outcome. If there is a data breach, the incident response team will support and provide details. Crisis Management takes it from there.

In practical terms it may be necessary for information security to:

- Raise the need for a Crisis Management Program
- Help management identify which employees will be responsible
- Coach and mentor designated employees as they establish the program

A multi-generational plan will help foster a thoughtful and deliberate approach:

- <u>Year one:</u> Establish a Crisis Management Program and minimal holding statement templates
- <u>Year two:</u> Include crisis management within a cybersecurity tabletop exercise
- <u>Year three:</u> Continue to mature the Crisis Management Program

A proactive approach to crisis communications minimizes business impact and reputational damage. If such a function does not exist, now is the time to present a slide deck and to discuss with your executives. This is your time to demonstrate leadership. Do not leave that opportunity on the table.

Chapter 12

Control by governance

12.1 INTRODUCTION

This chapter provides practical advice to assert control through governance processes. Transition common information security tasks to a Governance, Risk and Compliance (GRC) Analyst (24 activities). Increase retention by focusing information security professionals on cybersecurity. Influence support and funding through a customized control framework. Implement activity task scheduling to ensure process execution. The chapter concludes with proactive measures to identify and mitigate risk such as issue management, security architecture reviews, system health checks and process governance. Governance oversight and separation from operations provides risk transparency to senior executives and the board of directors. These processes and management routines provide a pathway to Enterprise Risk Management.

12.2 GRC ANALYST

Onboard a GRC Analyst to offload the burden of administrative tasks from the security operations team.

Support model rationale

The rationale for this organizational change is based on a simple mantra.

Information security professionals should work on information security.

A GRC Analyst has utility within a mature control environment. There are at least four programs that can be supported (Figure 12.1).

Transition of common tasks

As an information security program matures the number of functions. Administrative processes and activities increase as well. Here are common tasks that can be transitioned to a GRC Analyst(s):

DOI: 10.1201/9781003543619-12

- **Training**
  - Security awareness training
  - Software security training
  - Role-based training
  - Privacy awareness training
- **Phishing test program**
- **Awareness communications**
  - Monthly activities
  - Security awareness month
  - Data privacy day
- **Document revisions**
  - Policies
  - Control framework
  - Process diagrams
  - Procedures manuals
- **Policies and procedures acknowledgements**
- **TPRM program support**
  - Assessment initiations
  - Vendor risk assessments
  - Vendor report analysis
  - Shared responsibilities matrices
  - Contract renewals
- **Audit and assessment support**
  - Trust center
  - Gathering artifacts
- **Risk register**
  - Expand beyond cybersecurity
- Facilitate remediation
- **Reporting and metrics**
- **Activity task scheduling**

Figure 12.1 Governance support model.

That listing is a menu of options. It helps to frame a conversation of what would be in scope. When management has options to select from that is inclusive and they feel ownership of the path forward.

A GRC Analyst can facilitate remediation of security issues within vulnerability management, third party risk management, privacy and compliance. That consists of following up on open issues, escalating when necessary and closing out tickets. That support would be welcomed by the operations teams.

That list has utility for onboarding the first GRC Analyst and can be used as criteria for an expanded program over time.

Business case - GRC analyst

Governance: Governance is a critical oversight function. It provides separation of duties and prevents conflicts of interest.

Expense: Specialized talent is expensive. It makes sense to focus information security professionals on their core duties, especially when considering the fully-burdened cost of salary, bonuses, taxes and benefits such as healthcare and 401K matching. The cost of a GRC Analyst is much less.

Retention risk: Employees want to work within their area of expertise. Peripheral administrative tasks reduce employee satisfaction. Information security professionals spend many years developing technical skills. They must keep current with changes in technology and the threat landscape. Consider the view from their side of the table. Employees with a technical skillset do not want to work on administrative tasks such as facilitating remediation, scheduling awareness training and manual reporting.

Turnover impact: When an employee leaves the organization, there is a loss of institutional knowledge. The team loses productivity as a replacement employee is onboarded, trained and acclimates their core duties.

Staffing strategy

A GRC Analyst is an entry level role. The Analyst would be exposed to information security, third party risk management, privacy management and regulatory compliance.

The Analyst could transition to one of those functions as the result of employee attrition or when capacity is exceeded and a new position opens (Figure 12.2).

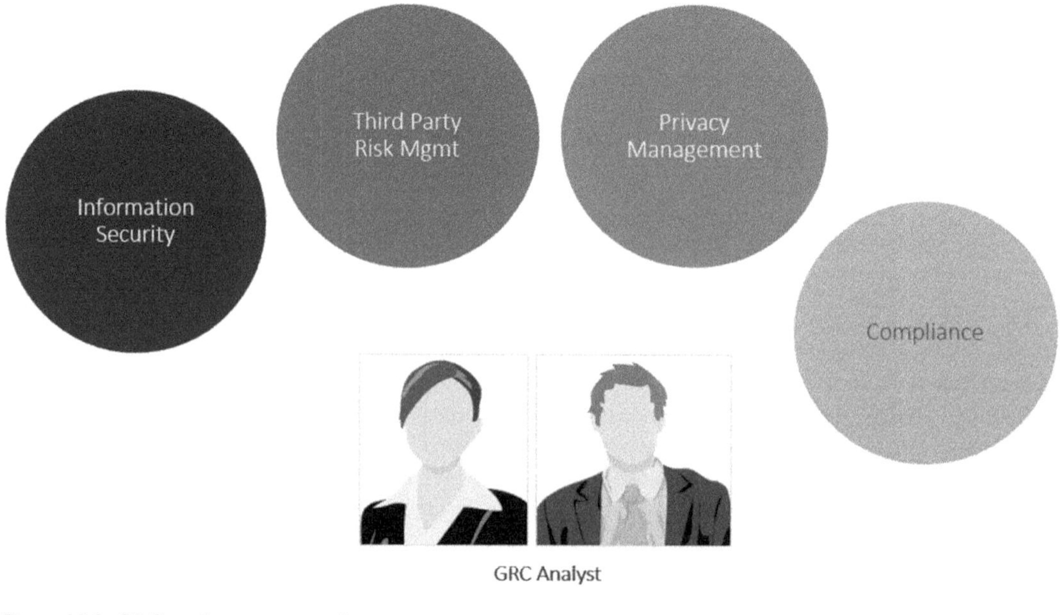

Figure 12.2 GRC analyst career path.

Next steps

Consider which functions should be supported by a GRC Analyst within your organization. Include transition of common tasks as a menu of options. Leverage the section headers and content above to create slides to discuss with your supervisor.

12.3 CYBERSECURITY GOVERNANCE

Hiring a GRC Analyst can be a proof-of-concept. The value-add will be clear with the first year. Assigning administrative tasks to an Analyst is an effective use of resources. In-scope operations teams will appreciate the support.

It makes sense to establish a formal program as demand for service increases. Be thoughtful and deliberate in your approach. Each new program must be customized to your organization. Conference room risk applies. Solicit input from affected leaders during the design phase.

Here is a visualization of cybersecurity in a GRC context (Figure 12.3).

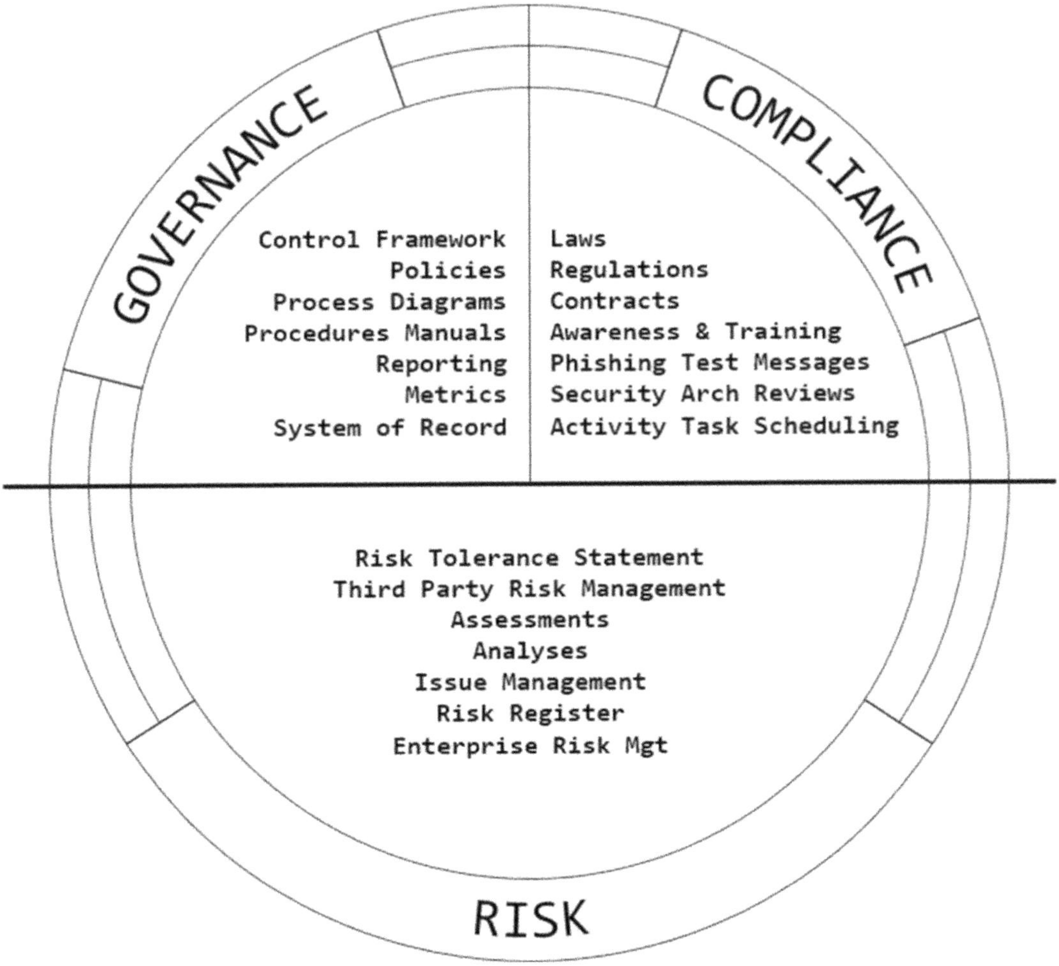

Figure 12.3 Cybersecurity GRC.

A governance program must be tailored to account for industry sector, assets, threat actors and applicable laws, regulations and contractual obligations. The design and implementation will depend on your organization. Make the new program your own.

12.4 FRAMEWORKS AND CERTIFICATIONS

Control frameworks contain reputable practices such as the NIST Cybersecurity Framework. Professional certifications are awarded to individuals that pass an examination such as the Certified Information Systems Security Professional (CISSP) (Figure 12.4).

C-level executives adopt control frameworks to implement reputable practices. That strategic direction results in stable and resilient operations.

Governance of a control framework comes down to either:

- The control is in-place and we are committed to maintaining it,
- The control needs to be implemented (risk mitigate),
- or the control will not be implemented (risk accept register entry)

Control frameworks provide risk transparency. C-level executives need that to make informed decisions. The board of directors needs transparency to conduct oversight.

Trust but verify. Conduct periodic assessments to determine current state and residual risk.

12.5 CYBERSECURITY RISK MANAGEMENT FRAMEWORK

Establish a control framework to identify and mitigate cybersecurity risk. The framework will be unique to your organization, designed to protect products, services, processes, information and assets.

Phase 1: Establish an initial framework

Leverage the NIST Cybersecurity Framework (CSF) to establish the first entries in your framework. NIST CSF is a reputable resource that provides a foundation of technical,

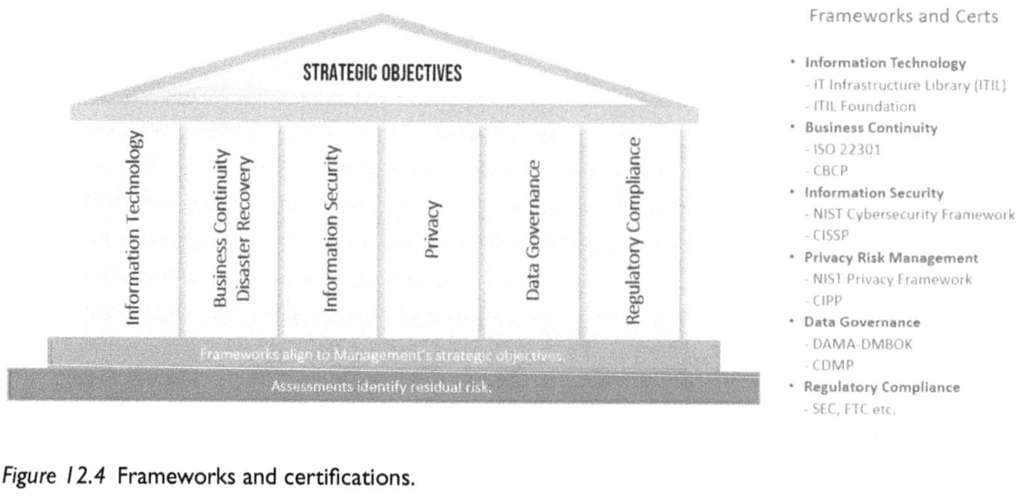

Figure 12.4 Frameworks and certifications.

administrative and physical security controls. Map cybersecurity controls from the NIST Privacy Framework to partner with your privacy officer. Layer on control requirements from applicable laws, regulations and contractual obligations (Figure 12.5).

Phase 2: Assign RACI designations

Add a RACI Matrix to the framework to designate who is Responsible, Accountable, Consulted and Informed (Figure 12.6).

Example:

PR.DS-11: Backups of data are created, protected, maintained and tested

Responsible: Backup Administrator Database Administrator Disaster Recovery Accountable: IT Manager	Consulted: CTO Informed: COO and board-level committee

Note that some controls may need to be assigned to multiple roles such as system hardening and encryption.

Here is an example of job functions for use within a RACI Matrix (Figure 12.7).

At this point we have a control framework with job functions assigned. Assign employees to those roles as a next step:

Control #	Control Description	Guidance	NIST CSF	NIST Privacy Framework
CSRM-0001	The organizational mission is understood and informs cybersecurity **and privacy** risk management	Ex1: Share the organization's mission (e.g., through vision and mission statements, marketing, and service strategies) to provide a basis for identifying risks that may impede that mission	GV.OC-01	ID.BE-P2
CSRM-0002	Internal and external stakeholders are understood, and their needs and expectations regarding cybersecurity **and privacy** risk management are understood and considered	Ex1: Identify relevant internal stakeholders and their cybersecurity-related expectations (e.g., performance and risk expectations of officers, directors, and advisors; cultural expectations of employees)	GV.OC-02	ID.DE-P2
		Ex2: Identify relevant external stakeholders and their cybersecurity-related expectations (e.g., privacy expectations of customers, business expectations of partnerships, compliance expectations of regulators, ethics expectations of society)		GV.PO-P4

Figure 12.5 Cybersecurity risk management framework.

Control #	Control Description	Responsible	Accountable	Consulted	Informed	NIST CSF	NIST Privacy Framework
CSRM-0001	The organizational mission is understood and informs cybersecurity **and privacy** risk management	CISO CPO	COO	CEO	Board-level committee	GV.OC-01	ID.BE-P2
CSRM-0002	Internal and external stakeholders are understood, and their needs and expectations regarding cybersecurity **and privacy** risk management are understood and considered	CISO CPO	COO	CEO	Board-level committee	GV.OC-02	ID.DE-P2 GV.PO-P4

Figure 12.6 RACI matrix fields.

- Application Developers
- AppSec Engineer
- Backup Administrator
- Business Continuity
- Business Leaders
- Change Management
- Chief Executive Officer (CEO)
- Chief Financial Officer (CFO)
- Chief Information Security Officer (CISO)
- Chief Operating Officer (COO)
- Chief Privacy Officer (CPO)
- Chief Technology Officer (CTO)
- Cloud Administrator
- Collaboration Platform Admin
- Computer Room Manager
- Crisis Management Team
- Cyber Threat Intelligence
- Data Governance
- Disaster Recovery
- DLP Administrator
- DNS Administrator
- E-mail Gateway Admin
- Encryption Key Admin
- Endpoint Protection
- File Integrity Monitoring
- GRC Analyst
- GRC Manager
- Human Resources
- Identity & Access Management
- IDS/IPS Admin
- Incident Response Manager
- Information Privacy Officer (IPO)
- Information Security Manager
- IT Asset Manager
- Legal Department
- Marketing
- PC/Laptop Administrator
- Penetration Testing
- Physical Security
- Procurement / Supply Chain
- Release Management
- Sales
- Security Awareness
- Service Desk
- SIEM Administrator
- SOC Analyst
- Storage Administrator
- TPRM Manager
- VM/Server Administrator
- VPN Administrator
- Vulnerability Management
- Web Content Filter Admin
- Web Server Administrator
- WebApp Firewall Admin

Figure 12.7 RACI job functions.

RACI Job Function	*Primary Contact*	*Alternate Contact*
Backup Administrator	Jane Smith	John Smith

A Cybersecurity Control Framework does not have much utility idling on an intranet website. Establish security awareness routines to communicate RACI task, advisory and oversight responsibilities. Inform each person in a RACI Job Function of their role and assigned controls. They may need role-specific training in some cases. Encourage each person to conduct a self-assessment of controls assigned to them. Those in advisory and oversight roles should have periodic meetings with the employees that perform tasks.

The benefits of a RACI Matrix become obvious as controls are assigned and communications routines play out. Some employees will be surprised by their role assignments. Others will balk and resist ownership. RACI designations help ensure that a control is in-place. Assignment of primary and alternate contacts reduces the potential for compliance jitter, where a control falls out of place.

Phase 3: Determine current state

Schedule working sessions with IT operations, information security and privacy teams at a minimum. Review the newly established framework from top to bottom. Discuss which controls are in-place and which controls need to be implemented. It may take 3-5 60-minute meetings to reach the bottom of the framework. This is not assessment or audit activity so we will not know as a statement of fact. This is a planning exercise, especially in a regulated environment. Provide risk transparency up the leadership chain using established routines such as a risk register process and a cybersecurity committee.

In cases where a new requirement requires minimal effort, open a service desk ticket for tracking with the risk rating set to an appropriate severity. For requirements that require significant effort, establish a project or an annual program goal. Consider the potential impact of new controls, such as staffing capacity, the need for funding and reliance on IT for implementation. IT and business units will not support unfunded mandates. Give them time to submit budgetary requests as necessary. Establish the new control framework and identify gaps in year one. Implement new processes and controls in year two.

Phase 4: Add controls based on the threat landscape

Continue to mature the framework and the information security program by establishing new functions such as insider risk management and crisis management. Add control requirements based on threat actor tactics and newly adopted technologies. Leverage reputable resources within cyber threat intelligence and the MITRE ATT&CK Framework. Leverage the maturity model within NSA's seven zero trust pillar documents. Select controls from CIS Critical Security Controls, the NIST 800 series and NIST 800-53. While your organization may not be required to comply with these resources, they represent a catalog of controls to choose from and reputable practices to cite.

Add controls to the framework thoughtfully and deliberately. The need for each control must be defensible from risk management and cost perspectives. Phase 3 should be an ongoing process over years. It takes time to influence change in an organization. Move at a moderate pace.

Benefits

There are numerous benefits to creating a control framework for your organization. The source control framework such as NIST CSF carries the support of senior executives, similar to a company policy. That means the controls will be implemented and there is a commitment to maintain support and funding for them year-over-year. Frameworks are reputable and are kept current by the information security community and government entities. Frameworks support metrics. An information security program is defensible when in-place controls adhere to a cybersecurity control framework, applicable laws, regulations and contractual obligations and reputable practices aligned to the threat landscape.

Enterprise risk management (ERM)

A Cybersecurity Risk Management Framework provides a foundation for an ERM program. If senior executives decide to go that route, it is relatively straightforward to add controls into the control framework and supporting processes. Start by adding privacy and fraud prevention controls. Senior executives will also require controls to manage business risk such as financial, credit and market risk. An ERM program provides a risk lens across the organization, with the ability to drill down into the details at any time. The end state of an ERM program may influence support and funding for earlier phases.

12.6 GRC SYSTEM OF RECORD

Consider the value-add of a GRC application for common areas of focus such as business continuity, disaster recovery, information security, third party risk management, privacy, data governance, regulatory compliance and internal audit.

Here is an overview of capabilities:

• Asset inventory	• Operational risk management
• **Business continuity**	• Policy management
• Compliance	• **Privacy management**
• **Control frameworks**	• **Risk assessments**
• **Dashboards and reporting**	• **Risk register**
• Incident response	• Risk scenarios inventory
• **Information security**	• **Technology integrations (APIs)**
• Internal audit	• Third party risk management
• **Issue management**	• Vulnerability management
• **Metrics - KPIs / KRIs**	• **Workflows**

A Governance Risk and Compliance (GRC) application may start as an efficiency play. It is time to leave spreadsheets and file-sharing behind when a program has been in production one year. A GRC application is a system of record that includes workflows, questionnaires and reporting built-in. It provides leadership with a top-down view of risk issues. (Figure 12.8).

GRC reporting can be used to display risk and compliance statuses for the organization. Leaders can drill down from a report chart into issue records. That gives them access to:

- Details of high risk issues
- Target remediation date
- Issue respondents
- Remediation activity
- Current status
- Last follow-up date

Access to issue records enables leaders to evaluate risk mitigation plans and the target date for closure. C-level executives participate in siloed committee meetings 3-4 times per year. A GRC application provides them with risk transparency on demand.

Cybersecurity issues should be risk rated and tracked to closure in order of risk severity. A GRC application supports that philosophy.

12.7 SECURITY ARCHITECTURE REVIEWS

Security Architecture Reviews evaluate technical controls within systems and networks. Develop Security Architecture Review criteria based on zero trust as an architectural framework and the NIST Cybersecurity Framework for mid-level details.

Here is a high-level view of Security Architecture topics for context (Figure 12.9):

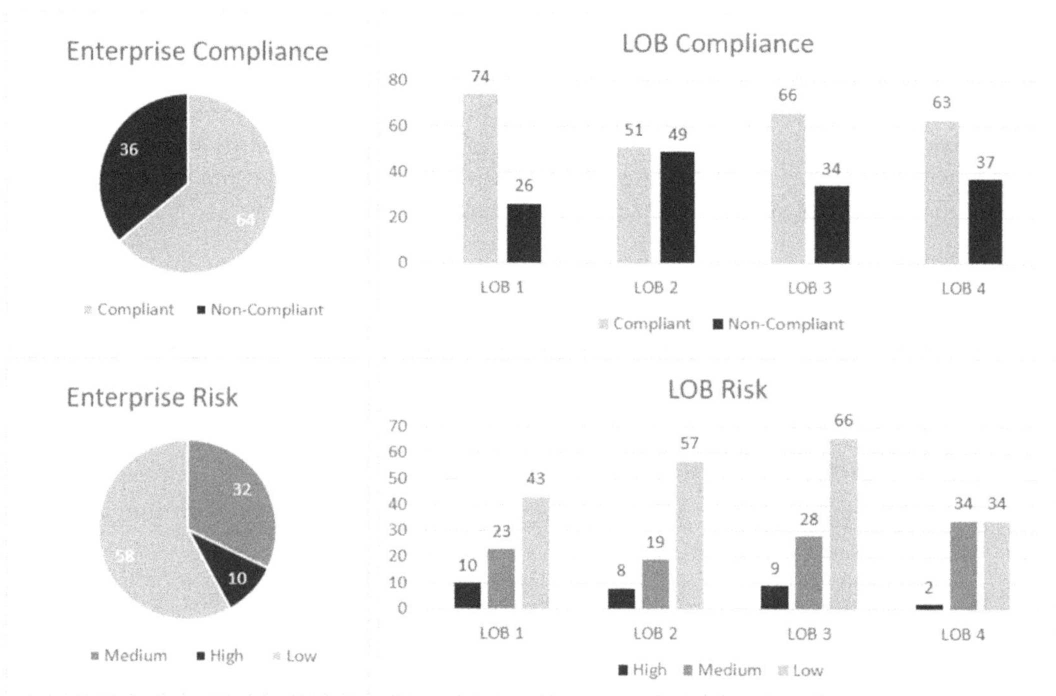

Figure 12.8 Risk and compliance reporting.

- AI agent accesses
- Alerts to clients
- API security
- Centralize logs
- Country data accessed
- Country data hosted
- Encryption-at-rest
- Encryption-in-transit
- Immutable backups
- Least functionality
- Least privilege
- Logs to clients
- Multifactor authentication
- Network segmentation
- No data for AI model training
- Offsite backups
- Patching
- Reauthenticate
- Security configurations
- Security operations center
- Separation of duties
- Shared security model
- SIEM log and event correlation
- Single-sign on
- Web application firewall

Figure 12.9 Security architecture topics.

Create a security architecture job aid. Insert security architecture reviews into existing processes such as project management, change management and TPRM. Establish architecture reviews within the procurement process as a mandatory requirement before a contract can be signed.

12.8 SYSTEM HEALTH CHECKS

Establish a process to conduct health checks of critical systems and software. Evaluate security configurations and monitoring. Identify in-scope technologies that must be evaluated (Figure 12.10).

Establish triggers for when health checks will be initiated such as when a new primary administrator is assigned and at least every three years.

- Evaluate
  - Security configurations
  - New features and functionality
  - Log and event replication to a centralized repository
  - Logging event codes and integration into the SIEM/SOC
  - SIEM alert configurations
  - Alert notification sent to SOC Analysts (not suppressed)
  - SIEM alert notification creates a service desk ticket
- Process
  - Open a support ticket with the above criteria
  - Review Admin and security configuration guides
  - Login and search the support site
  - Search the vendor's Internet exposed support documents
  - Conduct Internet searches
- Health check candidates
  - Active directory
  - Data loss prevention
  - Database software
  - E-mail security gateway
  - Endpoint protection
  - Network firewalls
  - Web app firewalls
  - Web content filter
- Potential resources
  - New primary administrator
  - Information security staff
  - IT operations partners
  - College interns

Figure 12.10 System health checks.

12.9 ISSUE MANAGEMENT

Assessments, scans, exercises and analysis populate a risk portfolio. Issue management influences mitigation in accordance with management's risk tolerance.

Inputs into cybersecurity tickets

Any process that identifies a cybersecurity risk should output tickets to enable issue management.

- Vulnerability management program
- SIEM security monitoring alerts
- Cyber threat intelligence program
- Cybersecurity team meetings
- On-site working sessions
- Cybersecurity tabletop exercises
- Cybersecurity control framework
- Iterative development
- Analyses and assessments
  - Zero trust controls analysis
  - Threat landscape and controls analysis
  - Failure mode and effects analysis
  - Cybersecurity risk assessments
- Intersection with privacy management and fraud prevention

Target dates

Issue Respondents may be reluctant to declare a target remediation date. When someone is not sure about a target date, ask 'Is it a year?'. They will respond 'of course not'. Then ask, 'Is it six months?'. Use that approach and enter a timeframe they are comfortable with. Encourage Issue Respondents to put a stake in the ground, with conservative, attainable target dates.

Remediation standards

Within information security programs we use scoring built into vulnerability scanning tools to influence remediation by risk severity. Cybersecurity control analysis and program assessments findings are more subjective. Establish a process to label findings and risk issues by category, with each category assigned a risk severity tier and a remediation standard. Reference Figure 12.11 below for examples.

Category entries provide simple explanations for each risk issue. Metrics logically follow, similar to how vulnerabilities are tracked to closure. This approach provides risk transparency of issue management to senior executives and the board of directors.

Facilitating remediation

Information security team members need to follow-up with Issue Respondents to ensure the risk management process is moving forward.

Here are tips to influence remediation:

- Create a 'Last Follow-Up' date field to reflect how each risk issue is being managed to closure
- Follow up on each issue record at least monthly. Issue Respondents should be executing to a plan, to milestones for extended work efforts

Severity: Critical	**Remediation Standard: 7 days**	**Severity: Moderate**	**Remediation Standard: 60 days**
Remediation of an issue within a CISA known exploited vulnerabilities advisory		Establish a plan and reporting for backlog of issues in extended remediation	
Vendor software vulnerability allows network and/or operating system access		Block threat vectors partially mitigated by another control	
Acme vulnerability posted to the Internet (e.g. within an article or blog)		Document where sensitive data is stored, processed or transmitted	
Severity: High	**Remediation Standard: 14 days**	Assign security roles and responsibilities to the workforce (RACI)	
Configuration to prevent data exfiltration		Conduct role-based security awareness training for material risk employees	
Search for an Indicator of Compromise (IOC) from a reputable security advisory		Implement deception technology such as honeypots and honeytokens	
Block access to a threat vector likely to be exploited by an adversary		Maintain security reporting, metrics, KPIs and KRIs	
Severity: Substantial	**Remediation Standard: 45 days**	**Severity: Low**	**Remediation Standard: Best Effort**
Implement hardening configuration recommended by reputable source (e.g. CISA)		Maintain information security policies, standards, process and procedures	
Establish an alert that monitors for threat actor tactics (TTPs)		Communicate risk tolerance from senior executives	
Configure logging used for suspicious activity analysis		Conduct a health check by a security benchmark or risk assessment	
Data security control that restricts access to sensitive data		Conduct analysis from reputable practices	
Automate security incident response		Research a potential security control	
Conduct insider threat monitoring and response		Documentation of in-place controls	

Figure 12.11 Remediation standards - Issue management.

- Respond to e-mail within 24 hours. When questions are posed to the information security team, the Issue Respondent considers the ball to be in our court and the process stops
- Update tickets with follow-up activity and as new information becomes available. The GRC system is used to generate reporting and may be used to respond to status requests from leadership

Facilitate remediation in a timely manner. Escalation is appropriate when a request exceeds a reasonable timeframe for completion:

	Request/Action	*E-mail Addresses*
Day 1	Request support to remediate a security issue or to follow-up on current status	To: Issue Respondent
Day 7	Follow-Up	Same
Day 14	Follow-Up	Add the Supervisor to the Cc
Day 21	Follow-Up	Add the Information Security Manager to the Cc

Keep the e-mail thread intact, starting with the request and including the follow-up messages.

Escalation to the Information Security Manager is also appropriate when remediation progress has slowed dramatically or has stalled.

12.10 ACTIVITY TASK SCHEDULING

Task scheduling enables the team to focus on day-to-day operations, projects and annual goals. Recurring activities are entered into a scheduling application which provides automated reminders and escalations. Here are task scheduling categories for inspiration:

• Access control reviews	• Risk assessments
• Awareness and training	• Risk management documentation
• Control testing	• Risk transparency communications
• Crisis communications	• Scans and security testing
• Meeting routines	• Security communications
• Policies and procedures	• Specialized training
• Program documentation	• System documentation
• Response exercises	• System hardening
• Response planning	• Third party risk management

This approach helps ensure consistent program execution by tracking reoccurring tasks (monthly, quarterly, etc.). Scheduling can be used to distribute workload across the year. It enables the team to focus forward on projects and goals.

12.11 PROCESS GOVERNANCE

Organizations with a high level of maturity conduct process governance. Process diagrams document how teams work together. When a diagram is initially created and discussed, teams may learn what each other are actually doing or how procedures have changed throughout the years. Process risk assessment proactively identifies operational risk before it results in business impact.

Process chevrons

Process chevrons are intended to convey the basic details of a process. It is similar to the concept of an 'elevator pitch', where you only have a minute to provide an overview of a topic (Figure 12.12).

Mid-level process diagram

A mid-level diagram documents an end-to-end operational process. It is typically comprised of 10-20 process symbols. The diagram should fit on two 8.5"x11" sheets of paper. A mid-level diagram can be used to evaluate a process from risk and efficiency perspectives. It also has utility to train newly onboarded personnel. Reference this technical remediation process diagram as an example (Figure 12.13).

Sub-process diagram

A sub-process diagram is used to provide more details. That may include a process before or after the activities depicted in the current diagram. Escalation and peripheral activities are also documented as sub-processes.

Process scope

Start by determining which business process will be documented. Establish a general consensus of the process' boundaries. Consider which business functions are involved and where the process starts and stops. Process design is time consuming. It is best for a person familiar with the process to draft a diagram alone and review with a broader audience later.

Process diagram elements

A process diagram contains swim lanes named by the roles or functions participating in the process, a starting point, process steps and decisions connected by arrows and an end point (Figure 12.14).

Critical control points

A Critical Control Point is a safeguard that identifies or mitigates risk at a crucial point in process execution. Control points are necessary where a process step failure would have significant business impact. Control points often require supporting documentation such as a sub-process diagram or corresponding narrative in a procedures manual. Control point examples are included in Figure 12.15 below.

Figure 12.12 Process chevrons.

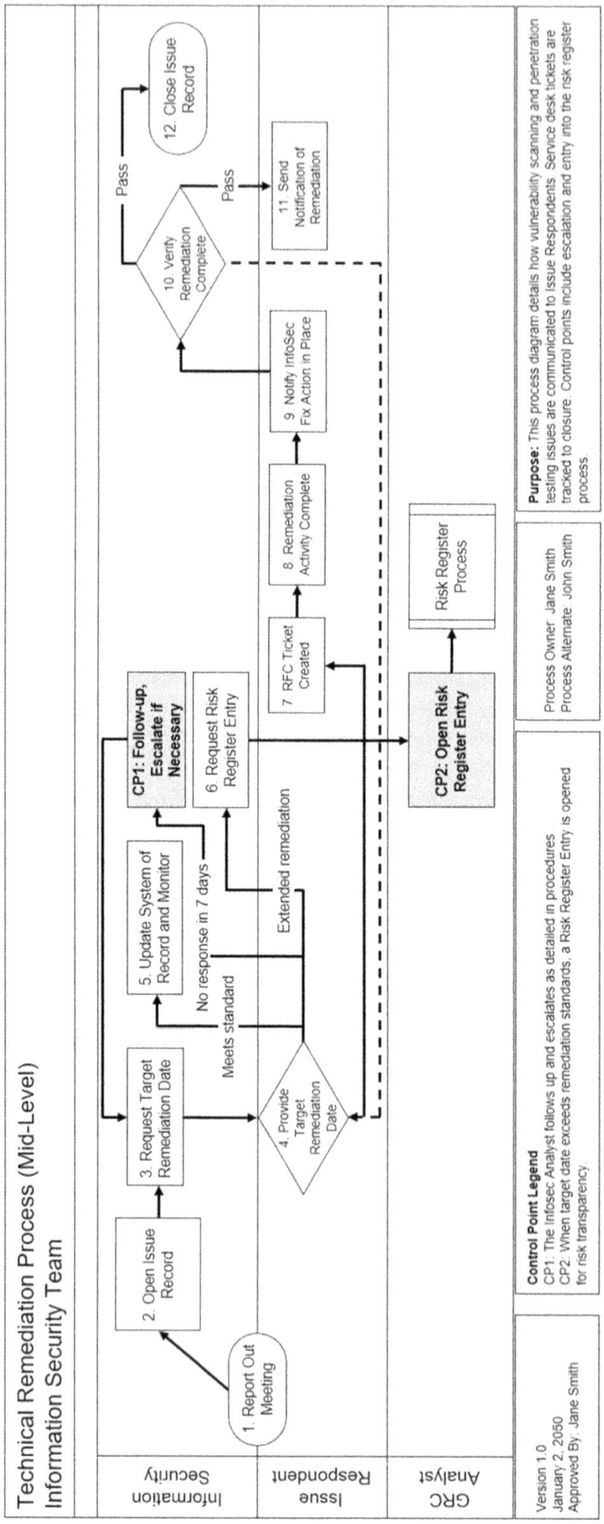

Figure 12.13 Mid-level process diagram.

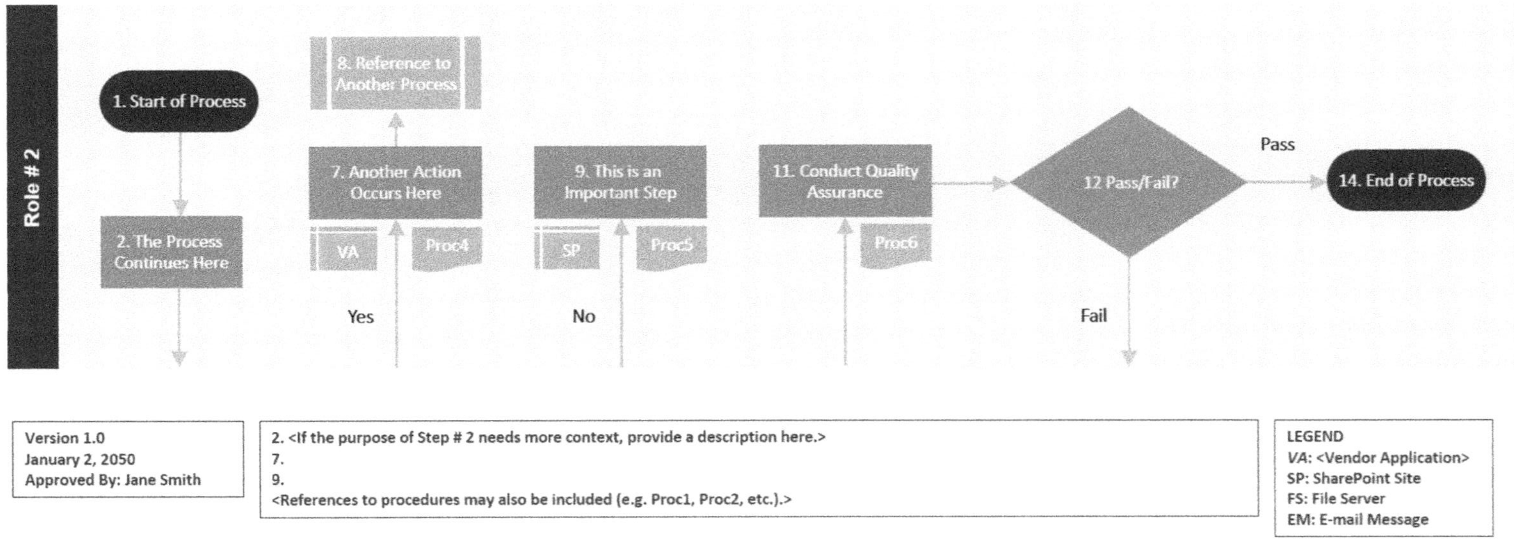

Figure 12.14 Process swim lane example.

Risk Scenario	Control Point(s)	Risk Category
Third party risk	Assessment	Cybersecurity and operational risk
Change in wiring instructions	Multi-factor authentication	Cybersecurity and social engineering
Authentication of a wire transfer contact fails	Escalation	Cybersecurity and social engineering
Funds disbursement	2-person integrity (separation of duties)	Fraud
Fraudulent transaction attempted	Fraud data feed	Fraud
Fraud has been committed	Fraud response plan	Fraud
Human error	Quality assurance	Operational risk
Scheduling error	Quality assurance	Operational risk
Failure to execute	Quality assurance	Operational risk
Refusal to participate	Escalation	Operational risk
Natural disaster	Business continuity plan and exercises	Operational risk
Process design change results in a privacy violation	Privacy compliance review	Privacy risk

Figure 12.15 Control point examples.

Policy

Establish a Process Governance Policy that explains what process design is and why it is important from a business perspective. The policy should require diagrams for all critical business processes. Provide an explanation of critical process criteria, such as 'a workflow or activity that supports delivery of a product or service provided by the organization'.

- Identify customer services
  - What are the core service offerings provided to customers?
  - What would be a 'bad day for the company' if a service went down?
- Identify operational risk
  - Which IT processes are required for service delivery?
  - Which back-office processes are required for service delivery?
  - Which business unit processes are required for service delivery?
  - Which services process sensitive data?

Process diagrams provide line of sight into processes that span across teams and functions. The act of documenting processes fosters discussion, evaluations and improvement. Provide details of required process documentation at a high level. End-to-end processes should be documented for critical processes. Process documentation should include high-level diagrams to provide an overview. Mid-level processes provide an end-to-end view, with control points and sub-process diagrams for greater detail.

Processes have a function of identifying and mitigating risk. Evaluate potential for fraud throughout processes. Address insider threat through least privilege, separation of duties and two-person integrity. Account for sophisticated adversaries as a threat when sensitive data or valuable assets are in scope.

Inventory

Establish a Process Diagram Inventory to ensure processes are documented and kept current. Consider the following elements:

• Process Number	• Approved By
• Process Diagram Name	• Process Owner
• Function/Business Unit	• Process Alternate
• Version Number	• Purpose Statement
• Revision Date	

Training

Establish process design documentation for training purposes. Conduct on-the-job training as processes are evaluated, maintained and created.

Governance

Establish a Process Governance function to review processes annually and ensure they are kept current. Track which processes have been established for critical business functions. Ensure processes are versioned and kept current. Ensure Primary and Alternate contacts for each process remain in place. Confirm that processes are revised annually and when significant changes are made operationally.

Process risk assessment

Process diagrams are typically documented as the process should function or by how business is conducted today. Operational risk exists as workflow crosses between functions.

Processes should be evaluated by:

• People that do the work	• Privacy management
• Information security	• Data governance
• Business continuity	• Fraud prevention
• Disaster recovery	• Third party risk management

Leverage Failure Modes and Effects Analysis (FMEA) to identify and mitigate risk. FMEA considers the potential for failure in each process step. Reference Section 1.11 for additional information.

Benefits

Process diagrams and assessments mitigate risk in the areas of access control, data minimization, data leakage, insider threat and fraud. Process diagrams feed into privacy impact assessments, failure mode and effects analysis, data actions inventory, business continuity and disaster recovery.

Appendix

A.1 GOALS AND WORKING SESSIONS

It can be challenging to establish goals and working sessions starting with a blank sheet of paper. Here is a list of sample meeting topics to inspire you. Reference Chapter 2 for associated content.

- Active directory assessment
- Activity task scheduling
- AI risk management
- Alerts based on adversary toolkits
- Application allowlisting
- Automate endpoint isolation
- Backdoors & breaches
- Behavioral monitoring
- Budget 2050 - Information security
- Business impact assessment
- CISA red team reports
- Cloud security strategy
- Communications plan
- Control monitoring
- Crisis communications plan
- Critical business processes: <Bus. unit # 1>
- Cyber threat intelligence
- Cyber threat intelligence program
- Cybersecurity and privacy policies
- Cybersecurity risk assessment
- Cybersecurity risk mgt framework
- Data actions inventory
- Data breach notification matrix
- Data exfiltration by employee or contractor
- Data governance, privacy and cybersecurity
- Data governance health dashboard
- Data leakage investigation techniques
- Data retention
- Deception technologies
- Digital rights management
- Disaster recovery site
- Executive reporting - Cybersecurity
- Fraud prevention and cybersecurity
- New version of <law, regulation, standard>
- NIST 800-53 analysis
- NIST cybersecurity framework
- NIST incident response practices
- NIST privacy framework
- Patching: Scheduling, delays and pauses
- Penetration testing methodology
- Physical security
- Plan of action and milestones
- Procedures manual - <Sub-program>
- Privacy and cybersecurity
- Process governance
- Process risk assessment
- Program goals 2050 - <Sub-program>
- Program goals 2050 - Information Security
- Program overview deck
- Program refresh - <Sub-program>
- RACI matrix - Cybersecurity
- Ransomware preparedness
- Remediation standards - Issue management
- Restricting lateral movement
- Risk management routines - Cybersecurity
- Risk register process
- Risk scenario inventory
- Risk tolerance statement
- Security architecture reviews
- Security awareness program
- Security monitoring alert configurations
- Security operations center
- Security response automation
- Shared responsibilities matrices
- SOC 2 due diligence process
- Staffing capacity - Information security

(*Continued*)

- GRC application
- Hardening standard - <Technology>
- Health checks
- Holding statement templates - Cybersecurity
- Incident disclosure rules
- Incident response automation
- Incident response tabletop exercise - Cybersecurity
- Insider risk monitoring process
- Insider risk program Phase I.
- Insider risk program Phase II.
- Integrate into ERM program
- Materiality within crisis communications
- Maturity model - <Sub-program>
- Metrics, KPIs and KRIs
- Multi-generational plan 2050
- Network segmentation analysis
- Suspicious activity monitoring
- SWOT analysis - Information security
- System and application inventories
- Tactics, techniques and procedures
- Third party risk management program
- Threat hunting
- Threat landscape and controls analysis
- Unstructured data scanning
- Vendor AI risk assessment
- Vendor contract security requirements
- Vendor cybersecurity questionnaire
- Verizon data breach report
- Web content filter
- Why or why not? - Cybersecurity controls
- Windows ## security features
- Zero trust controls analysis

A.2 INSIDER THREAT PERSONAS

The Accidental Insider - Insider Threat Persona # 1

The accidental insider

An accidental insider exposes an entity to loss or exploitation by mistake. This can be due to a lack of security training or awareness provided by the entity.

Not being aware of obligations does not exempt you from investigations or prosecutions for misconduct or criminal conduct.

Red flags

- Poor or incomplete training provided by the entity
- Unrealistic workload or time pressures
- Inadequate management or oversight

Examples

- Clicking on a malicious link received by email
- Mistyping an email address and sending security privileged information1 to the wrong recipient
- Responding to a fraudulent request believing they are engaging with a legitimate colleague or stakeholder

Case study:
Accidental insider

Meena worked for a large government healthcare provider. She and other staff received an email with a link directing them to a Microsoft Office 365 login page which asked for their login details. Meena and some of her colleagues thought the email was legitimate as they used Microsoft products in the workplace. They were unaware staff were not permitted to click on links in emails without first consulting the cyber security team.

The link directed Meena and her colleagues to a fake webpage. By entering their login details, scammers were able to compromise their email accounts. As a result, the scammers sent hundreds of phishing emails to patients that appeared to originate from the healthcare provider, causing distress and financial loss to the victims.

The Negligent Insider - Insider Threat Persona # 2

The negligent insider

A negligent insider exposes an entity through willful carelessness. They are familiar with security and information policies. But they choose to ignore them, either because they are in a hurry or think they are irrelevant.

Key motivators

A 'win at all costs' workplace culture that disregards risks or unethical behavior or tolerates cutting corners or workarounds.

Red flags

- High error rates
- Failure to keep appropriate or accurate records or receipts
- Poor management and leadership practices
- Open disregard for attending training
- Unrealistic workload or time pressures

Examples

- Allowing someone to "piggy back" through a secure entrance point at work
- Failing to secure an entity-issued mobile phone or laptop containing security privileged information
- Ignoring messages to install software updates
- Sending privileged information to a personal email address

Case study:
Negligent insider

James was having trouble formatting an Excel spreadsheet at work. He was worried about meeting a deadline, and emailed the spreadsheet to his wife's personal email address in the hope she would help him resolve the issue. James had recently attended security awareness training and knew staff were not supposed to email anything work related to personal email accounts. But he thought because it was his wife, it would be alright.

The spreadsheet contained the personal information of 36,000 employees including employee ID data, places of birth, and accounting department codes. This resulted in substantial resources being diverted to mitigate the risks of personal information being exposed. For James, it led to the termination of his employment.

The Self-Motivated Insider - Insider Threat Persona # 3

The self-motivated insider

A self-motivated insider acts by choice rather than pressure, influence, or direction by a third party. They carry out malicious actions or behaviors and may groom other trusted insiders to facilitate desired action.

Key motivators

Financial gain, ideology, desire for recognition, ego, self-image, revenge, divided loyalties, adventure or thrill, compulsive or destructive behavior, personal circumstances, disgruntlement.

Red flags

- Conflicts with the entity's purpose, values or goals
- Code of conduct issues
- Financial hardship or unexplained wealth
- Addictions

Examples

- Helping someone be successful in a procurement process for financial gain
- Stealing data or intellectual property to 'advance' their career
- 'Bending the rules' to make a decision that aligns with their views
- Fraudulently re-routing invoice payments to personal accounts
- Submitting false timesheets or medical certificates
- Refusing to take personal or annual leave

Case study:
Self-motivated insider

Hannah realized vendor quotes were always less than what was budgeted for. She asked vendors she knew to submit quotes to her first, and then recommended they increase their quote before formally submitting it. This increase was used to finance kickbacks to Hannah to secure the contract. They were a combination of cash, cheques, EFT payments, and payments to third parties.

One of Hannah's colleagues noticed a photo on social media of Hannah at a vendor's Christmas party and informed their supervisor. Hannah resigned the day after being asked about her relationship with the vendor. Despite resigning, there was an investigation into the contracts awarded by Hannah which led to criminal charges.

The Recruited Insider - Insider Threat Persona # 4

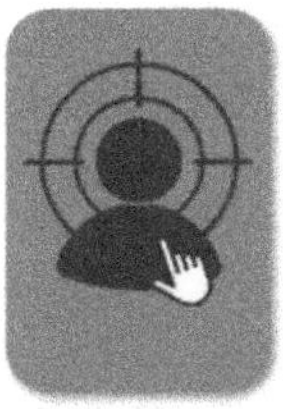

The recruited insider

A recruited insider is targeted by a third party to exploit their potential, current or former privileged access. This can be known as grooming. The insider may willingly assist the third party.

Key motivators

Financial gain, ideology, desire for recognition, ego, self-image, revenge, divided loyalties, adventure or thrill, compulsive or destructive behavior, personal circumstances, disgruntlement.

Red flags

- Unexpected wealth
- Attempts to access information unrelated to their duties
- Frustration in the workplace
- Displaying questionable loyalty

Examples

- An offer to split proceeds in exchange for downloading ransomware or providing access to systems
- A close friend exploiting their relationship to access privileged information or get around standard processes or procedures

Case study:
Recruited insider

Alex worked for a public service entity responsible for the biosecurity arrangements of imported cargo. Charlie, a new importer, contacted Alex for help navigating the inspection process even though the information was publicly available. Charlie started to send Alex lots of gifts, including alcohol and cash. Alex even accepted secondary employment with Charlie.

Charlie began requesting specific assistance and official information. Alex felt like he owed Charlie for his gifts and employment. He made a number of unauthorized disclosures, and self-assigned inspections to himself so he could waive the fumigation requirements for Charlie.

When the investigation into Alex's conduct commenced, he voluntarily resigned. Alex was convicted of criminal offences of bribery and unauthorized disclosure. Charlie was convicted for providing corrupting benefits to a Commonwealth official.

The Coerced Insider - Insider Threat Persona # 5

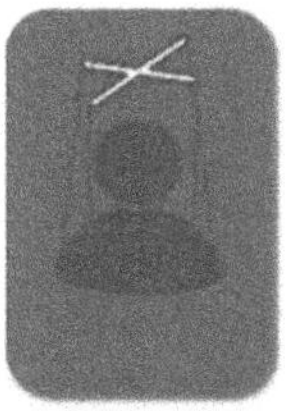

The coerced insider

A coerced insider is targeted by a third party to exploit their potential, current or former privileged access. The coerced insider cooperates due to pressure from the third party, often to avoid having private personal information exposed.

Key motivators

Vulnerability to blackmail, fear of secrets being revealed.

Red flags

- Attempts to access information unrelated to their duties
- Works outside normal hours without authorization, or accesses the network at odd times
- Has interest in matters outside their scope of duty
- Introduces electronic devices into secure work areas
- Fails to meet personal circumstance reporting requirements

Examples

- Someone threatening to release privileged information if a person refuses their requests
- Someone threatening physical safety or the safety of others if a person refuses their requests
- A supervisor or senior executive misusing their authority or influence to pressure personnel

Case study:
Coerced insider

Tracy worked for an entity that held privileged information. She was a well-respected senior manager with a good reputation. During her time at university, Tracy attended a party where she was involved in illegal activities. This was not disclosed to her entity during onboarding.

One night, she received a message from a stranger who told her they had an incriminating photo of her. They threatened to distribute the photo to her family, friends and work colleagues if she refused to cooperate.

Tracy was asked to take a thumb drive to work and download certain information. In exchange, they would destroy the photographic evidence. Tracy was distraught at the thought of her previous activities being exposed so she agreed. She waited for everyone to leave work for the day and copied the information.

When the leak was discovered, the entity's security team-initiated security protocols and traced the file access back to Tracy. Tracy lost her job and was investigated and subsequently charged.

Reference: Countering the Insider Threat: A Guide for Australian Government

The opinions expressed within this book are my own and not necessarily those of my current or past employers.

Bibliography

Advancing Zero Trust Maturity throughout the User Pillar-National Security Agency April 2023 www.nsa.gov

ATT&CK Matrix for Enterprise - The MITRE Corporation 2025 - https://attack.mitre.org

Boeckl, K. and Lefkovitz, N. (2020), *NIST Privacy Framework: A Tool for Improving Privacy Through Enterprise Risk Management, Version 1.0, Other*, National Institute of Standards and Technology, Gaithersburg, MD, [online], https://doi.org/10.6028/NIST.CSWP.01162020 (Accessed March 29, 2025)

Countering the Insider Threat: A Guide for Australian Government-Commonwealth Fraud Prevention Centre, Attorney-General's Department 2023 - https://www.ag.gov.au

Design Principles and Methodology for the Insider Threat TTP Knowledge Base - MITRE Engenuity 2022 - https://ctid.mitre.org/

Governing Through a Cyber Crisis - Australian Institute of Company Directors, the Cyber Security Cooperative Research Centre, and Ashurst February 2024 - https://www.aicd.com.au/risk-management/framework/cyber-security/governing-through-a-cyber-crisis-cyber-incident-response-and-recovery-for-australian-directors.html

Insider Threat Mitigation Guide - Cybersecurity and Infrastructure Security Agency November 2020 - www.cisa.gov

Pascoe, C., Quinn, S. and Scarfone, K. (2024), *The NIST Cybersecurity Framework (CSF) 2.0, NIST Cybersecurity White Papers (CSWP)*, National Institute of Standards and Technology, Gaithersburg, MD, [online], https://doi.org/10.6028/NIST.CSWP.29, https://tsapps.nist.gov/publication/get_pdf.cfm?pub_id=957258 (Accessed March 29, 2025)

The National Risk Index - Federal Emergency Management Agency (FEMA) 2025 - https://hazards.fema.gov/nri

Unrestricted Warfare - Qiao Liang and Wang Xiangsui, PLA Literature and Arts Publishing House 1999 - www.c4i.org

Index

Pages in *italics* refer to figures.

For Product Safety Concerns and Information please contact our EU representative GPSR@taylorandfrancis.com
Taylor & Francis Verlag GmbH, Kaufingerstraße 24, 80331 München, Germany

www.ingramcontent.com/pod-product-compliance
Ingram Content Group UK Ltd.
Pitfield, Milton Keynes, MK11 3LW, UK
UKHW052221190926
475702UK00006B/1146

* 9 7 8 1 0 3 2 8 4 2 3 3 2 *